ANGKOR

ANGKOR

Marilia Albanese

CONTENTS

2-3 Warriors in a gallery of Angkor Wat.
4 A devata at Angkor Wat.

ANGKOR

The Author

Marilia Albanese, a graduate in Sanskrit and Indology, with a diploma in Hindi Language and Indian Culture, is the director of the Lombardy Section of the Italian Institute for Africa and the Orient (I.A.O.) at the University of Milan. She has also pursued further studies in India, a country she has visited about 30 times since 1975. She held the chair of Hinduism and Buddhism in the off-campus branch of the Pontifical University Urbaniana (of Rome) in Monza located in the Seminary of the Pontificio Istituto Missioni Estere (Pontifical Foreign Missions Institute). Ms. Albanese has studied the psychological aspect of Buddhism in depth and has continued her studies in psychology even in the context of Western culture, specializing in *counseling*. For 10 years, she was president of the National Association of Yoga Teachers and she continues to give courses on Indian culture for this institution, which runs a four-year professional training program. She currently teaches Indian Scenic Art at the "Arrigo Pedrollo" Conservatory of Vicenza, attached to the Faculty of Extra-European Music. In addition to writing numerous articles and essays, she is the author of several books, including: *India Divina* (Be.Ma.) *Fiabe del Rajasthan*, edited by Maria Grazia Cella (Arcana); *Chakras*, written together with Fiorenza Zanchi and Gabriella Cella (Xenia Edizioni); *Mandala*, and *Kriya Yoga*, written together with Gabriella Cella (Xenia Edizioni); *Il Tantrismo* (Xenia Edizioni); *Lo Yoga* (Xenia Edizioni) *Cinque Volti dell'India*, under the auspices of the EEC for "Obbiettivo sul Mondo." For Edizioni White Star she has written *Lost Civilizations* (sections on India, Burma and Cambodia); *The Hidden Treasures of Antiquity* (sections on India and Cambodia); *Royal Palaces* (sections on India); *Treasures in Gold* (sections on India); *Northern India: an archaeological guide*; *Ancient India. From the Origins to the XIII Century A.D.*; *Angkor: Splendors of the Khmer Civilization*; *Siddhartha: the Prince who became Buddha*; and *Archaeology from the Sky* (Asia). She has also edited the scripts of five documentaries in the series "La Dea ferita" (The Wounded Goddess) produced by the Italian language Swiss Television, the result of a three-month working camp in India in 1998 to study the gap between the importance of goddesses in Indian civilization and the condition of women in everyday life. She has participated in the Radio 3 (an Italian National radio station) broadcast of "Uomini e Profeti" (Men and Prophets) on various occasions, and has taken part in specialized programs on India for Italian national television.

THE TEMPLES OF ANGKOR, AMONG THE MOST IMPORTANT CULTURAL MONUMENTS OF SOUTHEAST ASIA, ARE EVIDENCE, SCULPTED IN STONE, OF THE POLITICAL AND RELIGIOUS POWER AND THE CULTURAL HERITAGE OF THE KHMER PEOPLE.

Introduction

8 *A 12th-13th century Buddha. Musée Guimet, Paris.*

Introduction

FEW PLACES IN THE WORLD ARE AS FASCINATING AS ANGKOR, THE HEART OF THE IMMENSE KHMER EMPIRE THAT FLOURISHED IN INDOCHINA FROM THE 9TH TO THE 13TH CENTURY AND IS TODAY A MAGNIFICENT ARCHAEOLOGICAL PARK.

The Khmers, who lived in present-day Cambodia (the name derives from the masculine Sanskrit word *Kambuja*, the land of the "Offspring of Kambu," who was a mythical ascetic) exploited the special features of the Angkor plain and created an incredible hydraulic network of basins, canals and rice paddies that not only guaranteed subsistence for a million persons but also made it possible to accumulate a surplus used to finance innumerable constructions.

The Khmer kings were skillful and warlike rulers who, drawing inspiration from the Indian concepts of regality and from the local cults of spirits and deified ancestors, built monumental pyramid temples as reproductions and representations of the mythical cosmic mountain, Meru. What is more, every temple was reflected in a large pool that served the practical purpose of a reservoir and the symbolic function of a representation of the primeval ocean. The result was a liquid checkerboard dotted with temples, wooden buildings and bamboo huts and swarming with markets, carts, dugout canoes, animals and people. This animated life is depicted with clarity and freshness in the bas-reliefs that line the walls of the Bayon, perhaps the most powerful monument to absolute royalty that the artistic genius of the Khmers ever produced. Convinced that their rule stemmed from divine right and that they themselves were part of the essence of Divinity, the Khmer kings left to posterity in their temple inscriptions their ideas and the celebration of their feats.

Another extremely valuable source of information for the reconstruction of the Khmer world in the last phase of its golden age are the *Notes on the Customs of Cambodia*, written by the Chinese emissary Zhou Daguan, who was in Angkor from August 1296 to July 1297.

10 A dancing apsara in the Bayon style.

The only remains of Angkor, the great capital city consisting of numerous urban areas that rose up over the centuries, are its temples, invaded by the luxuriant vegetation. The plant world has regained possession of what were once human settlements, bursting through the stones in a suffocating maze of branches and lianas; indeed, the presence of this greenery that adds to the ineffable artistic beauty of the Angkor temples a magical atmosphere of distant times and remote worlds. Whether listening to the dawn voices of the forest from the top of the Phnom Bakheng, strolling beside the pools of the Royal Palace or among the ruins of Preah Pithu at sunset, seated to contemplate the reflections of the Srah Srang in the moonlight, one is overwhelmed by a subtle enchantment that goes well beyond aesthetic pleasure.

11 Angkor Wat reflected in the northwest basin.

Itineraries

The itineraries recommended here are based on the quality rather than number of visits and, whenever possible, on the chronological order of the sites and the best time to visit them with regard to sunlight. The Archaeological Park is open from 5:30 a.m. to 5:30 p.m. Visitors can purchase entrance tickets for 1 day, 3 days, or 1 week; at present they cost US$20, US$40 and US$60 respectively. Visitors must have a passport-size photograph with them. Getting around on foot is out of the question because of the distances between the sites, but you can rent bicycles or use motorbikes with drivers, 'cyclos,' 'motor rickshaws,' motorcycle taxis, taxis and minibuses.

12 A modern Buddha seated on a naga at Tep Pranam.

Tour 1: One-day Tour

The sites that must not be missed

Morning: Angkor Wat. If there is time, Baksei Chamkrong and/or Prasat Kravan and/or Thommanon as well. *Afternoon*: Angkor Thom: South Gate, Terraces of the Elephants and of the Leper King, Bayon. *Sunset*: Ta Prohm.

Tour 2: Two-day Tour

The most ancient and perfect examples of temple decoration and sculpture

1st day *Morning:* Roluos: Preah Ko, Bakong, Lolei. *Afternoon:* Banteay Srei. *Sunset:* Pre Rup.

2nd day The same as Itinerary A.

Tour 3: Three-day Tour

Temples with a tortuous course and so large they include residential areas

1st day The same as Itinerary B.

2nd day *Early morning:* Angkor Wat. If there is time, Thommanon, Chau Say Tevoda and/or Takeo, and Spean Thma as well. *Afternoon:* Preah Khan, Neak Pean, Baksei Chamkrong. *Sunset:* Phnom Bakheng by elephant.

3rd day *Early morning:* Angkor Thom: Gate of Victory, Bayon, Aphou, Terraces of the Leper King and of the Elephants, Royal Palace, Pools, Phimeanakas; if there is time, Preah Palilay. *Afternoon:* Prasat Kravan, Banteay Kdei, Srah Srang. *Sunset:* Ta Prohm.

Tour 4: Four-day tour

All the most important sites to grasp the spirit of Angkor

1st day *Morning:* Roluos: Preah Ko, Bakong, Lolei. *Afternoon:* Prasat Kravan, Mebon orientale, Ta Keo, Spean Thma, Baksei Chamkrong, Bei Prasat. *Sunset:* Phnom Bakheng by elephant.

2nd day *Early Morning:* Banteay Samré. *Afternoon:* Banteay Samré. *Sunset:* Pre Rup.

3rd day *Morning:* Angkor Wat. If there is time, Ta Prohm Kel, Thommanon, Chau Say Tevoda. *Afternoon:* Ta Som, Preah Khan, Prasat Prei, Banteay Prei, Krol Ko. *Sunset:* Neak Pean.

4th day *Early morning:* Angkor Thom: South Gate, Bayon, Baphuon, Terraces of the Leper King and of the Elephants, Royal Palace, Pools, Phimeanakas and, if there is time, Tep Pranam and Preah Palilay. *Afternoon:* Banteay Kdei, Srah Srang. *Sunset:* Ta Prohm.

Tour 5: Five-day Tour

The joy of discovery

1st day *Morning:* Roluos: Preah Ko, Bakong, Lolei. *Afternoon:* Baksei Chamkrong, Bei Prasat, Prasat Kravan, Bat Chum, Mebon, Leak Neang. *Sunset:* Pre Rup.

2nd day *Early Morning:* Banteay Srei, Kbal Spean. *Afternoon:* Thommanon, Chau Say Tevoda, Spean Thma, Ta Keo. *Sunset:* Ta Prohm.

13 *Buddha seated on a naga (12th century). National Museum, Bangkok.*

3rd day *Early morning:* the Bakheng River at dawn; Angkor Wat, Ta Prohm Kel. *Afternoon:* Ta Som, Preah Khan, Prasat Prei, Banteay Prei, Krol Ko. *Sunset:* Neak Pean.

4th day *Early Morning:* Angkor Thom: South Gate, Bayon, Baphuon, Terraces of the Leper King and of the Elephants, Royal Palace, Pools, Phimeanakas and, if there is time, Tep Pranam and Preah Palilay. *Afternoon:* Victory Gate, East Gate (on foot or on motorbike, since cars cannot negotiate the paths), Prasat Suor Prat, Khleang, and any monuments not visited in the morning. *Sunset:* Preah Pithu.

5th day *Early Morning:* Phnom Bok, Banteay Samré. *Afternoon:* Ta Nei oppure Prasat Chrung e passeggiata sulle mura, Banteay Kdei, Kutishvara. *Sunset:* Srah Srang.

15 The faces of Jayavarman VII in the Bayon.

Itineraries outside the Archaeological Park

In Siem Reap: Wat Preah Indra Kaorsey.
The West Baray, with Ak Yum and West Mebon.
Phnom Krom and Tonlé Sap, 6.8 miles (11 km).
Chau Srei Vibol, 1.5 miles (2.5 km).

Angkor National Museum

The Angkor National Museum was inaugurated in 2007 and it is considered to be the crowning achievement in the study of Cambodian art, because of the fine selection of artifacts and also the evocative multimedia support.
We recommend that you commence your visit on the upper floor with Gallery A, which offers an overview of the origins and evolution of the Khmer civilization. In Gallery B, the daily life and beliefs of the people are illustrated, while Gallery C is dedicated to the most honored kings.
Before going down to the lower floor, you will come to the Gallery of the 1,000 Buddhas, which offers one of the finest collections of statues of the Enlightened One.
Gallery D, at the entrance level, reveals the glories of Angkor Wat, while Gallery E brings Angkor Thom back to life.
Gallery F houses a selection of inscriptions of fundamental historical importance, while the numerous statues on display in Gallery G trace the evolution of costumes and jewelry.
The museum is open daily from 9.00 to 20.00 and tickets cost $12.

14 Floral volutes around a praying figure, Angkor Wat.

Angkor Wat

1 Ak Yum
2 The West Baray
3 The West Mebon
4 Baphuon
5 Phimeanakas
6 The Royal Palace
7 Prasat Chrung
8 Preah Palilay
9 Tep Pranam
10 Terrace of the Leper King
11 Prasat Suor Prat
12 Victory Gate
13 Preah Pithu
14 Angkor Thom
15 Khleang
16 Bayon
17 Terrace of the Elephants
18 Krol Romeas
19 Banteay Prei
20 Prasat Prei
21 Preah Khan
22 Thommanon
23 Spean Thma
24 Chau Say Tevoda

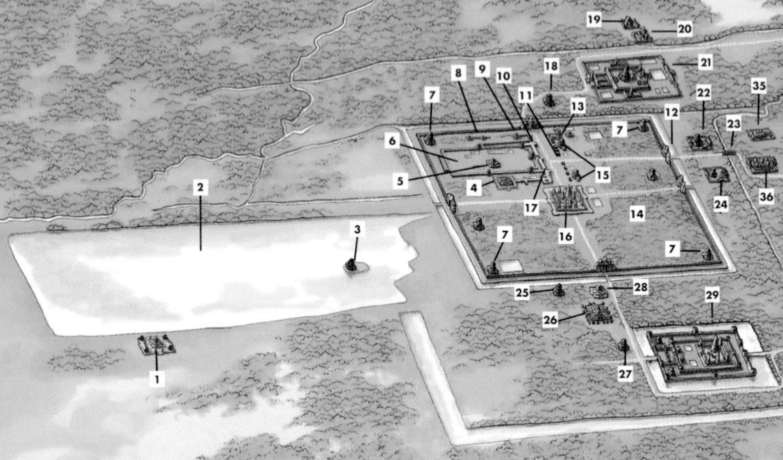

25 Bei Prasat
26 Phnom Bakheng
27 Ta Prohm Kel
28 Baksei Chamkrong
29 Angkor Wat
30 Phnom Krom
31 Kbal Spean
32 Banteay Srei
33 Krol Ko
34 Neak Pean
35 Ta Nei
36 Ta Keo
37 Ta Prohm
38 Kutishvara
39 East Mebon
40 Pre Rup
41 Banteay Kdei
42 Prasat Kravan
43 Bat Chum
44 Srah Srang
45 Ta Som
46 Prasat Leak Neang
47 Banteay Samré
48 Phnom Bok
49 Lolei
50 Preah Ko
51 Bakong
52 Chau Srei Vibol

Note to the Reader

For the visits to the temples the best itineraries have been recommended, but they are certainly not the only ones. Some reservoirs and moats are dry during the hot seasons and filled with water right after the monsoon season, making certain recommended tours somewhat difficult. The names of the temples are those presently used by the locals. Since it is impossible to provide a detailed description of all the most important bas-reliefs, a selection has been made from among them. The Sanskrit terms are written in a simplified transliteration in which the diacritic marks have been eliminated to make for easier reading. The name Cambodia derives from the Sanskrit Kambuja, which means "(Land) of the Kambu."

18 *Bronze head of the Bodhisattva Maitreya (8th century). National Museum, Bangkok.*

The Pre-Angkor Period

The area of present-day Cambodia was already inhabited in the 3rd millennium B.C., but it was it was not documented historically until the beginning of the Christian era, when there rose up along the Gulf of Siam a kingdom that Chinese chronicles describe as Funan, from the Khmer word bnam, or "mountain."

The Kingdom of Funan

The foundation of Funan may be ascribed to a certain Kaundinya who, inspired by a dream, presumably went from India to Cambodia, where he married Soma, a local princess who was one of the Nagas, mythical beings that were part cobra. The son of Soma and Kaundinya was supposedly the founder of the first Kaundinya dynasty of Funan. In the 5th century a second Kaundinya arrived from India to revive the Indianized customs that had gone by the wayside, and beginning with King Kaundinya Jayavarman (478-514) the rulers of Funan became more defined in a historical sense. Vyadhapura, their capital, is considered by some scholars to have stood at the foot of Ba Phnom. In 514 Rudravarman ascended the throne and chose Angkor Borei as his capital, where he probably lived until after 539. In The most distinguished artistic production in this period is sculpture, which was part of the so-called **Phnom Da style** (540-600), named after the sacred rise near Angkor Borei, south of Phnom Penh.

For the most part the sculpture works, in schist or sandstone, consist of portraits of Vishnu and figures connected to him, since Vishnuism must have been the religion of the sovereigns. However, Shivaism is documented by numerous *lingams*, and this period witnessed the first representations of Harihara, half Shiva and half Vishnu. However, the arch and fillets that support the head and arms of the portraits betray the lack of confidence the

19 Stele (left) with an ancient Khmer inscription (10th century); a 7th-8th-century stele (right). National Museum, Phnom Penh.

THAILAND
Mt. Kulen
MAHENDRAPARVATA
RONG CHEN
AK
YUM
SIEM REAP
HARIHARALAYA
(Roulos)
Tonlé Sap
Mekong
CAMBODIA
Gulf of Siam

sculptors had in the stability of their work.

The first statues of Buddha make their appearance in this period; he is depicted standing, with his garment flowing down to his feet, which guaranteed stability to the piece and allowed the sculptor to avoid using supports. Of the 32 particular signs that according to the sacred texts distinguish Buddha, the ones most represented in Khmer art are the *ushnisha*, the cranial protuberance rendered by means of a roll or knot on the top of the head and which is the symbol of nirvana, and the elongated lobes of the heavy earrings Buddha wore before he renounced all worldly things.

Side by side with Buddha there were also the *bodhisattvas*, enlightened figures who remain in the world to help humans liberate themselves from suffering. The most famous of these is Avalokiteshvara, "He who looks from on high," known in the Khmer world as Lokeshvara, the "Lord of the World," and Maitreya, the Buddha of the Future.

Chenla and the First Khmer Kingdoms

The Khmers, who were probably vassals of Funan, came from the upper course of the Menam River and had reached the Mekong River via the Mun River Valley. Their first independent principality developed in the 5th century, north of Tonlé Sap Lake: the Chinese accounts call this kingdom Chenla and also mention

20-21 The circle in the map indicates the development of Angkor.

the kings Shrutavarman and Shreshthavarman, whose capital Shreshthapura must have been in southern Laos.

A major influence on the future history of Cambodia was wrought by the Khmer kingdom of Bhavapura, in the area of present-day Kompong Thom: its most important sovereign, Ishanavarman, completed the conquest of Funan in 612-628 and chose Sambor Prei Kuk as his capital, renaming it Ishanapura.

After some turmoil, Jayavarman I regained control of the kingdom in 657, but upon his death after the year 700 the kingdom broke up into numerous principalities, among which there emerged that of Shambhupura, or Sambor, on the Mekong River, whose ruler Pushkaraksha proclaimed himself king of all Kambuja in 716. According to the Chinese chronicles, in the early 8th century there were two Chenlas, a 'land Chenla' and a 'water Chenla'; the former was united and centered around the ancient territories of Chenla, while the latter consisted of several fiefs in the area that once constituted Funan. The son of King Pushkaraksha, Shambhuvarman, and his heir, Rajendravarman I, maintained control over most of 'water Chenla' up to the end of the 8th century, when the Malayans and Javanese gained dominion over many Khmer principalities.

Four artistic styles are ascribed to this period, the first of which, the **Sambor Prei Kuk style** (600-650), was named after the capital of Bhavapura, 22 miles (35 km) north of Kompong Thom and 87 miles (140 km) southeast of Angkor. This style laid the foundation for future Khmer architecture. The temple or *prasat* consists of a rather squat square or oblong *cella* (the space within the temple walls) with a single access and slightly protuberant pilasters on the outside walls, and surmounted by a pyramidal top with symmetrical steps. The play of recessed and protuberant elements gradually increases, thus augmenting the number of external pilasters. Besides the access, which almost always faces east, there are other false doors on the other sides of the prasat. The *cella* is covered with a structure made up of progressively smaller levels, each of which reproduces the façade of the temple.

The doors and lintels are made of sandstone. The openings framed by round colonnettes in which the upper bulb is in the shape of a turban fringed by garlands, are a legacy of Indian architecture. The lintels – fundamental in tracing the evolution of Khmer art – consist of an arch emerging from the jaws of two *makara*, aquatic monsters with a trunk and horns.

Inserted in the arch are three medallions with animals or divinities in relief, and in the lower register there are garlands of flowers and festoons of stylized leaves, as well as necklaces and pendants. In some cases the arched motif of the lintel is a *naga* or many-headed serpent and the *makara* is replaced by knights riding fantastic animals, while the lower register is filled with figures.

The sculptural production of Sambor Prei Kuk is noteworthy for the rendering of some anatomical features; the male figures have slim bodies and round faces illuminated by a faint smile. Here for the first time female figures make their appearance; with ample bosoms, they are wrapped in long dresses fastened under the navel, with or without a central series of folds.

23 Map showing the Kambuja kingdoms before the rise of Angkor.

24 The durga of Tuol Kamna (left, 7th century). National Museum, Phnom Penh; the Harihara from Prasat Andet (right, 7th century). National Museum, Phnom Penh.

25 The durga from Sambor Prei Kuk (7th century). National Museum, Phnom Penh.

Prevailing among them are the portraits of Durga, the consort of the god Shiva, who in the Khmer civilization was also considered to be the sister of Vishnu.

The number of female images increases in the **Prei Kmeng style (635-700)**, which takes it name from the temple on the southwest corner of the West Baray (a *baray* is an artificial reservoir), while new elements are the first images of Brahma and the widespread use of mobile metal attributes that the gods hold in their hands. The colonnettes become larger and are more heavily decorated and in the lintels the *makara* are replaced by large figures at the ends or in the middle of the composition, which is dominated by more rectilinear arches.

The **Prasat Andet style (7th-8th century)**, named after a locality near modern Kompong Thom, is marked by the development of the sculptural elements of the previous periods: great attention is paid to the anatomical details of the bodies, which are executed in the round without sustaining arches, and the faces of the male statues have thin moustaches. Vishnu, Harihara and Devi, the Great Goddess, are the most common figures represented.

The following **Kompong Preah style (706-800)**, centered near Pursat, shows a decline in the aesthetic quality of the statues: the limbs become heavy and the faces are rendered rather coldly. In architecture there is an increase in the rings of the cylindrical colonnettes that are decorated with delicate petals, while in the lintels medallions are no longer used and the garlands dominate the carved surface, with a central knot of vegetation among rows of leaves that become protuberant pendants in the lower register.

The Angkor Period

The 9th century witnessed the rise of Angkor art, that is, the art produced almost entirely in the vast zone of Angkor, the only exception being Koh Ker, a locality 53 miles (85 km) away. The history of the 'capital' – nagara in Sanskrit, from which the Khmer word angkor derived – began with the grandiose consecration ritual of Jayavarman II (790-850) in 802 on Mt. Kulen to celebrate the independence of Kambuja from Javanese dominion.

The Center of the Empire

That year marked the inauguration of the cult of *Devaraja*, the 'God King' who was the celestial counterpart of the terrestrial ruler with universal power, and the name of the **Phnom Kulen style (802-875)** derived from that of the mountain. The supporting arch was done away with for good, but the statues, which were now only of males, became more massive. In some works the eyebrows merge, lending intentness to the facial expression. Diadems appear for the first time. The buildings were made of bricks, while sandstone was used for the doors and windows. Together with the traditional colonnettes, square and octagonal ones began to appear, the former becoming a distinguishing feature of this style. Pendants are now an important element in the lintel garlands.

26 Detail of a Buddha in the Baphuon style. Musée Guimet, Paris.

The foundation of Hariharalaya near present-day Roluos was the first settlement in what would later become the empire of Angkor. When Jayavarman II died, his successor Jayavarman III (850-877) built the Prey Monti at Hariharalaya. But Indravarman I (877-889) was really the first in a series of great rulers who built major monuments. In 877, the excavation of the 'island' at the Lolei temple of the Indratataka *baray* was the beginning of hydraulic architecture based on the *baray*, the artificial reservoir that served both practical and symbolical purposes and that would mark the rise of Angkor. The same ruler also built the Preah Ko and Bakong sanctuaries.

The **Preah Ko style**, which prevailed during the reign of Indravarman I (877-889), is characterized by greater movement and animation, although the heaviness in the limbs remains. Collar-like beards and moustaches are characteristic features, and the faces are broad and inexpressive. The chignon is now a cylinder divided into stylized sections and the tiara extends in two bands on either side of the ears, decorated with complex patterns and, in the case of the god Vishnu, becoming a sort of octagonal pagoda. The knotted diadem on the nape of the neck is common. A particularly distinguishing feature is the bas-relief, the first examples of which are at Bakong.

The temples are surrounded by concentric enclosures, and the

27 Vishnu at Phnom Kulen (9th century). National Museum, Phnom Penh.

entrances have *gopuras* (monumental pavilions); the *prasats* are aligned on common platforms, while in the brick walls there are sandstone niches with male and female figures of *dvarapala* (temple guardians). This period also witnessed the construction of enigmatic structures known as 'libraries,' and the first temple mountain makes its appearance. This is also the period in which the most beautiful lintels in Khmer art were carved: two festoons of garlands held in the middle by the demon Kala, with two *makaras* facing backward at the ends and tiny figures riding horses or the three-headed *naga*. Another recurrent central motif is Vishnu on Garuda, the part bird, part man lesser deity that served as the god's steed.

At the time of King Indravarman's death, Khmer dominion had spread as far north as Ubon, Thailand and south as far as Phnom Bayang, at the southern tip of Kambuja. His successor Yashovarman (889-910) kept his father's possessions, built the East Baray to supply water for the new capital Yashodharapura and built its main temple on Phnom Bakheng as well as two others on Phnom Krom and Phnom Bok. The **Bakheng style (889-925)** accentuated and stiffened the faces of the statues, highlighting the eyes and mouth with a double stroke, while the continuous carved line of the eyebrow arch is in relief. The moustache and beard are pointed, and the overall impression is that of a formal and abstract solemnity. The architecture is marked by the development of the temple mountain and the increasing use of sandstone; on the octagonal colonnettes with their seven visible faces, more use is made of rings and foliage decoration, while the small figures no longer appear on the lintels.

King Harshavarman I (910-923), the successor of Yashovarman, ordered the construction of the Baksei Chamkrong and Prasat Kravan, while Ishanavarman II (923-928) was dethroned and from 921 to 944, following the usurpation of Jayavarman IV, the capital was moved to Koh Ker, about 56 miles (90 km) northeast of Angkor. Jayavarman IV (928-941) is to be credited for the rise of the **Koh Ker style (921-944)**. Here the artists show much more confidence in their means and experiment with large forms; of special interest are their abandonment of frontality and the introduction of the

28 A Bakheng style head of Shiva (10th century). Musée Guimet, Paris.

29 Combat between Valin and Sugriva, Koh Ker style (10th century). National Museum, Phnom Penh.

innovative representation of movement. The faces are made softer and more gentle thanks to a faint smile, and carved jewels replace the mobile parures, which suggests less wealth. Moreover, narrative scenes appear on the lintels.

After the brief reign of Harshavarman II (941-944), Rajendravarman II (944-968) returned to Angkor in 944 and, after clashing with the Cham kingdom, extended his authority to the east as far as the Annamite range, reaching Burma to the west and the Gulf of Siam to the south. This ruler and his famous architect Kavindrarimathana were responsible for the

30 Shiva and Uma, Banteay Srei (10th century). National Museum, Phnom Penh.

construction of the Pre Rup, the East Mebon, the Bat Chum and the Srah Srang reservoir. During the reign of Rajendravarman the **Pre Rup style** revived small figures and the static hieratic quality in sculpture. Belts become a common motif and the hairstyles are more elaborate.

The structures now imitate the former plastered brick constructions, while the long halls that surround the temples in this period prefigure the later continuous perimetral galleries. The first of these temples was the Ta Keo, attributed to Jayavarman V (968-1001), who founded the new capital of Jayendranagari.

In the meantime the Brahman Yajnavaraha had built the splendid Banteay Srei temple, after which a new period was named.

The **Banteay Srei style (960-1000)** effected a sort of revolution and was one of the most significant artistic styles in Cambodia. Tinged with archaism – a typical characteristic of Khmer art, which returned to the models of past several times – Banteay Srei production featured soft, delicate images, with fleshy lips and wide-open eyes; the men's faces have beards and moustaches, while the women's are pervaded with pensive, gentle calm. Elaborate jewels adorn the divinities, revealing the mastery and refinement of Khmer jewelry. The pediments are

31 A monkey guarding the Banteay Srei stairway (10th century). National Museum, Phnom Penh.

32 *Buddha seated on a naga, Baphuon style (11th century). Musée Guimet, Paris.*

now superposed and their deeply carved relief sculpture becomes narrative, consisting of highly plastic statuary groups.

Lintels with garlands articulated in complex volutes at the ends and with a god in the middle alternate with others that hark back to the old division into quarters bearing elephant heads, *Kalas* and mythical figures. Cylindrical columns appear for the last time.

The Golden Age

The first decade of the 11th century witnessed the ascent to the throne of a powerful king, Suryavarman I (1010-1050), who unified almost all Kambuja and made southern Thailand and part of southern Laos his vassals. His reign was distinguished for the rise of the **Khleang style (1010-1050)**, which is clearly seen in the two groups of buildings of the same name, in the Royal Palace and its central temple – Phimeanakas – and, outside Angkor in Phnom Chisor, in certain parts of the Preah Khan at Kompong Svay, of the Preah Vihear and of the Wat Phu. Common features of the style are the continuous outer galleries with cruciform *gopura* entrances, in which the quartered lintels have a *Kala* holding large floral garlands in its hands. The faces of the statues have faint smiles and the braided hair is another typical feature of the Khleang style.

33 *Head of Buddha, Baphuon style (11th century). Musée Guimet, Paris.*

The construction of the gigantic West Baray begun by Suryavarman I was finished by his son Udayadityavarman II (1050-1066), who managed to keep his father's kingdom united despite several provincial revolts. Udayadityavarman II is also credited with the construction of the West Mebon and the huge Baphuon, after which the new **Baphuon style (1050-1066)** was named. This style produced smaller, more slender images that in some cases are almost thin when compared to the size of the head; the thinning out of the legs was made possible by the supports placed behind the heels. Much attention was paid to detail: the lips are tight and the eyes are carved in outline, and they may once have been decorated with semi-precious stones. The tip of the beard is pointed at the chin, which bears a characteristic dimple. The hair is braided, held together by a garland of pearls. The utter charm and spiritual gentility of the facial expressions are unequalled in all Khmer art. This is the period that marks the appearance of Buddha seated in meditation on the coils of the king of the *nagas*, the many-headed cobra Mucilinda, a motif that was extremely popular in the following period, so much so that it became one of the emblems of Khmer sculpture.

The middle of the *Kala* lintels is surmounted by a figure on a steed or by mythological scenes, while the pediments are filled by a maze of foliage.

34 *12th-century devatas at Angkor Wat.*

Suryavarman was succeeded by his brother Harshavarman III (1066-1080), who had to confront the neighboring Chams many a time; upon his death in 1080 the throne of Angkor passed on to Jayavarman VI (1080-1107), a prince from Mahidharapura, a fief that may have been situated in northeastern Thailand, who built the temple of Phimai in this area.

After Dharanindravarman I (1107-1112), who was a rather nondescript ruler, the throne was won by Suryavarman II (1113-1150), who was crowned in 1119. A warlike sovereign, he again unified Kambuja, tried several times to invade Annam and occupied Champa in 1144, going as far as the boundaries of the Burman kingdom of Pagan to the west, as far east as the sea and to the heart of the Malayan peninsula to the south. Suryavarman II built the temples of Thommanon, Chau Say Tevoda, Angkor Wat, Preah Pithu, and Banteay Samré, and, outside Angkor, Beng Mealea, some buildings of the Preah Khan of Kompong Svay and the Phnom Rung.

Architecture reached it zenith with the **Angkor Wat style (1100-1175)**: the *prasats* are surmounted by conical towers with curved profiles; the side galleries are linked by axial wings;

34-35 Suryavarman II at Angkor Wat, third gallery, south side, west wing (12th century).

the half-galleries are either purely ornamental or serve as buttresses; cruciform terraces and balustrades bordered by *nagas* connect the various buildings. The columns may have as many as twenty sides, and the lintels have floral decoration, narrative scenes, and crowned *nagas*.

Contrary to what one might expect, given the perfection of the architecture, the sculpture seems rather stereotyped. The charm and sweetness of the Baphuon style is replaced by the old frontality and stiff solemnity. The figures with square shoulders and puffed-up chests have rather clumsily carved legs and feet. In the faces, which for the most part are clean-shaven, the eyebrows are still connected and the eyes, highlighted by deep carving, are elongated in a mannered fashion. The female figures have more lively, characterized expressions than the males, especially the faces. The complex garments are coupled with equally complex hairdos, which are often supported by frames: except for some *devata* who gather their hair in a chignon, letting a braid hang free, most of the females seem to prefer boldly conceived, fantastic diadems under which the hair flows in braids or tufts.

Most of the jewels have floral motifs; these profusely decorate the divinities.

The Evolution of Dress in Khmer Art

Khmer culture appears at the apex of its splendor even in the various stages of evolution, and in the different styles of men's and women's clothing.

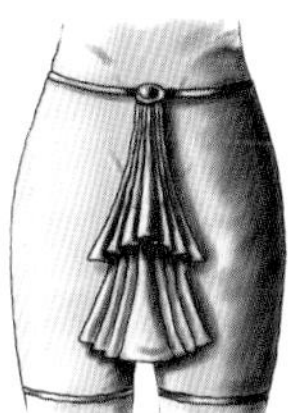

PHNOM DA STYLE, 540-600.

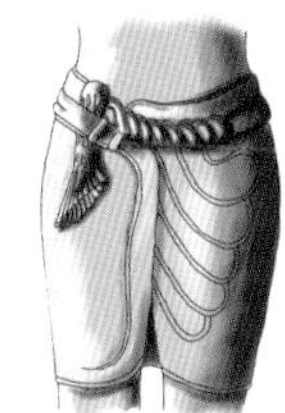

PHNOM KULEN STYLE, 802-875.

PREAH KO STYLE, 877-889.

BAKHENG STYLE, 889-925.

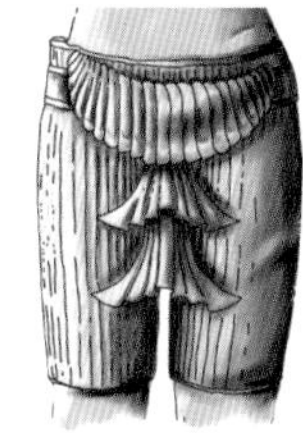

KOH KER STYLE, 921-944.

PRE RUP STYLE, 944-968.

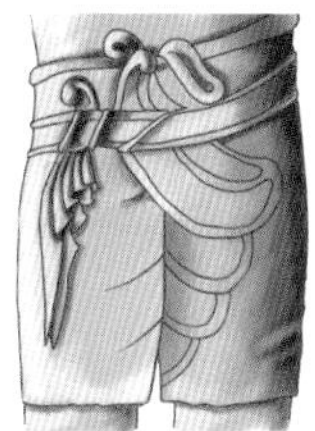

BANTEAY SREI STYLE, 960-1000.

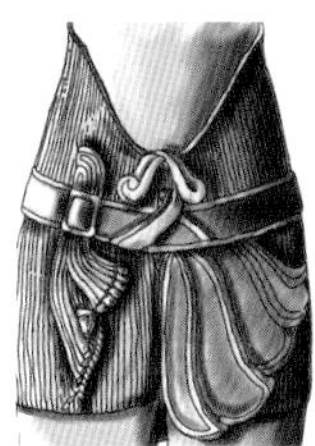

BAPHUON STYLE, 1050-1066.

ANGKOR WAT STYLE, 1100-1175.

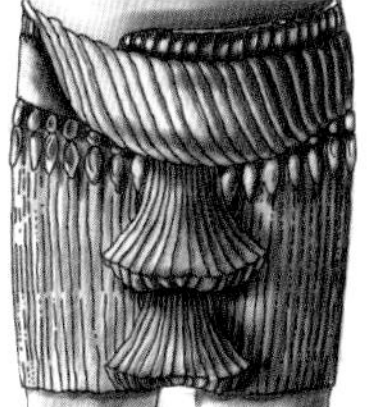

BAYON STYLE, 1181-1219/20.

The Evolution of Men's Dress in Khmer Art

36 and 37 bottom right A Kulen period Vishnu (9th century). Musée Guimet, Paris.

PRE-ANGKOR STYLE,
8TH CENTURY.

BAKONG STYLE,
9TH CENTURY.

BAKHENG STYLE,
889-925.

BANTEAY SREI STYLE,
960-1000.

BAPHUON STYLE,
1050-1066.

ANGKOR WAT STYLE,
1100-1175.

BAYON STYLE,
1181-1219/20.

BAYON STYLE,
1181-1219/20.

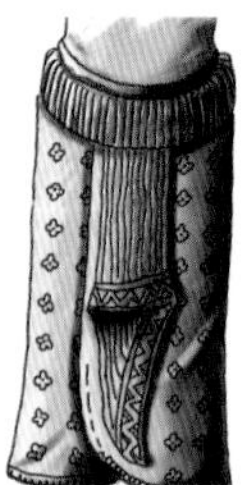
BAYON STYLE,
1181-1219/20.

The Evolution of Women's Dress in Khmer Art

38 bottom Detail of a female figure from Angkor Wat.

39 A devata from Angkor Wat.

40-41 Female figures in the southwest corner pavilion of the third gallery (12th century), Angkor Wat.

Suryavarman was succeeded by Dharanindravarman II (1150-1160) and then Yashovarman II (1160-1165).

In 1165 the usurper Tribhuvanadityavarman assassinated the legitimate king and, taking advantage of the prevailing turmoil, the Cham ruler Indravarman IV landed at Yashodharapura in 1177, sacked the city, killed Tribhuvanadityavarman, and settled in the Angkor area.

Decline in the Shadow of Buddha

The Chams were driven out and Kambuja was again unified by Jayavarman VII, who was crowned in 1181 when over 50 years old. This fervent Buddhist ruler replaced the cult of Shiva-*Devaraja* with that of *Buddharaja*, lord of the universe. Under Jayavarman VII the Empire attained its greatest area, including the Khorat Plateau, the Menan Valley and part of southern Malaya. The king annexed Champa and northern Laos, while the Burmese kingdom of Haripunjaya, Annam, and perhaps Java, became tributaries.

42 The goddess Tara, associated with Jayarajadevi, Jayavarman VII's consort. Musée Guimet, Paris.

An incredible builder, Jayavarman VII was responsible for Ta Prohm, Preah Khan at Angkor, Neak Pean, Banteay Kdei, Ta Som, Ta Nei, Srah Srang, Angkor Thom, Bayon, the Terraces of the Elephant and of the Leper King, the ponds of the Royal Palace and, outside Angkor, the Preah Khan at Kompong Svay and the Banteay Chhmar. The **Bayon style (1181-1219/20)** is known for the spread of huge religious complexes that were made mostly of laterite (a clay rich in iron that is easy to cut and becomes quite hard when exposed to the air) and were built hastily. The motifs in the lintels are either Buddhist or the decoration consists of a garland divided into four parts or by spirals of foliage and fringes of vegetation.

The new style abandoned the hieratic frontality and aimed at greater movement and plastic qualities in space. The fact that Buddhism became the state r eligion led to an aesthetic ideal that was more human and intimate. The faces are now characterized by inner smiles and mystical expressions. Furthermore, the tendency to deify ancestors and relatives and the identification of King Jayavarman VII with the *bodhisattva* Lokeshvara, led to the production of more realistic images that reflect the psychology of the figures portrayed. Jayavarman VII's delusions of grandeur are also manifested in the sculpture, some examples of which are simply colossal. The rows of giants that guard the entrances and the enormous faces of the king-*bodhisattva* looking out from the towers of Bayon are the most impressive examples of this tendency.

Two years after the supposed death of Jayavarman in 1219 or 1220, the Khmers evacuated Champa, while in the outlying areas of the empire acts of secession were becoming more frequent and the Thai menace was looming along the frontiers. The Brahmans stirred up a Shivaite reaction against the spread of Buddhism, but the Theravada, the 'Doctrine of the Elders,' also known as Hinayana or 'Little Vehicle (of Salvation)', an essential and more ancient form of Buddhism, eventually prevailed.

Little is known of the last rulers: Indravarman II (1218-1243) built the Prasat Sour Prat and Jayavarman VIII (1243-1295) was responsible for the Mangalartha. Under Shrindravarman (1295-1307), the Chinese emperor Timur Khan sent a mission to Kambuja in 1296: one of the emissaries was Zhou Daguan, whose chronicle provides us with information about the Khmer civilization. The last kings were Shrindrajayavarman (1307-1327) and Jayavarman Parameshvara (1327-?). In the meantime the first large Thai state, Sukhothai, had occupied much of the western and northern territories of the Khmer empire. In 1430 a Thai king, Paramaraja II of Ayuthya, swept into the Angkor plain and began a siege of the capital, conquering it in seven months. From that moment on abandon and decadence set in.

When the Khmer empire came to an end, the sculptors resumed working in wood and the growing power of the Thai kingdoms influenced the artistic production of the following centuries. This period produced the 'decorated Buddha,' that is, covered with jewels. This image was conceived sometime between the 9th and 10th century in the Indian monastery of Nalanda and then spread more in Indo-China than in India. This curious use of jewels (Buddha had made a vow of poverty) is to be explained by the desire to emphasize the pre-eminence of the Enlightened One who, having attained spiritual supremacy, was associated with the *cakravartin*, the universal sovereign, one of whose prerogatives is to wear jewels.

43 Head of Jayavarman VII (12th-13th century). National Museum, Phnom Penh.

Basic elements of the Khmer Temple

There are more than 1,000 sandstone temples and shrines scattered all around Angkor: a living testimony to the artistic heights reached by the Khmer people. The buildings and their particular design features, including the plan, the low-reliefs and the sculptures, all had their religious importance.

44 top Detail of a pediment at Angkor Wat.

The Prasat - a Sanctuary Tower

The Khmer temple or *prasat* is a tower structure that reproduces the cosmic mountain. Whether it be mythical Mt. Meru, Mandara or other sacred mountains such as Kailasa, the dwelling place of the gods is the center of the universe as well as the focal point around which the world is laid out in an orderly, rigorous fashion, emerging from the primordial chaos. As an axial symbol, the mountain links the sky, earth and, upside down, the underworld in the shape of a funnel underneath the mountain. Its peaks – either one, three, or five, according to the various mythical versions – are the home of the deities, one of whom in particular is associated with mountains: the god Shiva, who prefers the recesses of the Himalayas.

As a mountain the *prasat* is an almost totally solid mass with the small, dark cavity of the *cella*, which is square because this form represents perfection in Hindu and, consequently, Khmer geometric symbolism. The Sanskrit appellation *garbhagriha*, or embryo chamber, underscores its role as the 'womb' of primeval nature, in which the world is enclosed in its potentiality, ready to evolve. In its function as a tabernacle, the temple houses the sacred image, the formal manifestation of the Absolute that becomes divine Presence.

The ceiling of the *cella* is a

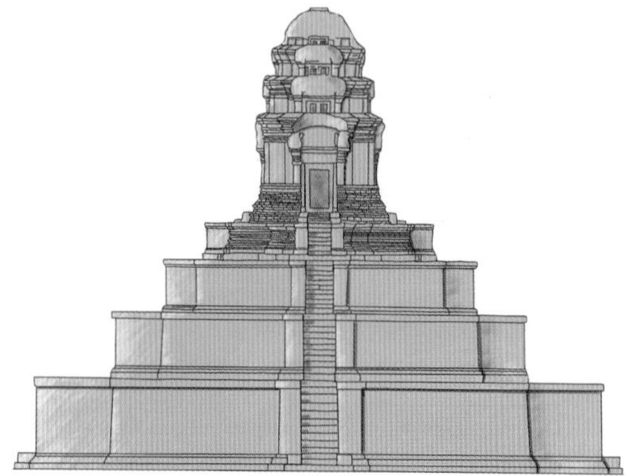

44 bottom The temple mountain or prasat of Baksei Chamkrong lies on a stepped pyramid.

corbelled vault, that is, made with corbeling, which consisted in embedding bricks or stones in a progressively protuberant manner in order to bear weight and stress, and then rounding them off to give the impression of a true vault, with a small opening affording a bit of light under the crown. A cloth ceiling – employed up to the 10th century – and a wooden lacunar ceiling concealed the stone or brick intrados of the *prasat*.

45 The central prasat of Angkor Wat is cross-shaped and has vestibules and porticoes.

The exterior of the *prasat* consists of superposed, progressively diminishing levels or 'stories,' usually four in number, that reproduce the body of the ground floor with a gate, lintel and cornice. In a later period miniature reproductions of the entire edifice were placed on the corners of the upper levels as antefixes. The top of the temple has a round motif in the shape of a vase or a lotus bud, on which metal pediments were probably placed.

The *prasat* never touches the ground, but stands on a platform with one or four access stairways. The most ancient temples have a single entrance; in later periods a blind door stood on each of the other three sides of the edifice and their stone frames were reproductions of the wooden models. A further step in the evolution of the temple was the

***46 top** The stories of the prasat imitate the molding of the foundation.*

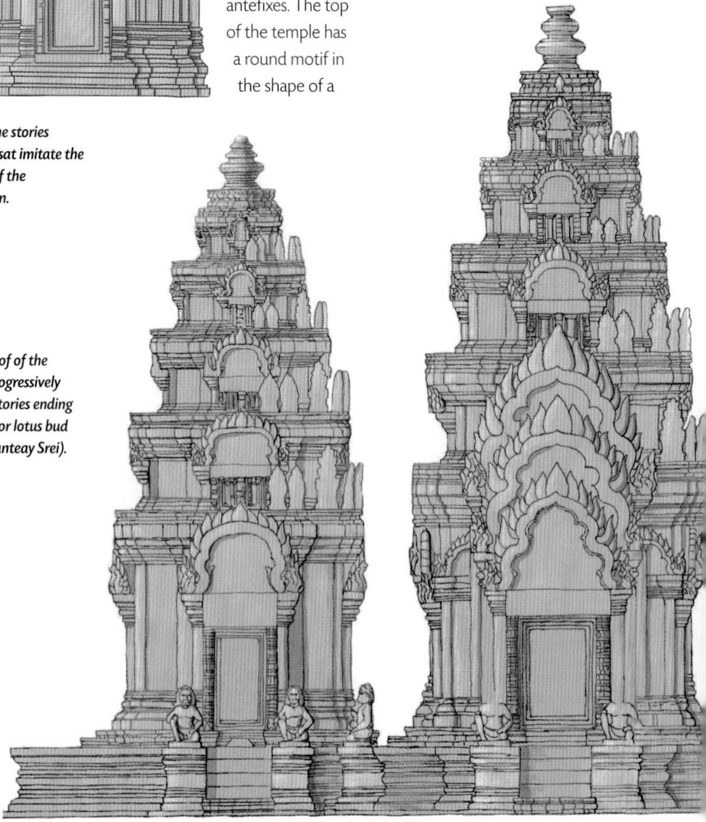

***46-47** Roof of the prasat: progressively receding stories ending with vase or lotus bud motifs (Banteay Srei).*

addition of protruding structures that served as porticoes.

The outside walls were decorated with bands of bas-reliefs and had niches framed by jutting pilasters that contained statues that were in such high relief they were almost freestanding. Solemn, armed figures of young men served as *dvarapalas*, the 'guardians of the doors' that were placed there to protect the temple from evil powers: there were two *dvarapalas* for each door, the one at the right generally having a benevolent attitude, while the aspect of his counterpart is threatening. Poised female figures, the *devatas* or goddesses, smile enigmatically. The upper corners of the walls consist of *nagas*, serpents with three, five or seven heads that were a legacy of Indian civilization, to which the Khmer added some special elements, such as the crest, which made them more similar to the dragon of Chinese origin.

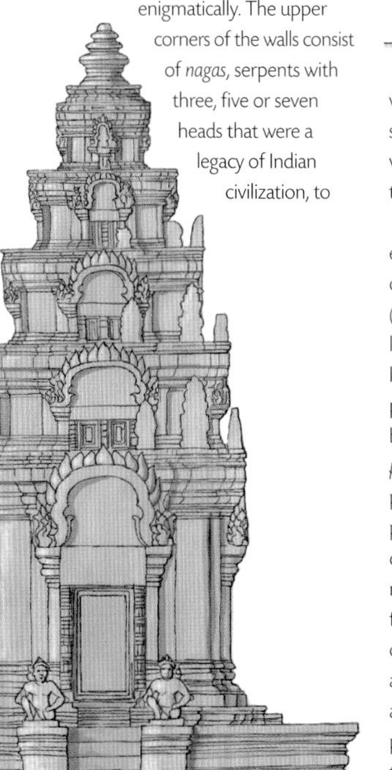

***47 top** A cruciform prasat with vestibules connected to the galleries.*

The *prasat* is the principal element of two different complexes – the pyramid temple (or temple mountain) and the longitudinal temple. The former lies on natural rise or an artificial pyramid. At first isolated and later built in groups of three or five, the *prasats* on the last terrace of the pyramid become the mountain peaks which are the abode of the deities. The theatrical quincunx mountain temple, that is, with five towers, four of which are on the corners of the square and the other in the middle, is an architectural type that achieved perfection at Angkor Wat and that represents the peaks of Mt. Meru.

Other Structures in the Temple Enclosures

The temple lies in one or more enclosures whose entrances are surmounted by *gopuras*. Initially rectangular entrance chambers with a superstructure rising above the side walls, the *gopuras* were later transformed into monumental cruciform pavilions, with side entrances, porticoes and halls that extended along the walls. At first covered with beams and roof-tiles, they later had corbelled vaults made of brick and sandstone.

In the innermost enclosure, access to the temple is afforded by long paved avenues flanked by balustrades in the shape of *nagas*. The balustrade is a symbolic link between the city and the temple, that is to say, between the world of humans and that of the gods, and refers to the rainbow that links the sky and the earth, and to rain, which is borne by the *nagas*. The *naga*-rainbow motif is also often to be seen in the temple pediments. The access causeways, which are sometimes elevated on a series of colonnettes that serve as stilts, may be flanked by monolithic stelae similar to pillars with a base and capital, crowned by voluminous cusps.

The enclosure walls of the longitudinal temple are replaced in the pyramid temple by

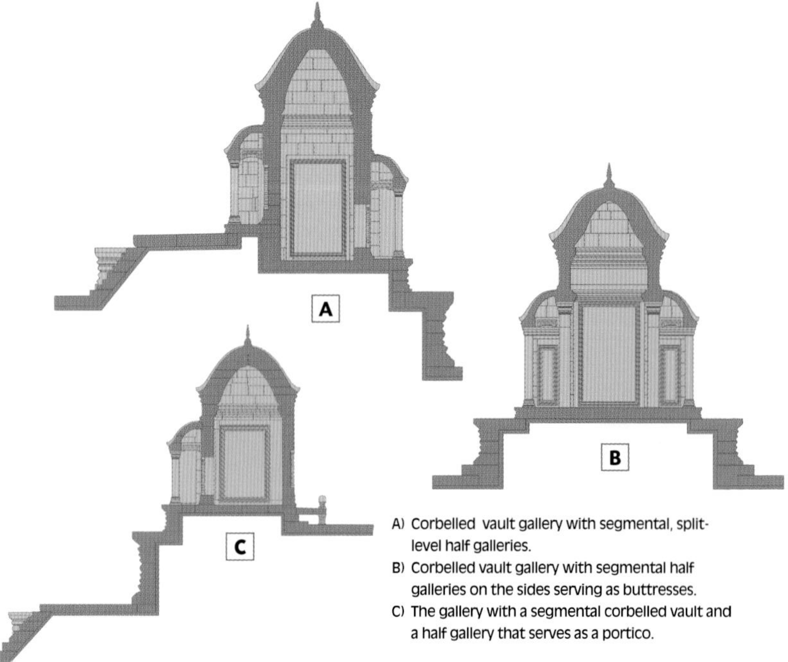

A) Corbelled vault gallery with segmental, split-level half galleries.
B) Corbelled vault gallery with segmental half galleries on the sides serving as buttresses.
C) The gallery with a segmental corbelled vault and a half gallery that serves as a portico.

concentric galleries that run along the perimeter of the stepped terraces. These galleries are probably derived from the merger of rectangular edifices whose purpose is unknown and that were originally separated from one another. Seen from above, the galleries of the mountain temple create concentric enclosures that delimit areas of different sacred significance. In the 11th century the galleries became part of the longitudinal temples as well. Of various types, they consist of an outer wall with or without blind windows, while the inner wall may have open chambers or be a colonnade with square pillars. In the most elaborate cases the main gallery, with a colonnade on one or both sides, is flanked by one or two columned half-galleries that serve as buttresses: in the latter case a sort of hypostyle hall is created. At the corners of the galleries are towers that are reproductions of the *prasat*.

Initially the galleries had tile roofs set on a wooden framework, but later they were crowned by corbelled bricks and then by corbelled vaults made of stone.

Plan of the gopuras:
1) Single rectangular chamber
2) Cruciform chamber with extension side halls.
3) Cruciform areas with double porticoes and extension halls along the walls.
4) Five-chamber cruciform structure with extension halls.

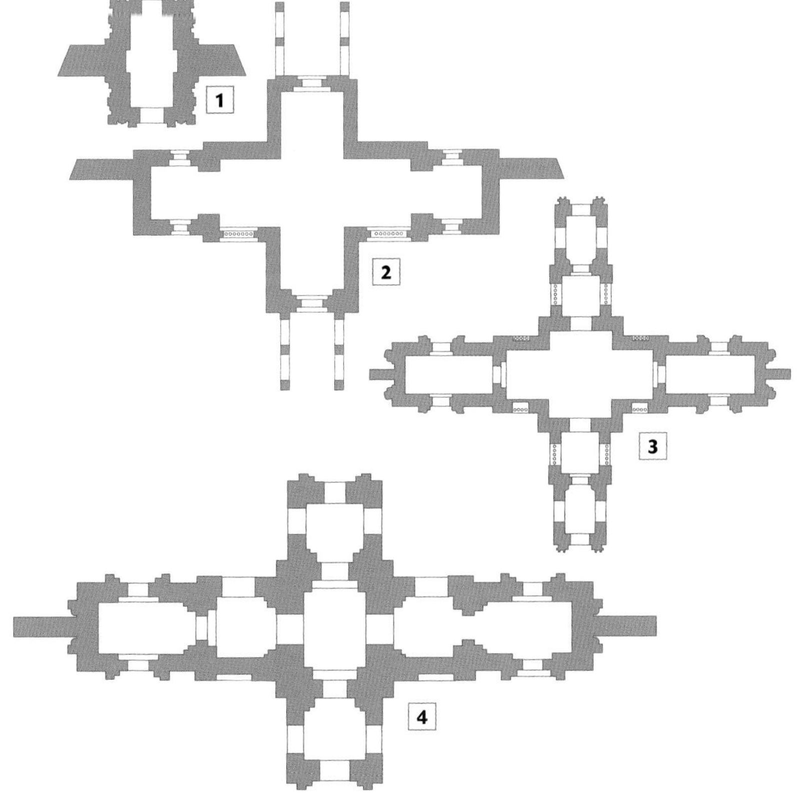

50 top and 50-51 Blind windows with small freestanding columns and superposed cornices (Angkor Wat).

The windows in the walls of the galleries have sort of grilles consisting of thin columns derived from secular architecture. These columns may be cylindrical or octagonal, depending on the period, with several coils and elaborate decoration. A feature of the windows made in the last Khmer period is the reproduction in stone of curtains and mats that are half lowered, obviously to save work time.

In the longitudinal temples that reproduced the Indian type, other structures are added to the *prasat*: the *mandapa*, the antechamber from which the faithful could enjoy a 'view' of the deity; the *ardhamandapa*, used as an entrance porch, usually placed to the east; the *antarala*, the access to the *garbhagriha* or *cella*. In the more complex temples the central shrine is preceded by porticoed halls, topped by wooden roofs that were later made of stone. The exterior of these roofs do not consist of mere smooth slabs, but reproduce ribbing and imitation tiles, the edges of which had lotus buds and acroteria with crest and pinnacle motifs. These elements derived from the older wooden architecture, as did the triangular pediments with volute stiles and carved scenes in the tympanum.

51 bottom Windows and portals of a gopura at Banteay Samré.

The evolution of the frame colonnettes and windows

1) door frame columns at Prei Kmeng; 2 and 4) door frame columns at Trapeang Phong.; 3) door frame columns at Sambor Prei Kuk.

Courtyards and cloisters house the annexes of the temple, among which are the structures known as 'libraries' – despite the fact that their purpose is still unknown – which were built first on a square plan with thick brick walls and a single door or opening and illuminated by loopholes. In a later period the 'libraries' were made of laterite or sandstone in keeping with a rectangular plan imitating a triple nave, with foreparts on pillars and imitation doors.

5 6 7 8 9

5) window colonnettes at Preah Ko; 6 and 7) window colonnettes at prasat thom at Koh Ker; 8) window colonnettes at Preah Vihear; 9) window colonnettes at Angkor Wat.

Building Materials and Techniques

53 Detail of a colonnette at Baksei Chamkrong.

Brick was the building material the Khmers first used. Their bricks were usually as large as 14 inches long, 6.2 inches wide and 3.9 inches thick (30 cm long, 16 cm wide, 10 cm thick). They were smoothed so there were no rough or uneven surfaces, and were then laid carefully and fixed with a binder made of lime, palm sugar and liana sap. Once laid, the bricks were carved and then covered with plaster

55 Construction with dovetailed blocks (Bayon).

made of lime and sand, which was fastened through pegging or by means of holes carved in the wall surface. The use of plaster, documented from the 9th century on, was widespread in the 10th century, after which time it became less popular. To save on hand-finished material, the inner part of very thick walls was filled with broken bricks and earth.

Later on, laterite and sandstone were used as building materials. Laterite was used for the foundations, platforms, the terraces of the pyramids, and the enclosure walls. The laterite was cut into uniform, well-connected blocks

54 Roof with imitation tiles and acroterion (second gallery of Angkor Wat).

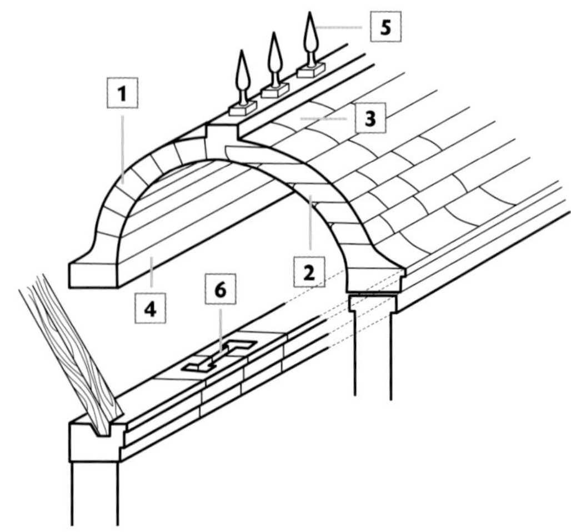

The construction technique of the corbelled vault:

1) Round vault
2) Corbelled Khmer vault
3) Extrados
4) Intrados
5) Acroterion
6) Anchorage

56 left Fediment framed by nagas whose odd-numbered heads create the corners (Angkor Wat).

56 right The elephant Airavata between two garudas on a lintel at Banteay Srei.

that were about 17.7 inches thick, usually from 12 to 19.6 inches wide, and 23.6-31.5 inches long (40 cm thick, 30 to 50 cm wide, 60-80 cm long) though the length was sometimes as much as 6.5 feet (2 meters). Sandstone, once extracted by means of fire, was cut into blocks that could weigh as much as four tons and were laid without mortar and rubbed smooth while dry. The stones were transported by means of barges on the canals or by wagons on land, and they were laid with the aid of elephants: the holes that can be seen in the stones were used to secure the ropes for carrying them.

The Khmers were not great engineers: they built their edifices with rather shallow foundations made of a layer of laterite rubble, and the stones were not always laid in the best fashion.

The static cohesion of the structures was based on the force of gravity and was achieved with carpentry techniques: large blocks or monoliths were adopted with iron anchors,

57 The tympanum of a 'library' at Banteay Srei.

The evolution of the lintels

Arched with three medallions and side makaras (pre-Angkor style).

Naga supported by a central mask and with makaras at the ends (pre-Angkor style).

Garland festoon (Preah Ko style, 9th century).

Spiral festoon supported by a central kala; Khleang style, first half of 11th century.

Lintel with a mythical scene, Baphuon style (second half of the 11th century).

Festoon with floral volutes including figures and with a kala in the middle (Bayon style, 12th-13th century).

59 top A sandstone tympanum from Banteay Samré.

59 bottom Detail of a garland.

cramps, joints and braces. The stones were laid horizontally instead of being staggered vertically, which would have avoided the creation of spaces between one block and another. On the other hand, the Khmers were exceptional architects and adopted stereometric techniques to obtain the correct optical perception of the monument: they imperceptibly decreased the height and width of the roofs of the *prasat* and the pyramid terraces and steps of the stairways, applying the law of the proportional reduction of scale to make the structures look taller than they actually were. Furthermore, they recessed the terraces in the opposite direction of the entrance so that the monument would not appear to jut forward; and they studied the proportions of the different parts of the monument in order to impart the greatest possible theatrical effect.

Iconographic Sources

The sources of Khmer iconography were the great Indian epic poems: the *Mahabharata* and the Ramayana, the collections in the Purana, and the 'ancient stories' that celebrated the gods and their exploits.

The *Mahabharata*, written during the period from the 4th century B.C. to the 4th century A.D., describes the primordial conflict between the gods and demons, which ends with the triumph of the former. The narration is fast moving and consists of various parallel stories. Vyasa, the future compiler of the *Mahabharata*, is the secret son of Satyavati, who married King Shantanu and had two children, both of whom died without offspring. The queen then forces Vyasa to copulate with the two widow princesses in order to ensure the continuation of the royal stock. Thus are born Dhritarashtra and Pandu, respectively the fathers of the 100 Kaurava brothers and the five Pandava brothers. In fact, the latter are the children of the gods, because Pandu can no longer have relations with his two wives because of a curse and therefore asks one of them, Kunti, to use a magic formula she knew to persuade the gods to have children with the queens.

60 From the Ramayana, the Battle of Lanka. Angkor Wat, third gallery, west side, north wing. The scene is dominated by a central, catalyzing figure.

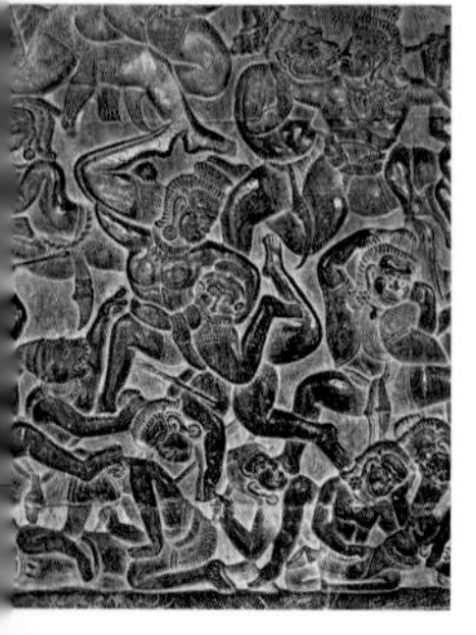

Pandu dies because he had relations with the younger wife, who has herself burned at her husband's funeral pyre, and the widow Kunti goes with her children to live in the court of her brother-in-law Dhritarashtra, so that the five Pandavas are raised with their cousins. Bitter rivalry divides the youngsters and the Pandavas, who, having survived several ambushes laid by the Kauravas, end up getting involved in a bogus game of dice and are thus sent into exile. Twelve years later they return to claim their kingdom, but the Kauravas refuse to grant it, thus triggering war. Krishna, the incarnation of the god

Vishnu and a relative of both the rival groups, offers to help either with his person or his soldiers: the Kauravas choose the army and the Pandavas choose Krishna. The battle ends with the victory of the Pandavas, who, after a long and prosperous reign, ascend with their common wife Draupadi to Heaven.

The *Ramayama* narrates the exploits of Rama, another incarnation of the god Vishnu, and was written between the 2nd century B.C. and the 2nd century A.D. by the legendary Valmiki, who participated directly in the events of the poem, since he is the hermit who takes in Sita, the wife repudiated by Rama. However, in the Khmer area there were partial or different versions of the official Hindu poem, and these were the inspiration for of the *Reamker*, the Cambodian version of the feats of Ream, or Rama, which was

***60-61** From the Ramayana, the Battle of Lanka. Angkor Wat, third gallery, west side, north wing. Note the corsets with floral decoration, which may be leather armor.*

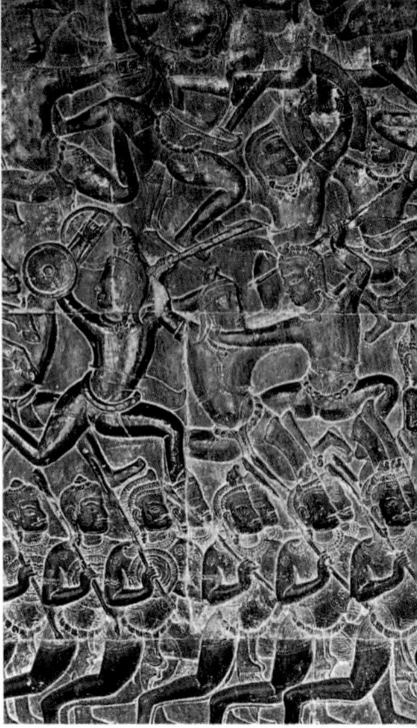

62-63 From the Mahabharata, the Battle of Kurukshetra. Angkor Wat, third gallery, west side, south wing. A warrior on a chariot, the favorite vehicle of the mythical heroes.

compiled in the 17th century and is still quite popular.

After a palace conspiracy hatched by one of the queen mothers, Rama, the official heir to the throne, is sent into exile in the forest. Sita, the beautiful wife whom the prince won during a joust, decides to follow her husband and is joined by Lakshmana, Rama's younger brother.

While in the forest the two meet the female demon Surpanakha, who first tries to seduce Rama and then Lakhsmana. The latter, quite annoyed, cuts off the witch's ears and nose. Surpanakha, thirsting for revenge, goes to her thousand-headed brother Ravana, the invincible lord of the island of Lanka, begging him to kill Rama and deviously extolling the divine beauty of Sita.

Ravana secretly goes to the forest, where he is struck by the princess. Having sent Rama and Lakshmana with a ruse, he approaches Sita in the guise of an old, errant ascetic and kidnaps her. Rama and Lakshmana search desperately for the princess and in the meantime they help Sugriva, the deposed king of the monkeys, to defeat his rival Valin and regain his throne. Sugriva promises to help Rama and sends Hanuman, who is the son of the god of wind can thus fly, out on a reconnaissance mission, and he discovers that Sita is being held

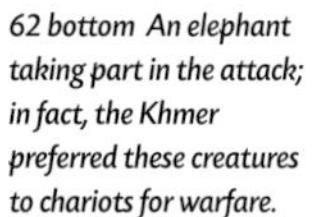

62 bottom An elephant taking part in the attack; in fact, the Khmer preferred these creatures to chariots for warfare.

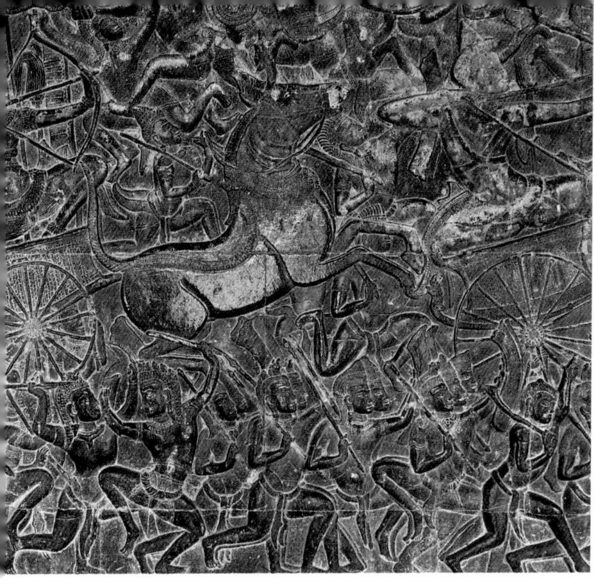

63 Detail of the battle.

prisoner on the island of Lanka. The monkeys then build a bridge to link the island to the mainland and go to the enemy city.

After days of bloody combat Rama and Ravana face each other and the demon is killed. Rama returns in triumph to his capital Ayuthya and ascends the throne, but Sita has to prove she is still pure with a trial of fire, since she lived with another man. Emerging from the flames is Agni, the god of fire, who proclaims the woman's chastity and gives her back to her husband. But shortly afterward the people speak out against the queen and Rama is obliged to repudiate his wife, who finds refuge in the hermitage of the wise man Valmiki, where she gives birth to twins. A few years later the two boys happen to meet their royal father, who immediately recognizes them and takes them to his palace. Rama also decides to have Sita at his side once again, provided she agrees to undergo another trial. Sita calls upon the goddess Earth to testify to her chastity, and the goddess, having ascended the throne, takes the hapless queen away.

Another myth that was a recurrent motif among the Khmer artists is the so-called "Churning of the Ocean of Milk" narrated in the *Mahabharata* and in some *Purana*.

Before the world began the gods were continuously menaced by the demons and they asked Vishnu to help them. This god advised them to gather some *amrita*, ambrosia that guaranteed immortality. This prodigious nectar lay in the depths of the ocean of milk, and in order to extract it the gods needed the aid of the demons, to whom they promised a share of the ambrosia. After the agreement had been made, the Mandara, the cosmic mountain, was placed in the ocean with the Vasuki serpent tied around it to as to make a churn. The two groups began to pull the snake, the gods holding onto its tail and the demons its head, thus

64 top From the Mahabharata, the Churning of the Ocean of Milk. Angkor Wat, third gallery, east side, south wing. Top: the left end, with the head of the demons supporting the serpent Vasuki.

causing the mountain to spin like a beater, but the mountain began to sink, so Vishnu, having assumed the guise of a turtle, descended into the ocean to become a foundation for Mandara.

During the churning, marvelous beings and objects of creation emerged from the ocean, as well as a poisonous miasma, which Shiva immediately swallowed in order to save the universe. At last the physician of the gods appeared, holding the cruet of ambrosia. The demons shouted for their share of the nectar, but at that moment Vishnu appeared in the guise of Mohini, a splendid girl, and distracted them with her fascinating beauty so that he was able to distribute the ambrosia among the gods, who, now strengthened, were able to defeat their adversaries and become lords of the universe.

64 bottom The demons.

65 top The celestial cohorts at the left end observe the scene.

65 bottom Vishnu is in the middle, on the turtle.

Hindu Deities

The three fundamental phases of the universe – creation, preservation and destruction – are controlled by three deities that are not separate entities but rather different aspects of the single, ineffable and unfathomable Absolute. This *Trimurti*, the 'Triple Form' of the Divine, consists of Brahma, Vishnu and Siva.

Brahma, whose primary function is to create the world, is depicted with four faces, because he is the lord of the origin and hence governs the expansion of space toward the four cardinal points, and also because from his mouth there emerge the four *Vedas*, the most ancient and sacred Hindu texts. Besides his four heads, another distinguishing feature of this divinity is the circle of pearls around the lower third of his chignon.

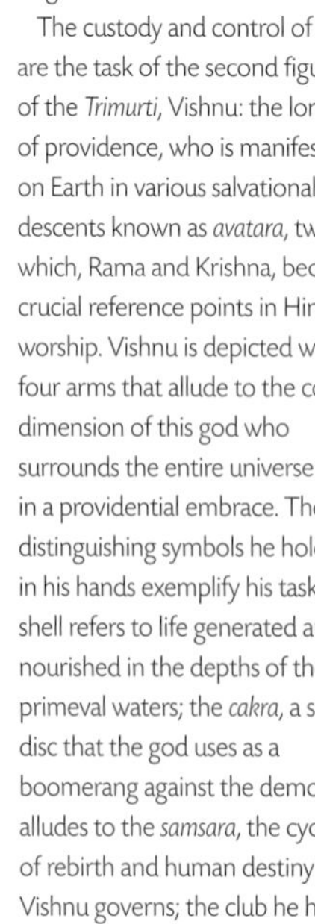

The custody and control of life are the task of the second figure of the *Trimurti*, Vishnu: the lord of providence, who is manifested on Earth in various salvational descents known as *avatara*, two of which, Rama and Krishna, become crucial reference points in Hindu worship. Vishnu is depicted with four arms that allude to the cosmic dimension of this god who surrounds the entire universe in a providential embrace. The distinguishing symbols he holds in his hands exemplify his task: the shell refers to life generated and nourished in the depths of the primeval waters; the *cakra*, a sharp disc that the god uses as a boomerang against the demons, alludes to the *samsara*, the cycle of rebirth and human destiny that Vishnu governs; the club he holds is both a scepter and a cudgel, underscoring the function as both guide and judge typical of a ruler; lastly, the globe represents the Earth. Vishnu's head is crowned by the *mukuta*, a miter whose shape has varied over the centuries.

When the time has come for the

66 A 10th-century representation of Shiva. Musée Guimet, Paris.

66-67 The four-headed Brahma, creator of the Universe (10th century). Musée Guimet, Parigi.

universe to be reabsorbed into the cosmic night, the god Shiva, the third component of the *Trimurti*, dissolves it so that another world can rise up.

Shiva, celebrated in Khmer culture with many names, is the principal deity, distinguished by his trident, a weapon that refers to the numerous triads in the Hindu world: the three deities of the *Trimurti*, the three levels of the universe (Earth, atmosphere and sky), the three dimensions of time, and so forth. His third eye lies in the middle of his forehead, symbolizing omniscience that transcends the duality represented by the other two eyes, and his hair is twisted into a *jatamukuta*, the tall chignon worn by ascetics, decorated with the crescent. In order to avoid the curse by which it was doomed to disappear, the moon had taken refuge on Shiva's head and in exchange was able to regenerate itself periodically. Besides his human aspect, Shiva was very often depicted in his symbolic and phallic guise as the *lingam*, and this essential image harked back to the ancient stones of Khmer animistic religion. Placed in the fields as the emblem of the *genius loci* that supported the soil and guaranteed fertility, the *lingams* were means of communication between the earth and the sky, between the ancestral world and

68 Lakshmi, the wife of Vishnu (12th-13th century). National Museum, Phnom Penh.

69 Harihara, the syncretic form of Vishnu and Shiva (7th century). National Museum, Phnom Penh.

70 Vishnu, the protector of the universe (11th-12th century). National Museum, Phnom Penh.

the world of the living. The axial, phallic and royal symbolism of the *lingam* was therefore rather common in the local context. Often consisting of three parts – square, octagonal and round – it combined the three deities of the *Trimurti*. Furthermore, the *snanadroni*, the round base of the *lingam*, which ends in a lip, was the symbol of the *yoni*, the female Principle or matrix, and thus referred to the Great Goddess. And the purpose of the *snanadroni* was to contain and channel the ablutions made on the *lingam*.

Vishnu and Shiva shared the favors of the sovereigns and the people. The two divinities, however, were never in conflict; on the contrary, they eventually merged into Harihara, the syncretic form of Hari, or Vishnu, and Hara, or Shiva.

Vishnu's consort is Lakshmi, the beautiful goddess of fertility and abundance, also known as Shri, or Prosperity, who accompanies Vishnu on his many descents to the Earth in various guises.

Shiva's consort, more than any other female divinity, embodies the ambivalence of the primeval Great Goddess: she is Uma, a sweet and devoted wife, but is also Durga, the female warrior who exterminates demons. Despite their voluptuous bodies, the female figures are extremely poised and, one might say, almost virginal. Besides the Great Goddess there are the *devata* or goddesses, a generic name for what are probably celestial nymphs, the Indian *apsaras*, even though this term is used in Khmer art to indicate images of female dancers.

Among the other principal Hindu divinities worshipped by the Khmer is Ganesha, the elephant-headed god who is the son of

Parvati; Skanda, the war god generated by Shiva; Indra, king of the gods; Varuna, lord of the ocean; Agni, the fire deity; Yama, who judges the dead; Kama, the god of love. Of Indian provenance were the servants and attendants, the minor gods, the semi-divine beings, and the powers of evil. There are also the *vahana*, the 'vehicles' of the gods: Brahma and Varuna sit on the *hamsa*, the goose with a striped throat; Vishnu and Lakshmi fly on Garuda, the vulture with human features; Shiva and Uma ride on the bull Nandi; Skanda on the peacock, Yama on the buffalo, Agni on the rhinoceros, Indra on the three-headed elephant Airavata. The sacredness of these animals, inherited from very ancient times, is manifested in the feral features the gods sometimes have. For example, Vishnu also manifests himself as the boar Varaha, or as the man-lion Narasimha.

There are very few statues remaining in the Angkor temples; most of them are in Siem Reap Conservation Area and in the splendid National Museum of Phnom Penh.

71 left Vishnu, the protector of the universe (11th-12th century). National Museum, Phnom Penh.

71 right Ganesha, son of Uma and Shiva (7th-8th century). National Museum, Phnom Penh.

Archaeological Research at Angkor

Although it was no longer the capital, Angkor was never completely forgotten because Angkor Wat, which had been converted into a Buddhist monastery, continued to be a popular place of worship. The site was known to the first Portuguese and Spanish missionaries and adventurers in the 16th century, and was described in detail by the Portuguese Diogo do Couto.

Most probably the manuscript, written in 1614, was not an account of a trip made by do Couto himself, but a compilation of descriptions related by the Capuchin friar Antonio da Magdalena, who visited Angkor in 1585-88. Later on the site was mentioned in a letter by the French friar Chevreul, dated 1668.

The oldest map of Angkor Wat was drawn up sometime between 1623 and 1636 by a Japanese pilgrim who was convinced he had arrived at Jetavana, the Indian monastery where Buddha presumably spent most of his life. The map was copied in 1715 and was acknowledged as the plan of the famous temple only in the first two decades of the 20th century.

In 1858 the French missionary Charles-Émile Bouillevaux, who had stayed in Angkor Wat for two days in 1850, published a short account. That same year the French naturalist Henri Mouhot went to Indochina and traveled there until 1861, when he died in Laos. The material he wrote was published posthumously in English and French, and *Journeys in the Kingdoms of Siam, Cambodia, Laos and other Parts of Central Indo-China* was published in French in 1863 and in English in 1864.

72-73 View of Angkor Wat from the Picturesque Album, which was added to the Journey of Èxploration to Indochina by Louis Delaporte, published in 1873.

73 The reconstruction by Louis Delaporte of one of the gates of Angkor Thom.

Thus Europeans began to be interested in Angkor and the Khmer civilization. The German ethnologist Adolf Bastian stressed its links with Indian culture, the Scottish photographer John Thomson saw cosmological symbolism in the temples and his rich documentary material attracted the attention of the art historian James Ferguson, who included the Khmer temples in his *History of World Architecture* (1867).

In the meantime Cambodia had become a French protectorate, and in 1866 France had organized an exploratory expedition of the Mekong River, headed by the naval officer Ernest Doudart de Lagrée. After stopping at Angkor, which at the time belonged to the Kingdom of Siam (present-day Thailand), Doudart went as far as southern Laos, where he visited many Khmer monuments, which he described later. One of the members of the

expedition, the painter Louis Delaporte, executed the drawings in the *Picturesque Album* that accompanied the two volumes of the *Journey of Exploration in Indo-China*, an account of the expedition published in 1873. Enamored of Khmer art, Delaporte brought back many examples to Paris, where a few years later he managed to establish the Indo-Chinese Museum at the Trocadéro.

The material and drawings exhibited at the 1878 Universal Exposition in Paris stirred the interest of the most famous architects of the time, one of whom, Lucien Fournereau, went to Angkor in 1887 and 1888, where he took photographs, drew sketches and plans, made casts and gathered numerous finds.

The year 1879 witnessed the first decipherment of Sanskrit on the part of the Dutch scholar Hendrik Kern, whose work was continued by the Frenchmen Auguste Barthe and Abel Bergaigne, who in 1885 published a volume of inscriptions dating from the 5th century B.C. on. Their fellow countryman Étienne Aymonier – a naval officer and a scholar of the ancient Khmer language who was charged with drawing up the first archaelogical inventory in Cambodia – made 350 reproductions of engravings, which were published in 1900-03

in three volumes. Fundamental works were written by Louis Finot and above all by Georges Coedès, who published eight volumes of Sanskrit and ancient Khmer inscriptions that allowed scholars to reconstruct the salient stages of the history of Kambuja and to decipher between the lines, as it were, the political, social and cultural policies of the time.

At present there are about 1,200 inscriptions, most of which are sculpted in stone and written in Sanskrit, sometimes with poles inserted into the stone, and in ancient Khmer. The writings are in an alphabet derived from the one used by the Pallava dynasty of south India and from a 9th-century script from north India. The Sanskrit inscriptions are poems that celebrate the genealogy and feats of the sovereigns, as well as the monuments they built. The dates are based on the Indian Shaka era, which begins in A.D. 78. The epigraphs in ancient Khmer, which appear for the first time during the reign of Ishanavarman (early 7th century A.D.), are on the other hand written in prose and consist mostly of lists of persons, land and possessions of the various temples used to operate the sanctuaries and to support the priests and those persons responsible for religious services.

74-75 The reconstruction of Angkor Wat by the architect Lucien Fournereau exhibited in the 1889 Paris Salon.

The École Française d'Extrême Orient (French School of the Far East or EFEO) was founded in 1898, marking the beginning of organized archaeological research in the area. The architect Henri Dufour and the photographer Charles Carpeaux worked at Bayon and prepared the first monograph concerning this site. Siam gave Angkor and the adjacent provinces back to Cambodia in 1907, and the following year the Conservation des Monuments d'Angkor, the registry in charge of safeguarding the local monuments, was established, with Jean Commaille as its first registrar and curator.

The catalogue of the Khmer monuments was compiled by another military figure, the colonial infantry officer Lunet de Lajonquière, who is to be gratefully acknowledged for writing the *Archaeological and Descriptive Inventory of the Cambodian Monuments*, which was published in 1902-11 and lists 910 monuments, plus others marked as "bis." This work was gradually enlarged by Henri Parmentier, the EFEO archaeological services director, and in 1922 Erik Seidenfaden added the Khmer monuments in the Thailand provinces.

Unfortunately, this period also marked the beginning of spoliation, the most famous instance of which was carried out by André Malraux at Banteay Srei in 1924.

The Angkor Archaeological Park was founded in 1925 and two years later Philippe Stern, the art historian of the Musée Guimet in Paris, reconsidered and redefined the chronology of Khmer art and civilization by working from the inscriptions, without ever going to Cambodia. In 1929 Stern's work was elaborated and developed by George Coedès, the EFEO director, who established the definitive chronology of Khmer civilization and its artistic styles on the basis of the inscriptions. The second curator, Henri Marchal, who held this post from 1920 to 1933, began to utilize the technique of anastylosis, already adopted with success in Indonesia, for the restoration of the Khmer monuments. This procedure, which is still used, consists in totally disassembling an edifice – adding numbers to each piece and at the same time gathering all the fallen parts – and then putting it together again in keeping with a meticulous plan of reconstruction and consolidation. The missing pieces are replaced by others that blend in harmoniously with the edifice but that can easily be recognized as new because of special labeling. Brought to perfection by Bernard-Philippe Groslier, the technique of anastylosis was applied for the first time in 1931 on the temple of Banteay Srei.

Interest in Khmer civilization increased so much that in the colonial exposition of 1931, held in Paris, Angkor Wat was reproduced by the architects Charles and Gabriel Blanche, father and son, who spent six years to elaborate their work, and was decorated by the sculptor Auberlet.

In the meantime, the digs continued at Angkor: with Georges Alexandre Trouvé (the new curator who unfortunately died in an accident in 1935 at the age of thirty-three), the main well of Bayon was excavated, yielding the colossal Buddha that had been dumped there. Maurice Glaze, who was in charge of the digs from 1936 to 1945, reconstructed the *prasat* of Bakong, among other things. The EFEO was always a focal point for prominent, fascinating figures, from the architect Henri Parmentier, head of the archaeological service, to the Russian nobleman Victor Goloubeff who, making use of the airplane for the first time, was able to photograph the Angkor monuments from above and thus discovered in 1931 that Phnom Bakheng had been the center of the first Angkor. The painter George Groslier, an aficionado of Cambodian dance, promoted the School of Cambodian Arts with the aim of reviving local traditions and handicrafts and also established the original nucleus of the Archaeological Museum of Phnom Penh. His son Bernard-Philippe was the last curator in the 1960s, following Henri Marchal who had again worked at the EFEO in 1947-53 and Jean Laur, who was in charge from 1954 to 1959.

Devastated by the terrible genocide perpetrated by the Khmer Rouge from 1970 to 1975, Cambodia remained 'off-limits' until 1991. Once the situation had returned to normal after much difficulty, the country could again take care of its monuments. Angkor was made part of the UNESCO World Heritage List in 1992. At present many restoration works are being carried out with the aid of foreign countries and under the control of the Cambodian government body Autorité pour la protectione du Site et l'Aménagement de la Région d'Angkor, generally referred to as APSARA.

77 A group of French explorers among the ruins of Angkor in 1867.

ALL GUIDED TOURS LEAD TO THE FIRST EXAMPLES OF SACRED BUILDINGS IN KHMER ARCHITECTURE, CHARACTERIZED BY SHARP LINES AND BEAUTIFUL DECORATIONS.

The Refinement of the Early Period

78 Lintel of the Preah Ko, with a garuda in the middle.

Introduction

THE EARLIEST EXAMPLES OF KHMER ARCHITECTURE REFLECT HIGH-QUALITY WORKMANSHIP, NOT ONLY FOR THE HARMONY AND CLARITY OF THE LINES, BUT ALSO THANKS TO THE ELEGANCE OF THE DECORATION. FOR EXAMPLE, IN THE ROLUOS GROUP – PREAH KO, LOLEI AND BAKONG – THE LINTELS ARE AMONG THE MOST BEAUTIFUL IN ALL KHMER ART.

The suggested itineraries follow the development of the two basic types of sacred site: the 'longitudinal' temple and the 'mountain' or 'pyramid temple,' of which the second type was first built on natural rises, as is the case with Phnom Bakheng. The so-called longitudinal temples – Preah Ko, Lolei, Bei Prasat, Bat Chum, Leak Neang and Prasat Kravan – are articulated in a series of *prasats* that have different functions but are similar in structure, with the extraordinary exception of Prasat Kravan, the only temple in the entire Angkor area that has sculptural reliefs inside *cellae* that were once painted. These give us an idea of how splendid the wall

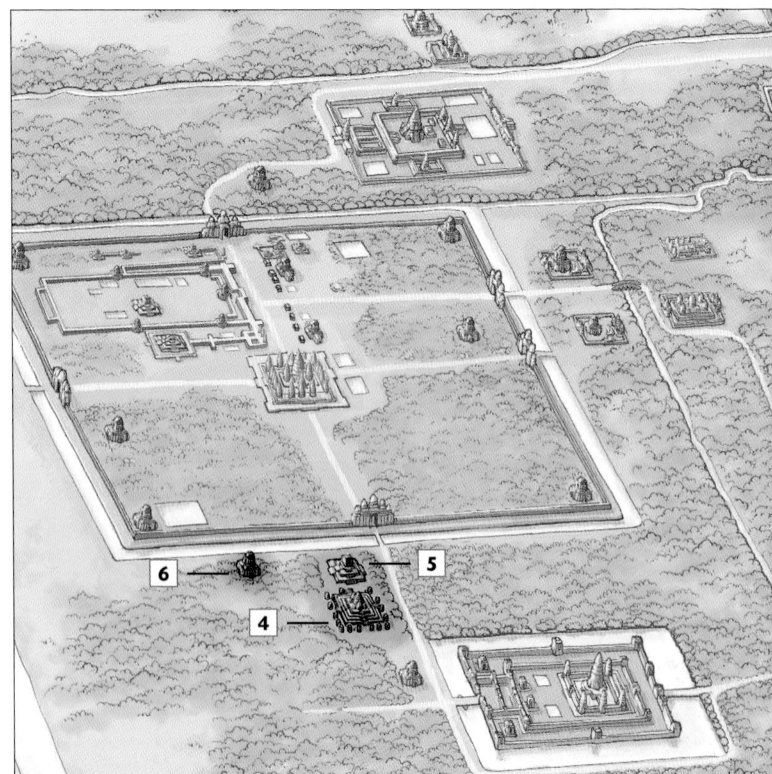

paintings must have been. At the same time the pyramid constructions gradually evolved from the Baksei Chamkrong, which because of its small size seems to be almost a prototype, to the elaborate complexes of the East Mebon and Pre Rup.

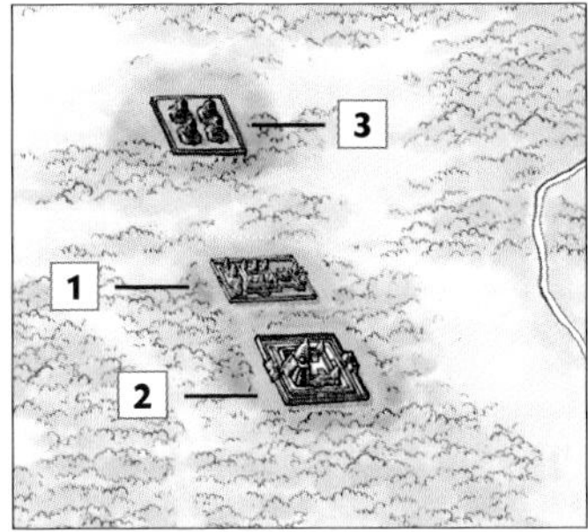

Legend

1 Preah Ko
2 Bakong
3 Lolei
4 Phnom Bakheng
5 Baksei Chamkrong
6 Bei Prasat
7 Prasat Kravan
8 Bat Chum
9 The East Mebon
10 Prasat Leak Neang
11 Pre Rup

Preah Ko

The Preah Ko, the temple of the 'Sacred Bull,' named after the three statues of Nandi located there that corroborate the temple dedication to Shiva, is situated in present-day Roluos, about 7.5 miles (12 km) southeast of Angkor.

The History

Here there once stood Hariharalaya, the 'Seat of Harihara,' which Jayavarman II dedicated to the syncretic divinity that incorporated Vishnu and Shiva; his grandson Indravarman I, who ascended the throne in 877, built the Indratataka here, the 'Pool of Indra' that guaranteed the water supply. After inaugurating the grandiose Khmer hydraulic architecture, in 879 the king had Preah Ko built in honor of his ancestors; it is located 984 ft (300 m) to the right of the main road.

Preah Ko was surrounded by a residential area of about 815 acres (330 hectares), which in turn was bounded by a moat 1312 x 1640 ft (400 x 500 m), including two ponds.

Visit

The temple proper is bounded by two enclosure walls with *gopura* entrances. The second enclosure, measuring about 311 x 324 (95 x 99 m), crosses eastward by means of a cruciform *gopura*, some parts of which have survived. Beyond it, along the access causeway there are two rectangular edifices that are perpendicular to the avenue and are preceded by porticoes. Two other similar structures made of laterite with the entrance facing east, run parallel to the causeway. Next to the southeast structure is a square brick 'library' with very thick walls and windows with brick grilles. The north and south sides of the second enclosure walls have one rectangular hall each, while two other similar constructions (with porches at the ends, however) extend to the west.

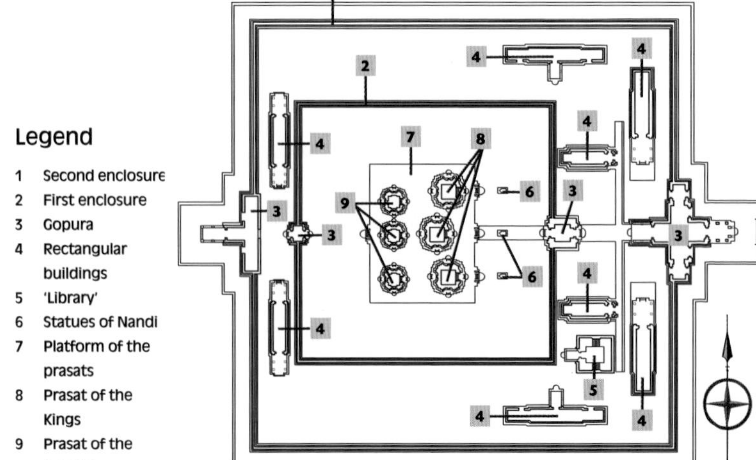

83 top The Preah Ko, preceded by statues of the bull Nandi.

83 bottom left Traces of stucco decoration.

83 bottom right Sandstone niche with a dvarapala, the 'gate guardian.'

The first enclosure, 193 x 197 ft (59 x 60 m), has almost totally disappeared: it houses a platform 82 x 101 ft (25 x 31 m), access to which is afforded by three stairways with guardian lions on the buttresses. Aligned on this terrace are six brick *prasats* on a sandstone platform that are oriented to the east and surmounted by four progressively receding stories.

84 top left Detail of lintel with cornice with praying figures.

84 top right The northwest prasat.

84 bottom Detail of blind door with grotesque mask.

The front towers, dedicated to the king's male ancestors, are larger than the three back ones, which are named after the consorts of three kings. The central *prasat* in the front row, the largest of all, housed the image of Jayavarman II in his posthumous and deified guise of Parameshvara. The north tower, to the right, contained the deified effigy of Rudravarman, Indravarman I's grandfather on his mother's side, and the south one had an image of Prithivindravarman, Indravarman's father. The respective wives of these kings – Narendradevi, Dharanindradevi and Prithvindradevi – were venerated in their divine form: in fact, the suffix devi means "goddess."

The outer walls were dressed with lime mortar, which was used like stucco to create highly refined decoration that is still visible in many points. In the wall recesses there are sandstone niches. On the *prasats* of the ancestors these contain figures of *dvarapalas* or gate guardians, and on the towers dedicated to the consorts there are *devatas*, female divinities. Sandstone is also the material used for the doors, which are flanked by beautiful, elaborate slender octagonal columns, with lovely floral decoration on the jambs of the false doors. The pilasters of the doors on the east *prasats* bear elegantly carved inscriptions. The lintels are among the most beautiful in all Khmer artistic production: the arch consists of a festoon whose ends have heads of *nagas* and *makaras* moving in different directions. Among the foliage are figurines of horsemen, and in the middle of the festoon is the

85 top Festooned lintel with knights and makaras at the ends.

grotesque mask of Kala, the all-devouring demon, or of the god Vishnu riding on Garuda, his half-human, half-bird vehicle. Above the lintel is a frieze representing mostly praying figures that acts as a connecting element with the pediment above it.

85 bottom Blind door with devata guardians in the niches.

Bakong

Bakong is the official temple mountain of the city of Hariharalaya; it lies about 1640 ft (500 m) past Preah Ko and was built in 881 at the behest of Indravarman I.

The History

Although there a couple of earlier examples, Bakong – the first to be built in sandstone, and larger and more articulated that its predecessors – is considered the prototype of the temple mountain. The outermost enclosure is bounded by a moat about 2624 ft (800 m) per side and included the residential area.

Visit

Having arrived by road at the north side of Bakong, it is advisable to go round the complex in order to enter via the east *gopura* in the second enclosure, which has some ruins of the laterite wall. Between the second enclosure, a rectangle 1312 x 1476 ft (400 x 450 m), and the first one there is a 197 ft (60 m) wide moat. The moat is traversed by two causeways on an east-west axis that are the extension of two of the four axial avenues of the capital city of Hariharalaya: your walk winds among the galleries of gigantic stone *nagas* that foreshadow the stupendous serpent balustrades of the Khmer classic age. In a strip of land about 82 ft (25 m) wide were the dwellings of the temple personnel, and the northeast corner has a modern Buddhist monastery built in the traditional Khmer style.

The first enclosure wall, made of laterite, bounds a rectangle 393 x 525 ft (120 x 160 m) that is accessible by way of four cross-shaped *gopuras* and which includes several edifices. Two rectangular structures built in laterite are perpendicular to the avenue of the east *gopura*; they were the prototype of the later continuous galleries. Both the northeast and southeast corners of the enclosure have two rather small *prasats* with a square plan and thick brick walls,

86 left Detail of the blind door of one of the prasats at the base of the pyramid.

86 right Panel with demons on the south side of the last step of the pyramid.

Legend

1 First enclosure
2 Gopura
3 Access avenue
4 Rectangular buildings
5 Chapels
6 Prasat with air vents
7 Prasat
8 Pyramid
9 Accesses to the stairways
10 Small prasat
11 Central prasat

while the northwest and southwest corners have only one *prasat* each. The best-preserved towers are those to the southwest. The ventilation openings in the upper part have led some scholars to advance the theory that these edifices were cremation chambers. At the sides of the access road

87 Acess causeway of the first enclosure, with the remains of a pedestal of a Nandi statue.

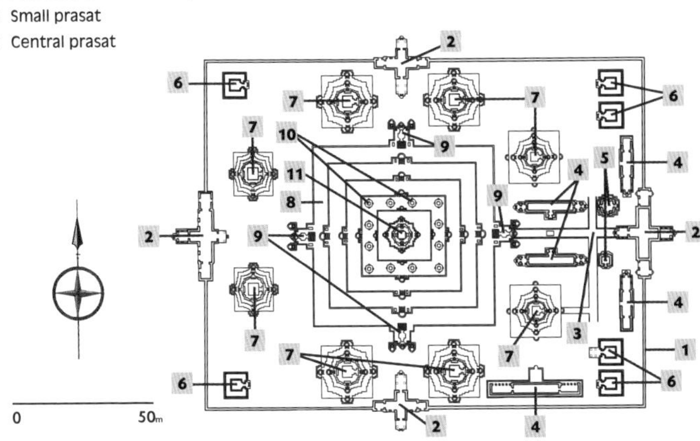

88 The central prasat surrounded by twelve smaller prasats.

entrance are the remains of two chapels; the foundation of the one to the north has been found.

Two other rectangular constructions with porches at either end and laid out horizontally along the avenue, were later additions; lying along the south wall are the ruins of a third tripartite structure that was constructed at the same time as Bakong. The destination of these edifices is unknown.

The other eight brick shrines arranged around the base of the temple pyramid were, as the foundation stele informs us, dedicated to the eight *murti* or 'aspects' of Shiva – the Sun, Moon, wind, earth, water, fire, ethereal space and the *atman* or soul. There may very well be cosmic symbolism in these monuments, as the number eight refers to the eight regions of space and the deities that protect them. The structure of the *prasats* is the usual one: a platform with four access stairways, the temple on a terrace base, progressively receding and smaller stories that reproduce the façade, tall pediments set over one another, and a lotus bud crowning the temple. In the interior the walls were covered with red plaster and the wooden ceilings concealed the intrados of the vault. Particularly noteworthy elements here are the lintels and the sandstone column frames of the freestanding doors, as well as the false doors, among which those on the northeast tower are especially interesting. There are *dvarapalas* and *devatas* in the niches, and the walls bear traces of stuccowork that reveal the mastery of the Khmer craftsmen: the best

preserved examples are on the *prasats* on the west side.

In the middle of the Bakong complex is an almost square pyramid, made of sandstone blocks; it is 220 x 213 ft (67 x 65 m) at the base and 65 x 59 ft (20 x 18 m) at the top, articulated in five tiers for a total height of 46 ft (14 m). This artificial mountain represents Mt. Meru and its five levels, each of which is linked to a category of mythical beings: *nagas, garudas, rakshasas* or demons, *yakshas* or tree deities, and *devas*, that is, the gods of the Vedic cosmogony. Four small rectangular structures give access to the axial

***89 top** One of the two halls at the sides of the access avenue.*

***89 bottom** A Lintel of one of the prasats at the base of the pyramid.*

90 top The central prasat guarded by lions.

90 bottom left North access pavilion of the pyramid stairway.

stairways: the northern one is the best preserved and should be carefully observed, partly because this kind of construction is unusual in Khmer architecture. An elegant threshold in the shape of a half-circle precedes the stairs, and guardian lions protect the flights. In order to create correct optical perception, the height and width of the stairways decrease imperceptibly as one ascends, since the Khmer architects made use of the law of proportional reduction, or false perspective, which up to that time had been applied only for the roofs of the *prasats*. For the same reason, that is, to correct the

90 bottom center Devatas of the middle prasat sculpted in sandstone.

90 bottom right Detail of the door frame colonnettes on the middle prasat.

perspective effect, each of the pyramid tiers recedes slightly to the west.

On the corners of the first three tiers of the pyramid there are statues of elephants celebrating the mythical animals that hold up the Earth: their presence aims at imparting magically to the construction the power and stability that distinguish them. Furthermore, the elephant is the mount of Indra, the king of the gods, and of the terrestrial sovereign. On the fourth tier are twelve sandstone tower shrines with entrances to the east surmounted by three stories, which once housed twelve *lingams.* The walls of the fifth and last tier were once completely covered with relief sculpture decoration, the first grandiose exploit of its kind: sadly, nothing has survived except a panel with effigies of demons on the south side.

The central *prasat*, reconstructed thanks to the skillful anastylosis effected by Maurice Glaize in 1940, is a 12th-century construction on a high platform and with a serrate plan, three blind doors and one real door, and a four-level top with an acroterion in the shape of a lotus: this housed the royal *lingam* Sri Indreshvara, which was consecrated in 881.

The Hariharalaya complex draws inspiration from Hindu cosmological symbolism: Bakong represents Mt. Meru, the first moat is the cosmic ocean from which the mountain emerges, the next dry area is the land inhabited by humankind, which in turn is bounded by mountain ranges – the city walls – and by another ocean – the second moat.

***91** Behind the guardian elephant are two of the prasats at the base of the pyramid.*

Lolei

Built by Yashovarman I in 889 in memory of his father Indravarman and his royal ancestors, the temple complex was the first in a series to be located on an artificial island, in this case in the middle of the Indratataka *baray*, which is now dry.

Visit

Lolei is about 8 miles (13 km) from Siem Reap and can be reached by turning left a little after the junction for Bakong and then proceeding for about 1968 ft (600 m).

On the terrace, which is 295 x 262 ft (90 x 80 m) and is traversed by rainwater drainage canals, are four towers. Scholars are not sure whether the architects had intended to build two other towers, as in Preah Ko. The brick *prasats* stand on sandstone foundations, face the east, and are surmounted by a four-tier pyramid structure. The workmanship of the doors is simply stupendous: the real doors are flanked by elegant slender columns, have inscriptions on the jambs and are topped by

92-93 The northeast prasat and the modern monastery in the background.

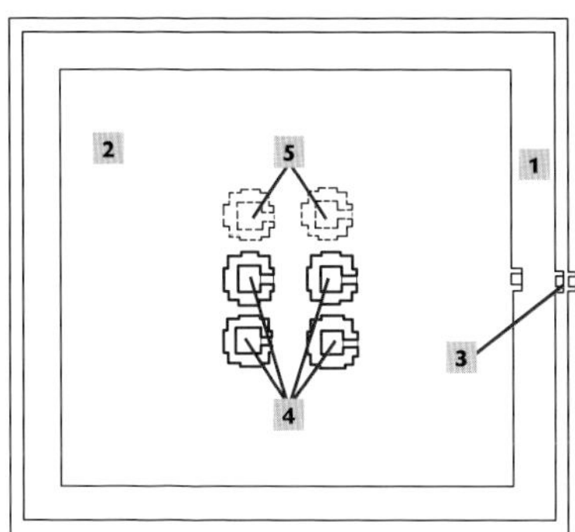

Legend

1 Artificial island
2 Platform
3 Stairways
4 Existing prasats
5 Supposed prasats

beautifully carved lintels, while the false doors have finely decorated stiles. The east towers are decorated with niches containing *dvarapala*, while those to the west have *devatas* with elegant folded garments. The modern monastery that has been built around the monument – the meeting hall on the left and the monks' wooden dwellings to the right – is in a certain sense the Buddhist spiritual heir of the *ashrama*, the ancient Hindu hermitage built together with the Lolei temple.

93 top Niches with dvarapalas and the east doorway, made of sandstone.

93 bottom Details of the decoration on a blind door.

Phnom Bakheng

Phnom Bakheng, the 'Strong Hill,' is a natural rise more than 230 ft (70 m) high on which was built the temple mountain of the same name, the center of Yashodharapura (the 'City that Bestows Glory'), which was the new capital of Yashovarman I, who was crowned in 889.

94 top The northeast 'library.'

The History

Surrounded by an enclosure wall 2.5 miles (4 km) per side and by moats that are 656 ft (200 m) wide placed between parallel embankments that served as elevated causeways, and with four axial entrances, this was one of the largest cities in the world at the time, even though it certainly included rice paddies and cultivated plots of land.

In order to supply his new capital with water, the king ordered the excavation of the Yashodharatataka, better known as the East Baray, which is more than 22,965 ft (7000 m) long and 5905 ft (1800 m) wide, fed by the Siem Reap River which, partly transformed into a canal, became the east moat of the city.

The seat of the royal *lingam* Yashodhareshvara, the 'Lord who bears glory,' the temple is accessible both via the original, steep stairway flanked by roaring lions and by the so-called Elephant path that starts off on the left (about a 20-minute walk).

Visit

Winding along the platform of about 393 x 607 ft (120 x 185 m) that supports the edifices, is the access avenue with the remains of pillars: after passing by a brick *stupa* and a small pavilion with Buddha's footprint, both of which date from later periods, you will come to the first laterite wall and another one that has the ruins of an entrance pavilion. Beyond the two sandstone 'libraries' is the temple

94 bottom left Brick tower at the base of the pyramid.

94 bottom right Small sandstone temples on the steps of the pyramid.

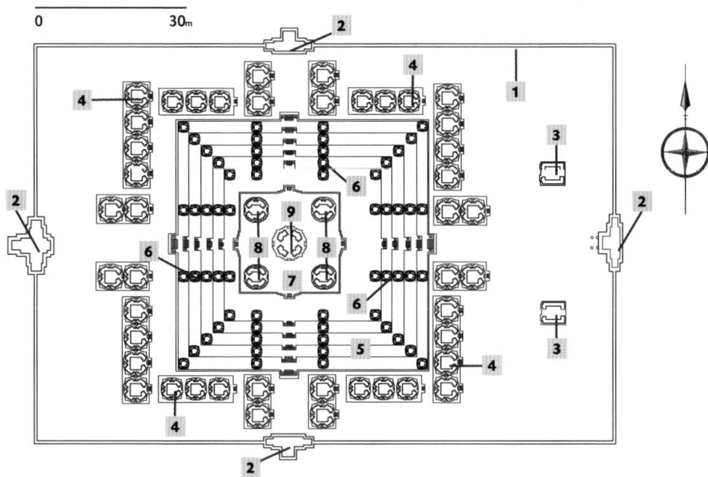

pyramid, which has five tiers that decrease in size as they go upward; they were cut out of the rock in the hills and were faced with sandstone, and have four axial stairways with ramps flanked by tall buttresses dominated by sculptures of guardian lions. All around the pyramid there stood 44 brick towers with the entrance

Legend

1 Inner enclosure
2 Gopura
3 'Libraries'
4 The 44 brick prasats around the base of the pyramid
5 Pyramid steps
6 Sandstone prasats, 12 on each level
7 Platform of the quincunx
8 Corner prasats
9 Central prasat

95 top Decoration in the central prasat.

94-95 Overall view of the temple.

***96 top** Small temple with four stories ending in lotus buds.*

***96 center** Bust of a guardian lion of the stairways.*

***96 bottom** Foundation and lingam on the last terrace.*

to the east and three blind doors, with the exception of the towers on the east side, which open out both eastward and westward, and the eight towers that flank the four stairways, which have one or two real doors. The best-preserved tower is on the west side.

When approaching the east stairway, you will note to the left a lovely statue pedestal near a foundation stone with holes. Facing each of the stairways was a Nandi bull: you can see the remains of these in front of the west and north stairways, while at the base of the south stairway a polychrome Nandi was recently restored.

The pyramid is 249 ft (76 m) per side at the base and 154 ft (47 m) at the top, and it is 43 ft (13 m) high. Each terrace has twelve sandstone shrines, four at the corners and two beside each stairway, with a single entrance facing east; these structures have four stories and are topped by a lotus bud.

On the fifth, top terrace a platform 101 ft (31 m) per side and a little more than 5 ft (1.5 m) high, with traces of molding, once housed five *prasats*; these were also made entirely of sandstone and laid out in a quincunx – four *prasats* on the corners and one in the middle – and all of them had four real doors. Very little remains of the corner towers: traces of the two are on the east façade and the *lingam*, since Bakheng was dedicated to Shiva.

The central *prasat*, which is larger and has stucco decoration, no longer has its superstructure, which was the same as that of the terrace *prasats*. Noteworthy are the sinuous plant ornamentation and, in the niches on the sides of the west and north doors, the *devatas* with their lovely pleated garments that were carved directly in the sandstone and no longer sculpted in stucco. On the east abutment of the north door, an inscription from a later period dates this temple to the year 907. Here from the top, to the southwest you have a fine view of the Angkor Wat reservoir and temple.

Bakheng is one of the most powerful representations of Mt. Meru and seems to encompass further magical-esoteric meaning. The total number of the *prasats* at Bakheng, which symbolically rotate around the central one, is 108 (44 at the base, 60 on the terraces, and four on the summit): this number alludes to the totality of the universe and is also the result of the multiplication of the number 27, the days of the sidereal month, by four, which stands for the four phases of the moon (new moon, waxing moon, waning moon, full moon). Furthermore, there are 108 principal names of Shiva and the same number of grains of the *mala*, the Indian crown-rosary.

The central *prasat* is the sum of all the others and, having the *lingam* in its *cella*, it refers to the *bindu*, the point-instant that gives rise to space and time, hence the universe. The *bindu* is the first manifestation of the Absolute Principle and the *lingam* is its image: by the same token, however, both allude to the reabsorption of the manifest

97 top Guardian lion of the stairways and small temples.

97 bottom The five terraces of the pyramid.

99 Detail of the stucco decoration showing praying figures among vegetation.

world, which returns to its origin and is dissolved in it. The central *prasat*, the supreme peak of Mt. Meru, is the beginning and end of the construction, as well as the symbol of the governing power that descends to the Earth, radiating from the *cella*, and of its guardian – the king – who upon his death is deified and ascends to the heavens.

An analysis of the distribution of the other *prasats* shows that each of the five terraces of the pyramid has 12 small towers, for a total of 60. In Indian tradition there are 12 signs of the zodiac and there are 12 animals in the Chinese astrological cycle, from which the Khmer drew inspiration. Moreover, it takes the planet Jupiter about 12 years to revolve around the Sun and pass through the entire zodiac, which the Sun traverses in a year. The cycle of Jupiter lasted 60 solar years, divided into five cycles of 12 years each, and this was also part of Khmer culture. Therefore, with its five terraces and their 60 *prasats*, Bakheng reproduces an entire Jovian year by utilizing the numbers 12 and 60.

Furthermore, the seven levels of Bakheng, that is, the base, the five terraces and the platform of the quincunx, refer both to the levels of Mt. Meru and to the *saptaloka*, the 'seven heavens' of the Hindu deities. Again, it seems that the particular placement of the towers and their different sizes are such that the viewer standing in the middle of each side, that is, in correspondence with the cardinal points, should see always and only 33 *prasats*; and in fact there are 33 principal Hindu divinities. Mt. Meru hosts the court of the gods, and its reproduction in the middle of human cities reasserts the king's desire to have his capital mirror divinity. The various inscriptions underscore this by comparing Yashovarman to Mt. Meru, to Indra the king of the gods, and to Brahma, Vishnu and Shiva, the divinities of the Trimurti.

98 left Niche with devata and stucco decoration on the central prasat.

98 right Devata on the ruins of one of the corner prasats of the quincunx.

Baksei Chamkrong

Baksei Chamkrong is located 820 ft (250 m) from the south gate of Angkor Thom, on the left-hand side of the road. The beginning of its construction is ascribed to Harshavarman I, but it was probably finished by his successor Rajendravarman in 947 and dedicated to Shiva.

100 top Niche with devata, east entrance.

100 bottom Detail of one of the three blind doors.

Visit

The name the locals gave to this temple means "bird with sheltering wings" and supposedly refers to a large bird that saved the life of a Khmer king by shielding him against his enemies with its wings.

Baksei Chamkrong is a relatively small monument, a little more than 42 ft (13 m) high, a square pyramid with four laterite steps, the first of which measures 88 ft (27 m) per side. The sanctuary single tower, which stands on a sandstone base with molding, is made of bricks and stucco, while the frames of the doorway and the blind doors are made of sandstone, as was customary.

The east lintel is particularly noteworthy: under the row of praying figures in the small arches, the god Indra on his three-headed elephant Airavata towers over two flower garlands that coil around the ends of the lintel; in the garlands is Ganesha, the god with an elephant's head, who is using his trunk as a mount. On the abutments of the doorway two exquisitely carved inscriptions relate the genealogies of the Khmer kings up to the year 947. The corners of the tower walls

Legend

1 Pyramid
2 Axial stairways
3 Platform
4 Prasat

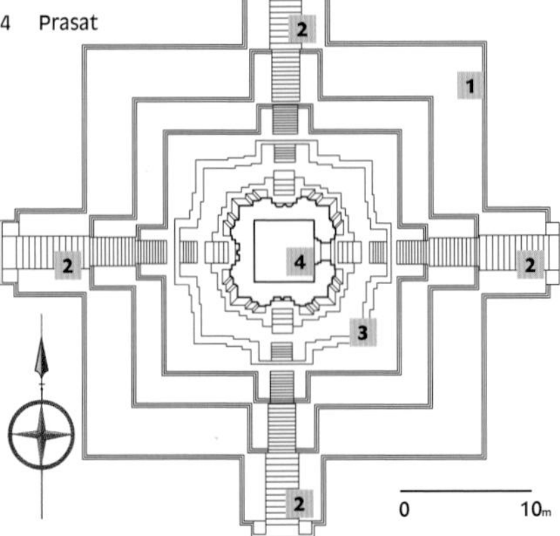

101 top In the interior is a recent statue of Buddha.

101 center An epigraph in ancient Khmer on the door.

100-101 The Baksei Chamkrong viewed from the east.

bear traces of *devatas*. The roof of the *prasat* consists of three levels that reproduce the façade. Four very steep axial stairways with massive buttresses lead to the summit of the temple, which was once in an enclosure whose entrance was surmounted to the east by a *gopura*.

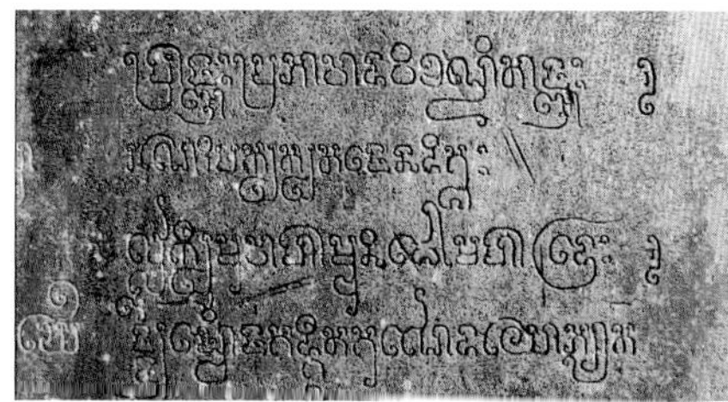

Bei Prasat

Just before taking the approach to South Gate of Angkor Thom, at your left is an agglomeration of ruins that culminates in the 'Three Towers' complex: Bei Prasat, built in the 10th century.

102 top Detail of a door.

102 bottom View of the three towers of the lovely prasats.

Visit

Once past a laterite foundation with the remains of a brick tower, you will come upon another one with a *lingam* and the frame of a sandstone door. Farther on, another platform made of laterite supports a central brick tower with three well-preserved levels that are progressively smaller, and two side towers without roofs, with sandstone doorways to the east and blind doors on the other sides. The precisely wrought five-sided colonnettes with pendants and garlands, and the floral lintel with Indra on the three-headed elephant Airavata on the central tower and with lions on the south tower, are in the 10th-century Bakheng style. The north tower is interesting because its unfinished lintel reveals the construction techniques employed.

Prasat Kravan

Prasat Kravan, the 'Cardamon Sanctuary' that was once surrounded by a reservoir, lies 2624 ft (800 m) before Banteay Kdei and is thought to date from the period of Harshavarman I.

Visit

The five brick *prasats*, which have been skillfully restored, are aligned on the same platform, which is 34 ft (10.4 m) wide and 115.4 ft (35.2 m) long and, like almost all the temples at Ankgor, have entrances to the east. The roof of the central tower has four progressively receding tiers with porticoes framing the blind doors, which emphasizes the vertical thrust of the monument. At the sides of the entrance gate you can see the outlines of large *dvarapalas*, the temple or gate guardians. Of the four side towers, only the southernmost still has its original two stories, while the others have only one.

Inside the central *prasat* there are splendid bas-reliefs, once covered with polychrome varnish, depicting various aspects of Vishnu, the Lord of Providence and second component of the Trimurti, to whom the temple is dedicated. On the left-hand wall the god is taking the three steps in the guise of Vamana, the 'dwarf,' an aspect assumed to destroy the power of King Bali. On the opposite wall Vishnu is depicted

103 top Detail of a figure adoring the Great Goddess in the north prasat.

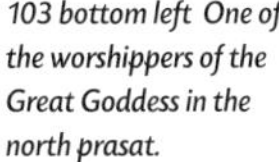

103 bottom left One of the worshippers of the Great Goddess in the north prasat.

103 bottom right Vishnu depicted on Garuda, north wall of the central prasat.

Legend

1 Central Prasat
2 Corner Prasat
3 Pedestals for the lingams
4 Bas-reliefsi

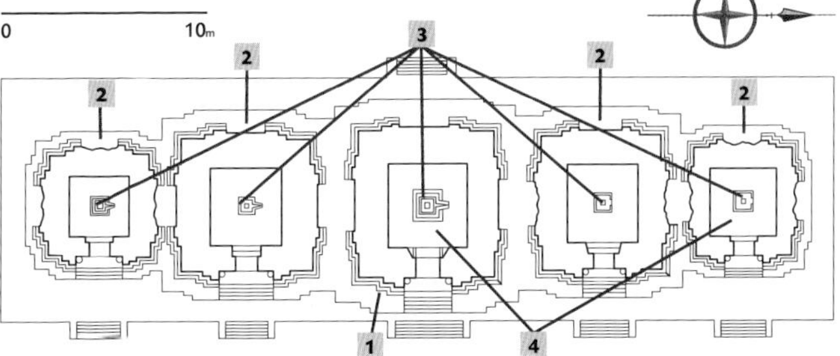

104-105 The five prasats viewed from the east side.

on his vehicle Garuda, part human and part bird of prey, with the disc, the shell, the earthen ball and the club-scepter, while on the central wall he is represented with eight arms in all his majesty, surrounded by praying figures and surmounted by an arch that frames a large lizard, perhaps an iguana, whose symbolism is yet to be determined.

The *cella* of north *prasat* has two female images, the one on the west wall with four arms and that on the north wall with two. Although these are portraits of Lakshmi, Vishnu's consort, the attributes she is holding – a disc, trident, prod for elephants and lotus – link her to the wife of Shiva and could therefore be identified as Devi, the Great Goddess.

104 bottom left Vishnu taking the three steps, south wall of the central prasat.

104 bottom right The Great Goddess on the west wall of the north prasat.

105 left Entrance to the central prasat, with a dvarapala in the niche.

105 right A worshipper in a detail of the bas-relief of Vishnu on Garuda.

Bat Chum

An unpaved road about 1312 ft (400 m) to your right after Prasat Kravan leads to this site. After skirting a pool you arrive at the temple, which is surrounded by an enclosure wall with a moat and a *gopura* to the east. About 1984 ft (300 m) from the sanctuary there was a pool considered sacred that was linked to the sanctuary via a paved avenue. A single foundation supports three brick *prasats* with an entrance facing east and blind doors. Consecrated in 960, the temple was built by Kavindrarimathana, the Buddhist architect of King Rajendravarman. On the door of every tower is a eulogistic inscription in verse praising the architect, composed by different authors. The colonnettes are extremely elegant. On the lintel of the central shrine a row of praying figures surmounts Indra riding an elephant between two lions; the lintel of the north sanctuary has floral volutes mounted by figures. On the floor of the central *prasat* archaeologists discovered a *yantra*, an esoteric diagram in seven parts that go to make up a checkerboard pattern with 49 squares containing the letters of the Sanskrit alphabet.

At present the temple is being restored.

The Myth

Despite the fact that he belonged to the lineage of the demons, Bali was a just king, but the great power he had acquired upon ascending the throne had disturbed the gods. They therefore asked Vishnu to help them, and he agreed. He had himself reborn in the form of a Brahman dwarf and went to Bali, asking him to grant a wish: a plot of land that he could measure with three paces. Surprised and amused, the king granted him his request and then Vishnu again took on his divine stature, and with the first step crossed over the Earth, with the second stride he traversed the atmosphere and with the third the sky, thus regaining the worlds of the gods, sending Bali to the underworld, which became his kingdom.

The East Mebon

The East Mebon, about 1 mile (1.6 km) north of Pre Rup, was built by the architect Kavindrarimathana for King Rajendravarman on an artificial island in the East Baray measuring 374 x 383 ft (114 x 117 m).

The History

Dedicated to Shiva in 952, it consists of a three-tier structure and could be reached only by boat. The presence of four landing stages made it impossible for the cruciform gopuras to have projecting elements, which were therefore set back slightly in the wall of the second enclosure, which could be reached by means of stairways guarded over by statues of lions. On the corners of the first and second terrace are the magnificent freestanding elephants, the best preserved of which is to the northwest.

Visit

Past the east entrance, running along the perimeter is a continuous series of rectangular edifices made of laterite whose purpose is unknown; they once had double-gable wooden roofs. The *gopuras* of the first enclosure are also indented, except for the west one, which is well worth seeing because of the beautiful lintel to the east with a sculpture of Vishnu as a man-lion disemboweling the demon Hiranyakashipu. On the second tier, on either side of every *gopura* there is a brick *prasat*, eight in all, that house the same number of *lingams* dedicated to the eight murti or "aspects" of Shiva: sun, moon, wind, land, water, fire, ethereal space and *atman* or "soul." Among the

Legend

1 Landing stages
2 Second enclosure
3 Gopura
4 First level
5 Rectangular edifices
6 First enclosure
7 Elephants
8 Second level
9 Brick prasat
10 Rectangular brick constructions
11 Third level
12 Corner prasats
13 Central prasat

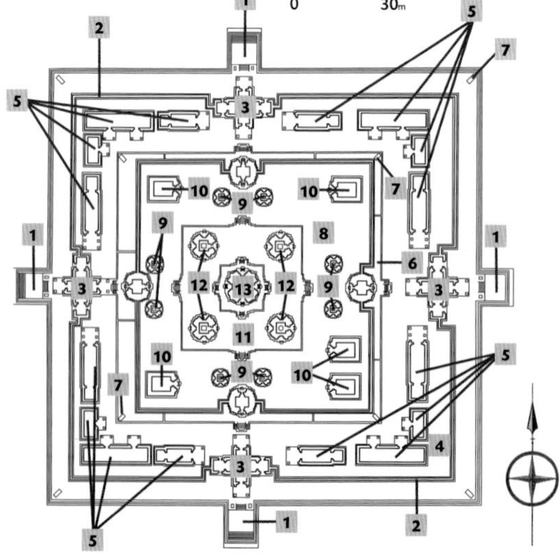

107 top Detail of a lintel with gods riding an elephant.

107 center Aerial view of the temple.

107 bottom left The west gopura in the first enclosure.

107 bottom right Detail of the wings of a blind door.

lintels on these *prasats* mention should be made of the two southern ones: the southeast tower on the east side has Garuda with a miter, and the southwest tower, again on the

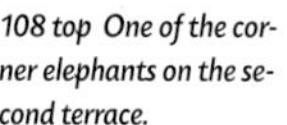

108 top One of the corner elephants on the second terrace.

east side, features Indra on the elephant Airavata in a beautiful swirling garland with small figures. Again on the second tier,

108 bottom The third terrace of the southeast prasat.

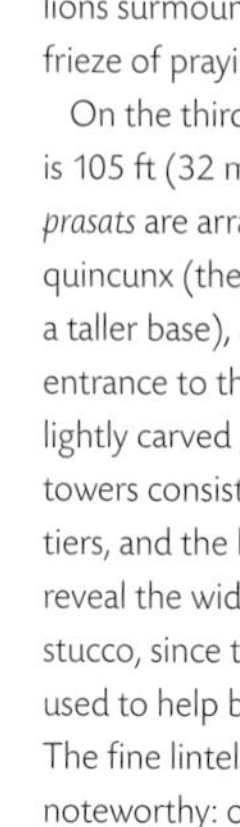

there are five rectangular constructions, four placed on the corners: the east lintel on the northeast one has three lions surmounted by a lovely frieze of praying figures.

On the third terrace, which is 105 ft (32 m) per side, five *prasats* are arranged in a quincunx (the central one on a taller base), all with a single entrance to the east flanked by lightly carved guardians. The towers consist of four receding tiers, and the holes in the walls reveal the widespread use of stucco, since the holes were used to help bind this material. The fine lintels are particularly noteworthy: on the middle *prasat* on the east side, Indra is riding on Airavata, while on the south side Shiva is on Nandi, and on the west one his son Skanda, the god of war, is seated on a peacock. The southeast *prasat*, with its beautifully wrought details, has a carving of Shiva and Nandi on the south lintel; on the east side of the northwest prasat we again see Indra as well as Ganesha riding on his own trunk, while the south lintel has a figure dancing on a lion and a row of praying figures. In the northeast *prasat* Indra once again dominates the east lintel, and there are two rampant lions on the south one.

Prasat Leak Neang

This is a small brick *prasat* that lies just beyond the Pre Rup, about 328 ft (100 m) immediately to the right. An inscription dates this monument at 960 and its only decoration is a lintel with Indra on the three-headed elephant.

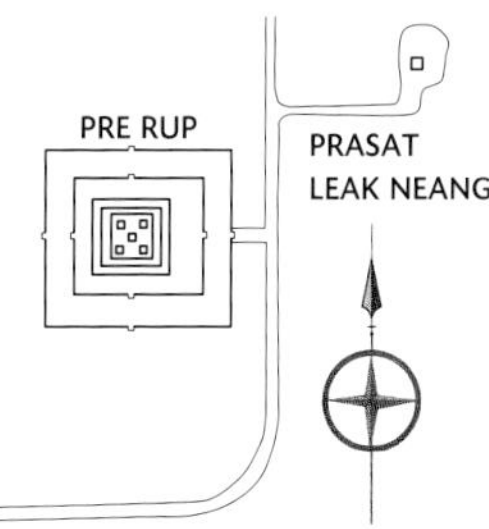

108-109 The third terrace of the southeast prasat.

Pre Rup

You arrive at Pre Rup 1.3 miles (2 km) after skirting the Srah Srang. A masterpiece of Kavindrarimathana, Rajendravarman II's architect, this is one of the most important temple mountains and marks the transition from the pre-classic to the classic period.

110 Devata with stucco decoration in the central prasat.

Visit

On the temple's east façade, between the first and second wall, are five brick towers; the sixth was never finished and only its foundation exists. These *prasats* were probably added at a later stage. They open out to the east and have slender columns and sculpted lintels, including the fine one on the southernmost tower representing Narasimha, the part-lion incarnation of Vishnu. On the three other sides of this first terrace there are rectangular edifices parallel to the inside wall.

This first enclosure, which measures 362 x 295 ft (80 x 90 m), contains four small *gopuras*: past the eastern one, you will come to the famous 'sarcophagus,' with the ruins of four columns per side that may have supported a wooden roof. Parallel to the 'sarcophagus' are two 'libraries' facing west, while along the wall are nine long rectangular buildings or galleries made of laterite that once had tile roofs with wooden frameworks. These long structures, whose purpose is still unknown, later gave rise to the development of

Legend

1 Second enclosure
2 Gopura
3 Prasat
4 First terrace
5 Long edifices
6 First enclosure
7 Second terrace
8 'Sarcophagus'
9 'Libraries'
10 Stele kiosk
11 Pyramid
12 Small prasats of the lingams
13 Corner prasats
14 Central prasat

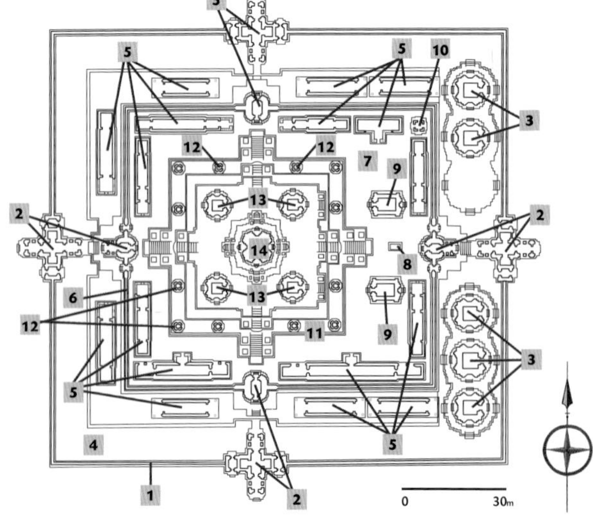

The History

Probably the site of a new capital, Pre Rup was built on an artificial rise made of laterite and was consecrated in 961 or the beginning of 962. Its modern name, 'Turning the Corpse,' derives from a 'sarcophagus' on the site that was supposedly connected to a burial ritual still practiced today, during which the shape of a body is created several times with the ashes of the deceased and oriented in different directions. It is more probable that the supposed sarcophagus was really a pedestal of Nandi, the bull that is the mount of Shiva, to whom Pre Rup is dedicated, even though there are grooves in the stone that seem to indicate the existence of a lid.

The temple consists of two terraces, on the second of which there is a three-tier pyramid made of laterite, and a series of walls, only two of which have survived. The outer wall, made of laterite and measuring 394 x 426 ft (120 x 130 m), was bordered by the moat. The four axial entrance pavilions topped by *gopuras* are made up of a cruciform body with two annexes and porches, a structure that became very popular in the classical period.

111 top Detail of a lintel with the three-headed elephant Airavata.

continuous outer galleries.

In the northeast corner of the enclosure is a small laterite kiosk that may have housed a stele, topped by a roof in the shape of a 'priest's hat' – i.e. a domed structure with a square plan – that ends in a lotus and has a corbeled vault in the interior. As there is a pool in the middle of the kiosk with a drainage canal, Cambodian

111 bottom Aerial view of the temple.

112 top Supposed stele kiosk.

scholars feel that the chamber was used to wash the bones left over after the cremation ceremony and that the stone element mentioned above was in fact a sarcophagus. Next to the kiosk, on the north side of the first enclosure, a hall – different from the other outer ones because it consists of a single chamber, not a tripartite one – up to some time ago housed the foundation stele of Pre Rup: 298 lines of text, which make it one of the longest existing compositions in Sanskrit.

The three-tier pyramid covers an area of 151 ft (46 m) per side at the base and 111 ft (34 m) at the top, and is up to 39 ft (12 m) high. On the first tier are twelve small *prasats* housing *lingams* and with a single entrance to the east. Both the first and second level are made of laterite, while the third one is cased with sandstone and on its east side the main stairway is flanked by two side stairways that lead nowhere and were inserted merely as decoration.

The towers of the quincunx are made of brick; the central *prasat* stands on a two-tier

112 bottom Overall view of the temple.

113 The 'sarcophagus' at the east base of the pyramid.

platform, with axial stairways guarded by lions, and it is surmounted by five stories that reach a height of 55 ft (17 m). The *cella* opens out to the east and there are blind doors on the other sides: this shrine once housed the Rajendrabhadreshvara *lingam*, in which the name of the sovereign was merged with that of Shiva Bhadreshvara, the ancient tutelary deity of Chenla. The plan of the central *prasat* is repeated in the four corner towers, which are smaller – 19.5 ft (6 m) per side instead of 26 ft (8 m). On the niche walls you can see guardian figures that were once covered with stucco made of lime mortar. The octagonal columns framing the entrances have elegant decoration and the sandstone doors are skillfully wrought.

Like the East Mebon, the Pre Rup temple seems to have had a two-fold function: the architectural features classify it as a temple mountain, the custodian of the tutelary *lingam* of the kingdom, but the dedication of the corner towers to relatives of the king also underscore its function as a shrine for ancestors. What is certain is that the King Rajendravarman wanted to transform it into his mausoleum. From that moment on it is quite probable that the temple of the *Devaraja*, with whom the living sovereign associated himself, became his tomb upon his death.

TOUR ITINERARIES LEAD TO THE TEMPLES THAT DISPLAY THE ART OF THE CHISEL AT ITS BEST. AT THE TEMPLE OF TA PROHM YOU CAN STILL IMAGINE PART OF THE ANCIENT SPLENDOR THAT ENRAPTURED THE FIRST EXPLORERS.

Masterpieces of Carving

114 Banteay Srei, nicchia con dvarapala sulle pareti del prasat principale.

Introduction

Divided into three parts – the portico, the pavilion of the worshippers and the *cella*, the longitudinal temples of Banteay Srei, Thommanon and its twin Chau Say Tevoda re-elaborate the Indian temple type with solutions of ethereal beauty.

At Banteay Srei the decorative genius of the Khmer reaches its zenith, favored by the small size of the buildings and by the particular type of sandstone used: all the available space is finely carved, and the plastic compositions of the pediments achieve unsurpassed expressive heights. A short distance away, a walk in the jungle in search of sacred figures sculpted in the bed of a river reveals the ancient Khmers' veneration of nature. By contrast, the impact of the bare walls of the Ta Keo temple, which was never finished on its high, steep pyramid, reveals the cyclopean framework of the Khmer temples and attests to the courageous determination of the builders, whose works of civil architecture have unfortunately disappeared almost entirely, with the exception of such bridges as the Spean Thma.

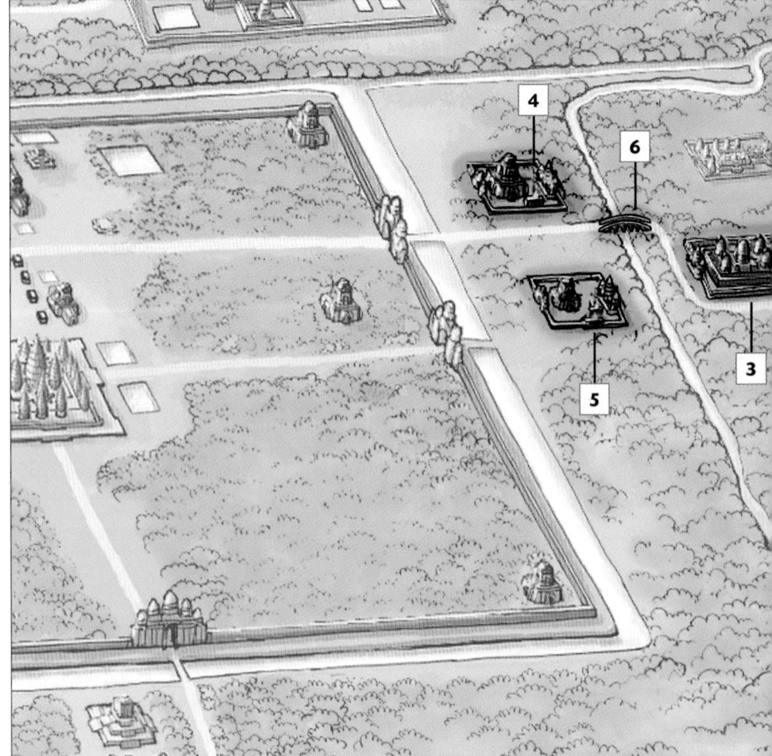

After the refined harmony of the small longitudinal temples and the austere power of the mountain temples, a visit to the chaotic and fascinating Ta Prohm, a veritable holy citadel, will rekindle the thrill and amazement of the explorers who first discovered this site.

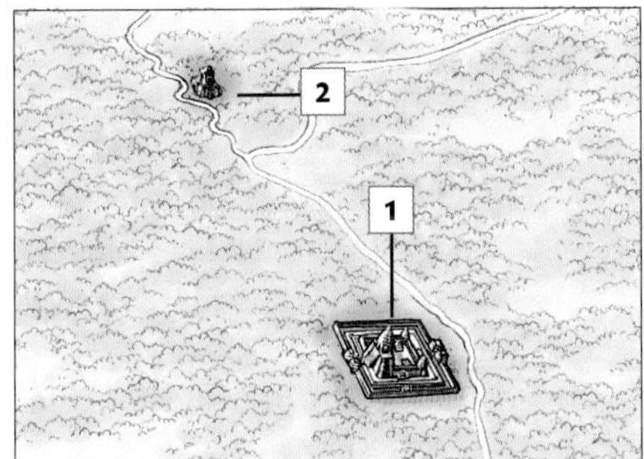

Legend

1 Banteay Srei
2 Kbal Spean
3 Ta Keo
4 Thommanon
5 Chau Say Tevoda
6 Spean Thma
7 Ta Prohm

7

Banteay Srei

The first of the Angkor monuments to be rebuilt (1931), it is now one of the best preserved.

118 top *Gopura of the second enclosure.*

Legend

1 Gopura
2 Processional avenue
3 Porticoes
4 Pavilions
5 Perpendicular pavilions
6 Third enclosure
7 Pools
8 Second enclosure
9 Long edifices
10 'Libraries'
11 Platform
12 Side prasats
13 Central prasat

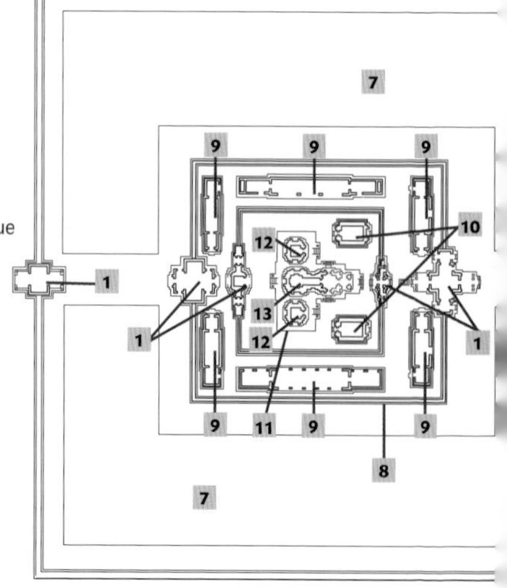

118 bottom *Typanum of the south 'library.'*

The History

Banteay Srei is situated about 12.5 miles (20 km) northeast of the East Baray: take the road 984 ft (300 m) south of the East Mebon and turn left at the village of Pradak; after about 11 miles (18 km) there is a fork in the road, where you again turn left. At the village of Banteay Srei, about 984 ft (300 m) past the Siem Reap River the temple will appear at your left.

The small and extremely elegant temple was not built by a sovereign but by two Brahmans, Yajnavaraha and his younger brother Vishnukumara, who were wealthy landowners in the area that at the time was called Ishanapura. The modern name Banteay Srei ("Citadel of the Women") was given by the locals, who were fascinated by the voluptuous devatas sculpted in the temple niches.

The complex was finished in 967: the total length, measured from the outermost east entrance pavilion to the western one in the third enclosure, is over 656 ft (200 m). The foundation stele (968) provides information concerning the patrons, especially Yajnavaraha, a highly cultured aesthete who commissioned a horizontally laid-out temple in the purest Hindu architectural tradition.

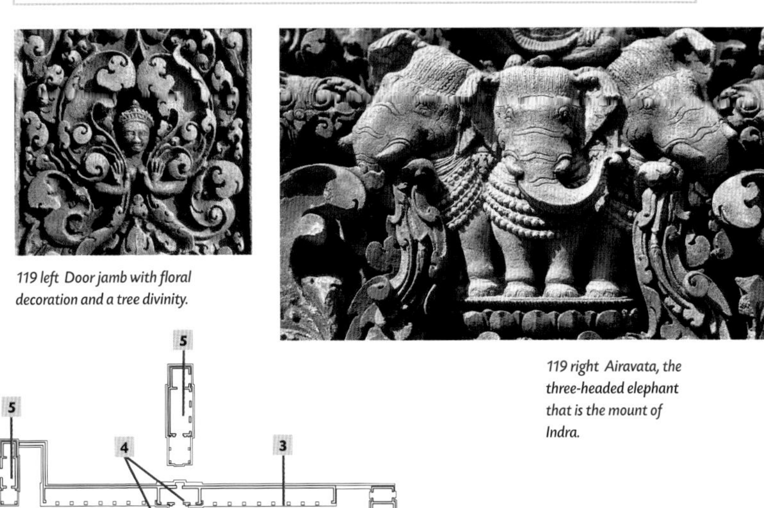

119 left Door jamb with floral decoration and a tree divinity.

119 right Airavata, the three-headed elephant that is the mount of Indra.

120 top Pool and access of the second enclosure

120 bottom Lintel of one of the tripartite edifices in the second enclosure.

Visit

Banteay Srei consists of three concentric enclosures preceded on the east side by a processional causeway 220 ft (67 m) long, accessible by means of a slightly cruciform *gopura*, with two porticoes and two small passages with very tall thresholds. There is no trace of a fourth enclosure; some scholars think a wooden one was associated to the pavilion, while others view the latter as a sort of propylaeum.

The access causeway winds between two wings with small pillars, flanked by arcades for its entire length. These edifices consist of a laterite wall whose outward side is blind and which has square sandstone pillars facing the inside. The arcades were once covered with a tile roof; they are interrupted at about their halfway point by two pavilions that each have two windows and a portico facing the causeway and an access facing outward on the opposite side. Perpendicular to these pavilions are, to the north (on your right), a construction with a portico, two windowed chambers, and a pediment with Vishnu in the guise of Narasimha, the lion-man, disemboweling the demon Hiranyakashipu; and to the south three similar edifices, the middle one of which is larger and the side ones having one more room. There is a sculpture of Shiva and his consort Uma on the bull Nandi in the pediment of the central building. The avenue continues and widens into a courtyard, lined with two small and perpendicular tripartite structures.

A cruciform *gopura* with two porticoes that once had a wooden roof and with inscriptions on the abutments, opens onto the third enclosure, a laterite wall which measures

312 by 360 ft (95 x 110 m), and contains the lake that surrounds the temple. The pediment lies on the ground at right and its carving narrates the demon Viradha's attempted kidnapping of Sita. The second enclosure, also made of laterite, surrounds a courtyard measuring 138 by 126 ft (42 x 38 m) that can be entered by way of another cruciform *gopura*, preceded and followed by porticoes and flanked by two side chambers with two entrances. The pediment, with flamboyant acroteria and spiral ends, is extremely elegant. The carving of Gajalakshmi in the tympanum under the portico is noteworthy. Beyond the *gopura* are the ruins of the sculpted bull Nandi. Little remains of the west gopura, which is a simpler structure in brick. Six laterite edifices flank the inner wall of the second enclosure, each with three chambers that once had tile roofs on a wooden framework.

The first enclosure, a square 78 ft (24 m) per side, was made of bricks but has virtually disappeared, while its east entrance pavilion is made of sandstone and has a tapered structure: the axial passageway with its corbeled vault is flanked by two rooms on each side that decrease in height and are so

121 top The south 'library' and gopura in the first enclosure.

121 bottom Gopura affording access to the processional avenue.

122 top 120 top One of the yaksha guardians of the temple platform stairways.

small that they are almost useless. For that matter, the temple itself is small, as was only proper for a structure built by anyone except the king. The east pediment has a carving of Shiva Nataraja, the Lord of Dance, while the west one shows his consort in the frightful guise of Durga on the lion which is killing the demon buffalo.

The west *gopura* in the first enclosure is rather unusual in that it has only one entrance and it is therefore probable that it was another shrine rather than an entrance pavilion.

In the southeast and northeast corners of the first enclosure are two 'libraries' made of sandstone with some laterite elements inserted in them, covered with corbeled bricks and a false triple nave made up of an imitation attic with real windows flanked by half-roofs with segmental barrel vaulting. Three lobate pediments inserted into one another lend a soaring effect to the two structures and also contain the most beautiful tympana in all Khmer art: on the east pediment of the south 'library,' Ravana, the thousand-headed demon, shakes Mt. Kailas, on which are seated Shiva and Uma; the scene on the west pediment depicts Kama, the god of love, about to shoot an arrow at Shiva, who is absorbed in meditation, so that he will notice his fascinating consort Uma. The east pediment of the 'library' to the north has a controversial scene: while there is no doubt that Indra, god of the sky, is on the three-headed elephant Airavata in the upper center, while the thick pattern of double oblique lines has been interpreted by some scholars as rain and by other as arrows. In the middle of the forest are Krishna and his brother Balarama, at right is Vishnu on a chariot, and at left Rama or

122 bottom left South 'library,' south side.

122 bottom right Gopura of the first enclosure, which no longer exists.

123 Mandapa of the main prasat, south side.

124 top Detail of a lintel, with a kala between two makaras.

Arjuna. On the west pediment, Krishna is killing his demon uncle Kamsa. The breadth of narrative invention, the dynamic plastic composition, and the profound psychological expression, have led experts to postulate works from an earlier period in wood, and above all paintings, that no longer exist.

The temple consists of three *prasats* aligned on a T-shaped platform with molding that is accessible by means of stairways with tall buttresses watched over by the kneeling guardians of the sacred site, splendid free-standing figures with the faces of a lion, monkey and genie whose originals are now kept in the Phnom Penh National Museum. The central *prasat* is made up of a portico affording access to a *mandapa*, a pavilion-antechamber with a brick roof that communicates, by means of the antarala or vestibule, with the *garbhagriha*, the *cella* with a serrate plan that has three blind doors and a real doorway. Next to the main *prasat*, which is dedicated to Tribhuvanamaheshvara, or Shiva

124 center North pavilion perpendicular to to the causeway.

124 bottom Detail of the trilobate east pediment of the south 'library.'

as the Great Lord of the Three Worlds, are two secondary *prasats*, simple towers with one doorway and three blind doors, the north one of which is consecrated to Vishnu and the southern one again to Shiva.

As was said above, the temple is small: the central *prasat* is less than 32 ft (10 m) high, and the *cella* itself is no more than 6.5 ft (2 m) wide, and since its door is only 3.2 ft (1 m) high, one must bend down to go in. The side towers are slightly over 26 ft (8 m) high. The roof of the three sanctuaries has four staggered levels in decreasing scale that reproduce the façade, surmounted by lotuses and water vases, with antefixes on the corners that reproduce the entire *prasat* in miniature. The arched pediments, which derived from the *kudu* – the horseshoe-arch motif of Indian architecture – are repeated and superposed on the four levels and also connect them with a series of arches.

The tympana and pediments are the most significant elements in the Banteay Srei complex. There are three types of pediment: triangular with flamboyant acroteria and broad lateral volutes, for the most part with a tympanum with floral decoration; lobate pediments with a particularly developed undulating profile and triple superposition that have mythical scenes; and arched pediments that derived from the *kudu*. The triangular pediments are related to the earlier wooden architecture and are used wherever the constructions have wooden or tile roofs. The lobate pediments have brick and sandstone roofs, especially in the case of the temple annexes, while the *kudu* ones are utilized mostly on the shrine itself.

All three forms are particularly elaborate at Banteay Srei: a fine example of this are the corners, which are made mostly with three-headed *nagas* emerging from the jaws of a lion or of a *makara* with

125 South 'library,' east pediment: Ravana shaking Mt. Kailas.

126 Pediment with Indra on the elephant Airavata.

127 top Side quadrant of a pediment, with garuda in the middle.

127 center Lintel and detail of the east pediment of the north 'library.'

127 bottom The combat between Sugriva and Valin on the east face of the west gopura in the second enclosure.

a very long trunk. Garudas with outspread wings are also used to transform the corners into a decorative element.

The entire surface of the three *prasats* is covered with elegant floral decoration that extends over the walls much like a tapestry and frames elaborate niches consisting of two slender columns topped by flamboyant arches, with two flying genies on the cusp. The young gate guardians and the *devatas* with their archaic style dress and hairdos smile enigmatically, almost as if they were engrossed in contemplation. For the most part the lintels consist of two arched festoons connected in the middle by a figure. The Lokapala, protectors of the regions of the universe, appear at the cardinal points assigned to them: Kubera to the north; Indra on Airavata to the east; Yama the god of the dead on a buffalo to the south; Varurna on the sacred geese to the west. Among the many beautiful works, because of its moving realism and pathos mention should be made of the duel between Sugriva and Valin, resulting in the death of the latter, on the east façade of the west *gopura* in the second enclosure.

The play of volumes, the skillful use made of stereometric effects, the high-quality sandstone with its warm pink hues that is so receptive to the changes of light, and above all the decoration, make Banteay Srei one of the masterpieces of Khmer art.

129 Niche with a devata on the west wall of the principal prasat.

Yajnavaraha had royal blood. He was the grandson of Harshavarman I, and had been the *purohita* or 'chaplain' of Rajendravarman and the tutor of his son Jayavarman V, who named him *vrah guru*, "most excellent spiritual master." His family dated back to Shivakaivalya, the Brahman who had officiated the grandiose ritual ordered by Jayavarman II on Mt. Kulen in 802. The post held by Shivakaivalya and his descendants entailed carrying out the *Devaraja* rituals as well as acting as the king's guru and the tutor of the heir to the throne.

Many hypotheses have been put forward regarding the *Devaraja* rituals and the cult of royalty in Khmer culture, and there is still no consensus among scholars concerning their reconstruction. Unfortunately, there are no inscriptions of Jayavarman II, and the information we have is based on the stele of Sdok Kak Thom dating to 1052, which was found 15.5 miles (25 km) from Sisophon. This inscription mentions the *Kamrateng jagat ta raja*, which the most recent studies indicate as a local Khmer divinity, a sort of *genius loci* and in this case the main deity among the many that must have been worshipped on a local level, in keeping with the archaic Indochinese cult of ancestors. The Khmer *Kamrateng jagat* ta raja or "Lord of the universe who is king," is translated in Sanskrit as *Devaraja*. Furthermore, the above-mentioned stele narrates that during the ceremony a *lingam*, the phallic stone symbolizing Shiva, was given by the god himself to the king as proof of the divine right of royalty. This marked the establishment of the cult of the *Devaraja*, which according to some scholars is the celestial counterpart of the terrestrial king. Although most of the temples celebrate Shiva as the supreme deity, hence the *Devaraja*, there are exceptions, the most famous of which is Angkor Wat, which is dedicated to the god Vishnu.

128 left Detail of a pediment with a flying genie.

128 right Detail of the panel decoration on the walls of the prasats.

Kbal Spean

This site is very evocative, and during your walk through the forest, when your eyes have become accustomed to the light, you will discover testimony of a faith so deep that it was manifested even in such unusual and isolated places.

130 top The four-faced Brahma seated on the lotus.

Visit

You arrive at Kbal Spean by going past Banteay Srei and proceeding on the road up to the parking area, where the path to the site begins. After about a 20-minute walk uphill you come to one of the tributaries of the Siem Reap River and, going down to its banks, you will spot the first sculptures on the surrounding rocks, as well as on the bed of the torrent. The area was inhabited by ancient hermits, who cut divine images and symbols everywhere in the rock during the reign of Udayadityavarman II (1050-66). Among the most fascinating sculptures is a large panel with

130 bottom left The central lingam is surrounded by eight others in a mandala arrangement.

130 bottom right Bas-relief of a makara transformed into a crocodile.

131 top A divinity emerging from the water.

Vishnu reclining on the serpent Ananta: emerging from the god's navel is a lotus flower on which is seated Brahma, the four-faced lord of the origin of the world. Next to this, Shiva and his consort can be seen on the bull Nandi. In front of this are a great many carved *lingams* under the surface of the water.

130-131 At left, Vishnu with Brahma on the lotus that was generated from his navel; center, the back of a lingam before Vishnu; at right, Shiva and Uma on Nandi.

131 bottom Three divinities bathing in a stream.

Ta Keo

A rectangular pyramid made of laterite and cased with sandstone, 147 ft (45 m) high and almost cyclopean in its unfinished state, this monument is one of the most fascinating examples of its kind.

Visit

Although one arrives at Ta Keo from the south, it is better to skirt it at the right in order to go to the east side, where the stairs are less steep than the others, despite their 55° gradient. Here you will see the remains of a processional avenue flanked by small boundary stones. The temple consists of two terraces surrounded by galleries and a three-tier pyramid with a quincunx. The first level is enclosed by a blind wall measuring 400 x 347 ft (122 x 106 m), with axial *gopuras*, the main one to the east; parallel to the east wall are two rectangular edifices preceded by porches and once covered with wooden and tile roofing.

The second level is at a height

The History

The most direct route to the Ta Keo is by crossing Angkor Thom and exiting from the Victory Gate and passing by the Thommanon and going for about a third of a mile. The temple mountain seems to have been the center of Jayendranagari, the "City of Indra the Conqueror" built by Jayavarman V as his new capital on the west side of the East Baray. Construction began in 985 and was resumed by the next king, Jayaviravarman; but the temple was never finished, perhaps because the latter ruler was defeated by Suryavarman I.

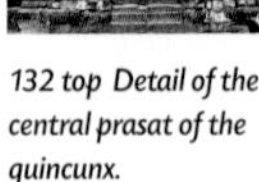

132 top Detail of the central prasat of the quincunx.

132 bottom Gopura and gallery of the second terrace viewed from the east stairway of the pyramid.

132-133 Aerial view of the Ta Keo complex.

of 18.79 ft (5.73 m) and has an innovative element, a continuous gallery 262 x 246 ft (80 x 75 m) with a corbeled vault made of bricks and with blind baluster windows on the outside and real windows facing inside, which also have balusters. The *gopuras* are incorporated into the walls, and at the corners of these latter the towers begin to take shape. Having been shaped by the compression of the preceding

Legend

1 Enclosure wall
2 Gopura
3 First level
4 Rectangular buildings
5 Enclosure gallery
6 Second level
7 'Libraries'
8 Pyramid

9 Corner Prasat
10 central Prasat

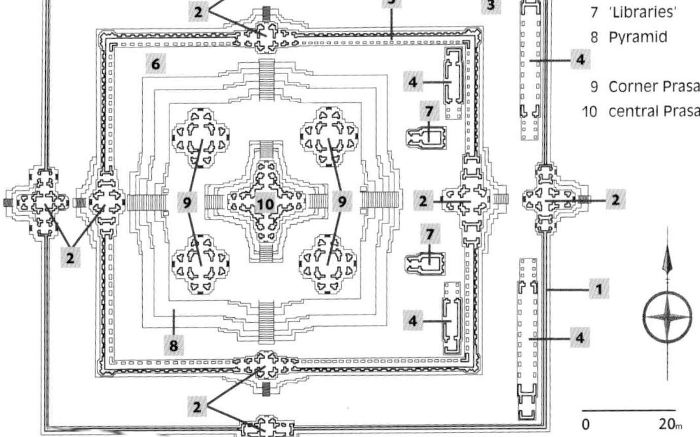

134 top View of the southeast corner.

134 bottom Gopura and gallery of the second terrace from the east stairway of the pyramid.

rectangular edifices, the gallery has no doors, which suggests it had a purely symbolic function. Inside the enclosure are two rectangular edifices that run along the east wall and two 'libraries' flank the access causeway; specifically in order to make room for these structures the east side of the terrace is larger than the other sides. The 'libraries' have a structure that was to become extremely popular and widespread:

135 top The northeast 'library' and corner rectangular edifice.

135 center The second level gallery and the terrace of the first level.

in the interior they have only one chamber, but at the exterior, because of two low segmental half-vaults placed against the outer walls, they seem to have three aisles or naves.

Set back toward the west, the pyramid, which has three sandstone tiers with splendid molding work, measures 196 x 190 ft (60 x 58 m) at the base and 147 x 150 ft (45 x 46 m) at the top – so it is almost square – and is about 46 ft (14 m) high. The *prasats* laid out in a quincunx pattern are entirely made of greywacke, a type of feldspar and quartz sandstone that is particularly hard. The four corner towers have a cruciform plan, with the *cella* opening out to the four cardinal points and preceded by four porches, and three progressively smaller stories above, for a total height of 55 ft (17 m), including the crown that must have stood on top of these structures. In the central tower, which stands on a cruciform platform 19 ft (6 m) high, between the *cella* and the porches are four vestibules with blind doors at the corners.

The inscriptions called the Ta Keo complex Hemashringagiri, or "Mountain with Golden Peaks," and it most probably was planned to represent the five peaks of the mythical Mt. Meru.

135 bottom Northeast prasat of the quincunx.

Thommanon

Rather small but most elegant, this temple was reconstructed thanks to the anastylosis undertaken in the 1960s. Not much remains of the laterite enclosure wall, which is 131 ft (40 m) wide and 150 ft (46 m) long.

136 Devatas on the south porch of the prasat cella.

Visit

You can get to Thommanon by crossing Angkor Thom, exiting by way of the Victory Gate and proceeding for about another third of a mile (0.5 km) until you spot it at your left. The name of the patron, the construction date and the purpose of this monument are still being debated, even though the architectural style dates Thommanon at the late 11th-early 12th century, therefore during the reign of Dharanindravarman I or Suryavarman II.

Arriving from the south, turn to the right of the temple to enter through the east *gopura*, which is preceded by a terrace. The entrance pavilion is a magnificent cruciform structure with two wings and a portico that faces the temple. The tower is tapered because the various levels decrease in size as they ascend; they are connected by a dome with a corbeled vault that covers the central chamber.

The west *gopura* is smaller and simpler, but the pediments have various mythical scenes, including, on the upper southern one, Shiva Mahayogin, or the "Great Ascetic." Even more interesting are those on the 'libraries' in the southeast corner, a rectangular building preceded to the west by a small portico and with a false door facing east: on the upper pediment of the entrance is a lovely image of the Churning of

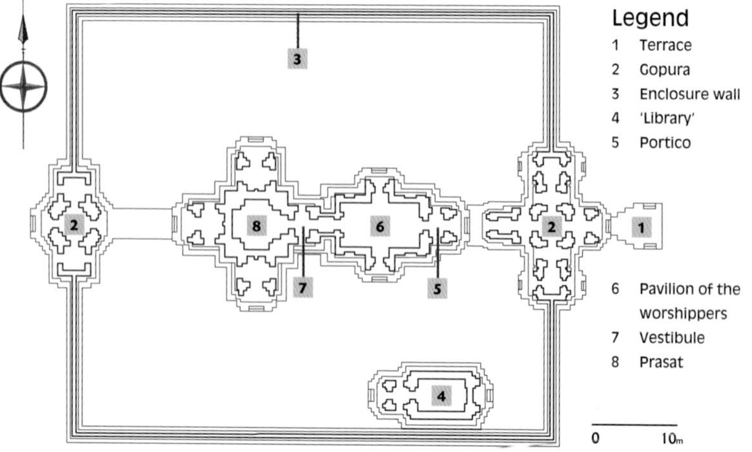

the Ocean of Milk – with gods at right, demons at left, and Vishnu in the middle – on a column that emerges from a lotus bud, flanked by the sun and moon discs; on the upper pediment of the back side are carvings of Sita, Rama, and Lakshmana – protagonists of the epic poem *Ramayana* – in the forest.

The *prasat* on a tall platform with profuse molding work has three porticoes with three exquisitely wrought blind doors, while the fourth portico to the east is the access to the *cella* and is connected to the west portico of the pavilion of the worshippers, which serves as a corridor. The east entrance portico of the pavilion almost merges with the projecting body of the east *gopura*. The *prasat* is surmounted by four levels and the stone extrados of the *mandapa* pavilion imitates tiles.

The wall decoration is a delicate flourish of floral motifs and the *devatas* smile from the niches with their elaborate tree backdrops. Inside the temple the lacunar ceiling was reconstructed in order to show what it was like when it was built. The interior lintels are striking, especially the one on the east entrance of the *prasat* depicting Vishnu riding on Garuda.

137 top Il Thommanon dal lato meridionale. Dright: portico, padiglione dei fedeli, vestibolo e cella del prasat.

137 bottom Detail of a niche with devata.

Chau Say Tedova

The temple is surrounded by a single wall 164 x 131 ft (33 x 42 m), only the laterite platform of which remains. Of the four gopura, the eastern one is the most spectacular.

138 Detail of the east gopura.

Visit

The Chau Say Tevoda site is reached by crossing through Angkor Thom, exiting from the Victory Gate and proceeding for about 1640 ft (500 m) until you see it at your right, opposite the Thommanon. Built by Suryavarman II or one of his high officials, the temple was probably accessible from the Siem Reap River, with which it is connected by means of a wide causeway bordered by stelae that leads to a cruciform terrace that in turn is connected to a passageway on stilts which, after a wider cross-shaped area, ends up in the east *gopura*.

The temple is surrounded by a single wall 164 x 131 ft (33 x 42 m), only the laterite platform of which remains. Of the four *gopura*, the eastern one is the most spectacular, its five-chamber central body flanked by two side entrances.

Among the pediments with sculptures of the epic *Ramayana* cycle, the one on the south doorway depicting the battle between Sugriva, the king of the monkeys, and the usurper Valin is particularly noteworthy.

A passageway supported by columns, flanked by two 'libraries' with their entrance pavilion to the west, leads to the temple, which consists of the two classic elements of temple architecture of Indian origin: the *mandapa* or pavilion of the faithful and the cella. The *mandapa* is preceded by a porch and has two other side entrances that are accessible via stairways; the west doorway leads to the *antarala*, a portico-corridor that goes to the *prasat*. This latter has a single entrance to the east and three blind doorways preceded by porticoes illuminated by windows with balusters. At present this monument is being restored; only part of it can be visited.

Legend

1 Terrace
2 Gopura
3 Enclosure wall
4 'Library'
5 Causeway on stilts
6 Porch
7 Pavilion of the worshippers
8 Porch-vestibule
9 Prasat

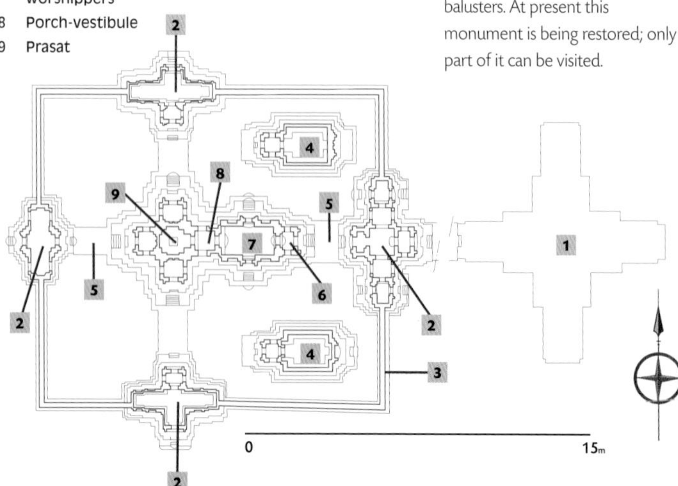

Spean Thma

The 'Stone Bridge,' as this monument is called in modern Khmer, lies to the left of the road leading from the Victory Gate to Ta Keo, where it crosses the Siem Reap River, whose present course has shifted toward the right. Built with materials taken from 15th-16th century temples, the 'bridge' is supported by piers made of stone piled up on one another to form arches with narrow corbeled vaults.

139 top The east side of the east Gopura.

139 bottom The spans of the bridge.

Ta Prohm

The temple is complex and difficult to interpret: according to the archaeologist-scholar Philippe Stern there were 39 prasats, 566 stone houses and 288 made of brick, and 260 divine images were housed there, not including those of Jayavarman's mother.

The History

Known as the temple of Brahma the Ancestor, Ta Prohm lies to the south of the southwest corner of the East Baray. It was consecrated in 1186 by Jayavarman VII, who dedicated it to his mother, deified as Prajnaparamita, the mother of all the Buddhas, Mistress of the "perfection of knowledge." Deliberately left in the midst of the jungle, 'choked' by two trees, the kapok and the sacred fig, this temple arouses in visitors the same emotion felt by the first explorers of Angkor. The decoration is typical of the Bayon period.

An inscription now kept in the Angkor Conservation Museum gives us an idea of enormous size of the complex, known during the reign of Jayavarman as "royal monastery" (rajavihara). Inside the enclosure lived no fewer than 12,640 persons, and the temple-monastery personnel included 18 high priests, 2,740 officiants and 2,232 attendants, including 615 women dancers; 3,140 villages helped to maintain the temple, and, including the villagers, 79,365 persons attended to the needs of Ta Prohm. Among the possessions of the temple were more than 1100 lbs (500 kg) of gold plate, 35 diamonds, 40,620 pearls, 4,540 precious stones, 876 Chinese veils, 512 silk litters, and 523 parasols!

Built in what was a residential area with a surface area of 148 acres (60 hectares), the Ta Prohm temple occupies 2.47 acres (1 hectare) and is encircled by a rectangular enclosure made of laterite that measures 3280 x c. 1968 ft (1000 x c. 600 m).

140 A gallery dominated by a ficus plant inside the first enclosure.

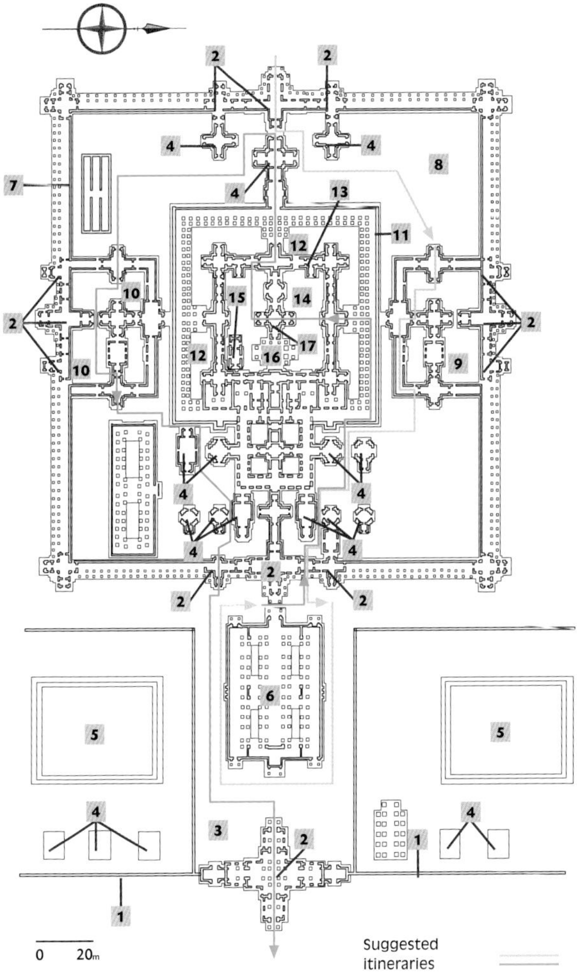

0 20m

Suggested itineraries

Legend

1 Fourth enclosure
2 Gopura
3 Fourth enclosure courtyard
4 Prasat
5 Pools
6 'Hall of the Dancers'
7 Third enclosure
8 Third enclosure courtyard
9 Northern complex
10 Southern complex
11 Second enclosure
12 Second enclosure courtyard
13 First enclosure
14 First enclosure courtyard
15 'Library'
16 Hypostyle hall
17 Central prasat

Visit

To complete the tour of this site you should enter from the west and exit from the east, making sure to have a vehicle waiting for you.

Past the west *gopura*, which is surmounted by the faces of Lokeshvara, you proceed along a path in the forest for 1148 ft (350 m) until you arrive at a cruciform terrace that serves as a bridge over the moats and leads to the entrance of the fourth enclosure, surrounded by a laterite wall 656 x 721 ft (200 x 220 m). Continuing along a causeway paved in sandstone, you will come to the third enclosure wall, which measures 351 x 364 ft (107 x 111 m) and is blind, with a double colonnade facing outward, corner pavilions, and triple axial gopuras. Here the

141 Niches with devatas and floral volutes.

142 top Terrace and east gopura of the fourth enclosure.

root systems of the trees literally strangle the edifices.

At this point, head left and, once past the northwest corner of the second enclosure, a square area 164 ft (50 m) per side bordered on the inside by a double colonnade, you enter the north complex dedicated to Jayamangalarthadeva, Jayavarman VII's guru. The lovely pediments of the central *prasat* more than justify this detour: keeping to the right, enter the south entrance pavilion and immediately turn left into the gallery until you exit once again into the courtyard of the third enclosure. You then pass through some small temples, go up a wooden stairway to your right, and follow the walkway that goes beyond the third enclosure.

The sandstone construction you will encounter may have been the Hall of the Dancers, bounded by walls with blind doors and with square piers in the interior that have sculpted panels of dancing *apsaras*. Access is difficult and you must be very careful: a similar structure can be seen much more safely at Preah Khan. Turning to the left of the pavilion, you will arrive at the stunning east *gopura* of the fourth enclosure: do not go past it, but keep it to your left in order to admire the scenes from the life of Buddha, which were unfortunately mutilated during the Brahmanic revival that occurred after the death of Jayavarman VII. Continue to go around the Hall of Dancers to retrace your steps; you will enter the cloister from where you exited (the wooden stairway), but instead of skirting the edifice of the right-hand corner from where you had come, take the first door in the laterite wall and go along the dark row of pillars until you come out through the north *gopura* of the first enclosure – a square area 98 ft (30 m) per side consisting of a wall with towers on the corners and four entrance pavilions –

142 bottom left The prasat in the third enclosure.

142 bottom right The kapok tree invades the gallery porticoes.

143 *East gopura of the fifth enclosure.*

and enter a cloister dominated by the huge roots of a tree.

In front of you is the central, cruciform *prasat*, which is rather small and is preceded by a hypostyle hall – which cannot be entered – flanked by a 'library' which is in ruins. The temple is connected to the west wing of the first enclosure by another corridor, also inaccessible. Here you enter the *cella*, which is austere and without decoration but may originally have had gilded stuccowork or was dressed with metal plates, as the holes in the walls seem to indicate. Cross through the *cella* and exit from the other side of the cloister, to the south; keeping to your right, you will see at left one of the pillars with a peg on the top whose purpose is still unknown. Go through the door on the

144 top The gopura in the fourth enclosure.

144 bottom Buddhas beheaded by thieves.

west side of the first enclosure and, taking the short passage at the right filled with stones, you will find to your left a wooden walkway that will take you outside the second enclosure.

Once you are in the third enclosure, instead of exiting, turn left to the south, once again skirting the second enclosure until you reach the southwest corner, where you will enter the southern complex, which is dedicated to Jayakirtideva, an older brother of the king. Passing through the west entrance, turn right and go around the central *prasat* until you come to the east *gopura*, on the west façade of which is the famous scene of the "Great Departure," when the future Buddha abandons his father's palace on horseback and the gods hold up the creature's hooves to muffle their sound.

Exiting from here is by no means easy: one past the enclosure you have to keep to your left, hugging the laterite wall of a columned hall in an area filled with rubble and ruins, in order to pass through it and reach the third enclosure by means of a narrow passageway between two *prasats*.

Having gone past the third enclosure you will again come to the Hall of the Dancers; skirt it by keeping it to your left until you arrive at the *gopura* in the fourth enclosure. Once you have exited, it is worthwhile stopping to have a good look at other Buddhist scenes, including the one on the lintel of the side entrance facing north depicting the goddess Earth wringing her hair soaked with human tears, driving away the tempter demon Mara, and the beautiful scene, on the side entrance facing south, of a badly damaged Buddha with a palace and a tree in the background.

A cruciform terrace is connected to the causeway that runs into the forest for 1640 ft (500 m), up to the east *gopura* of the fifth enclosure. At left is a 'house of fire'; this is a rectangular building made of stone, with a tower to the west, an entrance facing east, windows only on the south side, and with a representation of Lokeshvara on the south pediment. The function of this edifice is still being debated, even though the name given to it in the inscriptions connect it to the fire cult.

145 top Frieze of apsaras, heavenly Dancers.

145 center Bayon style devata.

145 bottom Blind doors in the 'Hall of the Dancers' in the fourth enclosure.

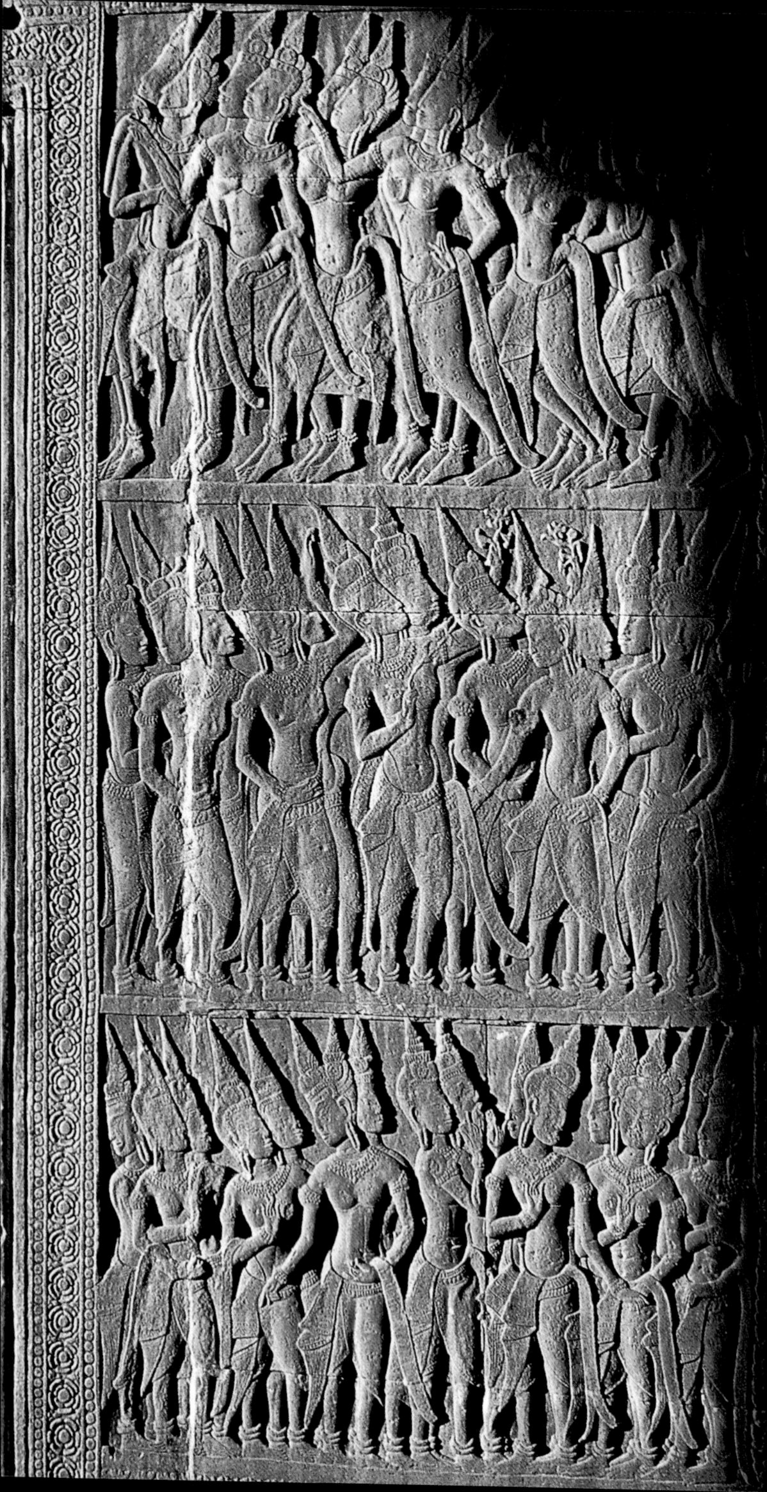

THE ROYAL TEMPLES AND PARTICULARLY ANGKOR WAT, THE LARGEST TEMPLE COMPLEX IN THE WORLD, ARE ABSOLUTELY UNIQUE IN THEIR GENRE AND VERY REPRESENTATIVE OF KHMER ART.

The Royal Foundations

146 Procession of devatas in the corner pavilion of Angkor Wat.

Introduction

THE KING IS THE PROVIDER AND GUARDIAN OF THE LIFE OF HIS SUBJECTS DURING HIS EARTHLY EXISTENCE AND THEIR DIVINE PROTECTOR AFTER HIS DEATH – THIS IS THE MESSAGE CONTINUOUSLY DIFFUSED BY THE SPECTACULAR KHMER ARCHITECTURE, OF WHICH ANGKOR WAT IS THE BEST KNOWN AND MOST SIGNIFICANT EXAMPLE.

The earthly paradise commissioned by Suryavarman II is an admirable fusion of the longitudinal and mountain temples in a unique and staggering complex. The great royal foundations of Jayavarman VII that followed – the most famous of which is the Preah Khan – revive the vision of the divine sovereign as a savior, who becomes

even more compassionate and concerned about his people because of his adherence to Buddhism: examples of this are the Ta Prohm Kel and the other hospital chapels, as well as the fascinating complex of pools at Neak Pean, which are known for their healing properties. A visit to Banteay Prei and Ta Som, which are much smaller and compact and therefore easier to interpret, will facilitate a better understanding of the structure of these foundations. The ruins of the Prasat Prei and Krol Ko illustrate the building techniques and their defects, while the Krol Romeas, a simple enclosure for animals, reminds us of the huge quantity of secondary buildings that with time have disappeared.

Legend

1 Angkor Wat
2 Ta Prohm Kel
3 Ta Som
4 Preah Khan
5 Prasat Prei
6 Banteay Prei
7 Krol Romeas
8 Krol Ko
9 Neak Pean

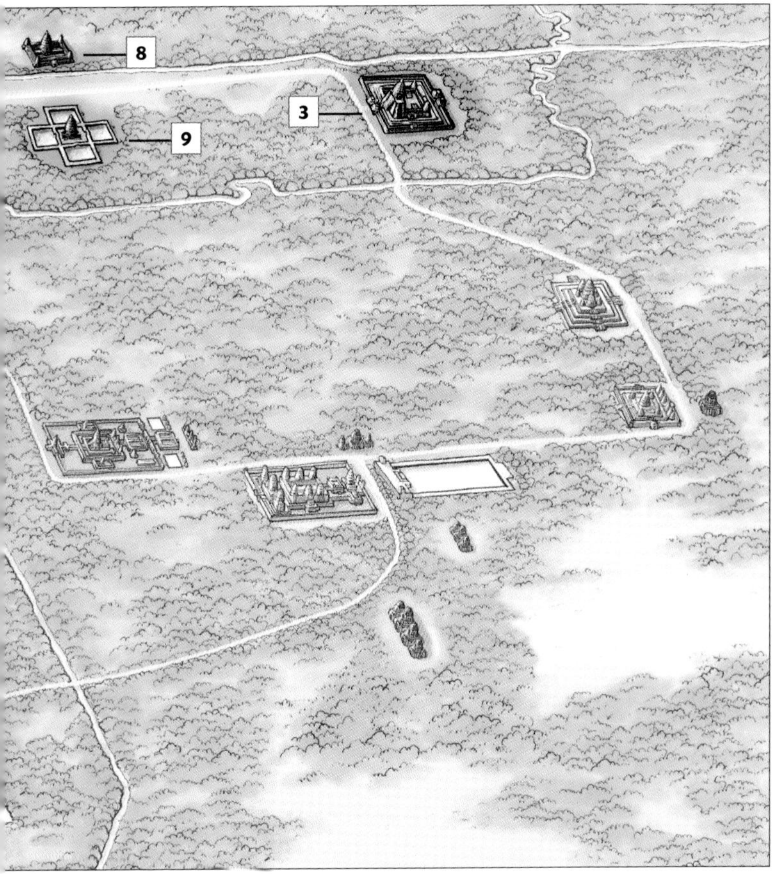

Angkor Wat

A visit to Angkor Wat, the most famous monument of Angkor, can be made by entering at the main entrance to the west and exiting from the secondary entrance to the east; if there is a large crowd it is advisable to reverse the order.

The History

Built by Suryavarman II from 1113 to 1150 and known in ancient times as Brah Bishnulok or Vrah Vishnuloka, the 'Sacred Abode of Vishnu' was dedicated to the second deity of the Trimurti, with whom Suryavarman identified himself. Indeed, upon his death, the great ruler was given the posthumous name of Paramavishnuloka, 'He who has entered the paradise of the supreme Vishnu,' and the temple became his mausoleum. The present name means "royal city [that is] a monastery," because after the religious revolution effected by Jayavarman VII in the 13th century the Khmer empire embraced Buddhism and Angkor Wat was transformed from a Vishnuite sanctuary into a Buddhist wat – a word of Thai origin that means "monastery."

Visit

The Angkor Wat complex, situated in the southeastern quarter of what was once the city of Yashodharapura, lies in a rectangle that is 4920 x 4625 ft (1500 x 1300 m), covering a surface area of about 0.4 sq. miles (2 sq. km). The fascinating moat surrounding the site, fed by a canal from the Siem Reap River, is almost 656 ft (200 m) wide and is bordered by broad terrace-steps that descend to the water. However, the stone edifices and annexes – 12,360 cubic ft

150 West side of the temple.

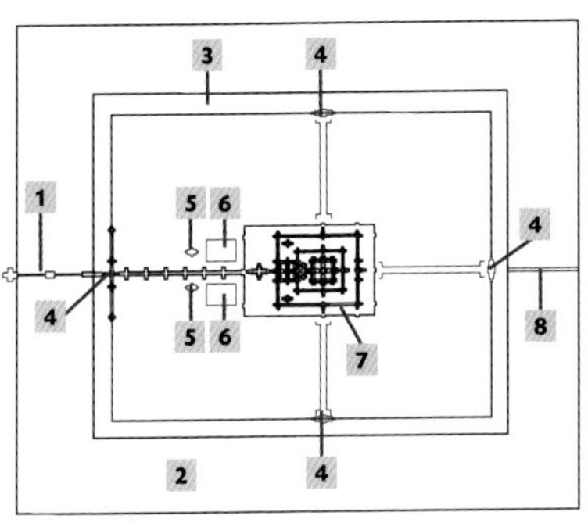

Legend

1 West dam and landing stage
2 Moats
3 Fourth enclosure
4 Gopura
5 'Libraries'
6 Pools
7 Temple platform
8 East dam

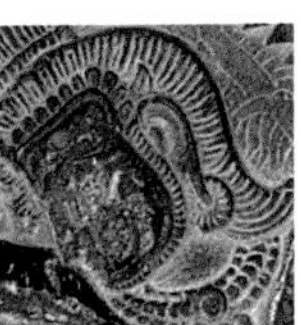

151 A guardian of the underworld.

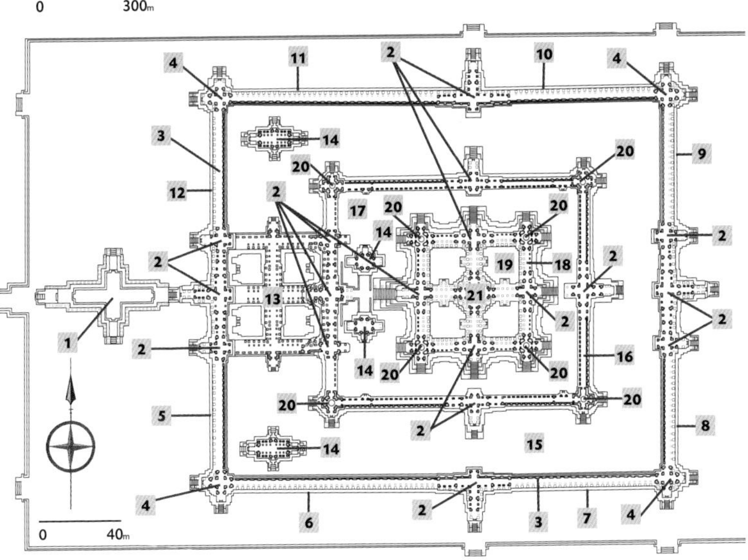

Legend

1 Cruciform terrace
2 Gopura
3 Third gallery
4 Corner pavilions
5 Bas-reliefs: the Battle of Kurukshetra
6 Bas-reliefs: the army marching
7 Bas-reliefs: the judgment of the dead
8 Bas-reliefs: the Churning of the Ocean of Milk
9 Bas-reliefs: Vishnu fighting against the demons
10 Bas-reliefs: Krishna combatting the asura Bana
11 Bas-reliefs: combat between gods and demons
12 Bas-reliefs: the Battle of Lanka
13 Cruciform cloister
14 'Libraries'
15 Courtyard of the first level
16 Second gallery
17 Courtyard of the second level
18 First gallery
19 Cloister of the third level
20 Corner prasats
21 Central prasats

152 top Platform with the temple, south side.

(350,000 cubic m) of material – occupy only 328,083 sq. ft (100,000 sq. m) of the vast stretch of land of Angkor Wat, since nothing remains of the structures made of wood and other perishable materials. The area surrounded by the outer wall of Angkor Wat housed the temple personnel as well as the king and his court, with all the people who revolved around it, perhaps as many as 20,000 persons.

The complex faces the west, in contrast with the ritual precepts of Hindu and Khmer architecture, which call for the temple to face the east. Scholars have provided various

152 bottom Southwest gopura of the fourth enclosure and landing stage of the west dam.

explanations for this unusual fact: the temple was dedicated to Vishnu, who is connected to the western quarter of the universe; it was also used as the king's tomb, hence the choice of the western orientation, since this cardinal point is the domain of the dead; the new complex was built in the already existing city of Yashodharapura and, if oriented to the east, it would have turned its back on the older urban settlement, which would have been most inauspicious.

The outermost enclosure wall, the fourth, is made of laterite and measures 3360 x 2674 ft (1025 x 815 m). It is possible to cross over the surrounding moat by means of two axial causeways: the one to the east is made of earth and must have been the service passageway; the western one, which is the more important, is an imposing avenue 820 ft (250 m) long and 40 ft (12 m) wide, paved with sandstone and flanked by a balustrade with raised *nagas*. These latter are serpents with five or seven heads and, although they are a typical Indian motif, they incorporate the local ancestral figure of the dragon of the waters, which brings rain and is the symbol of the rainbow that links the earth and the sky. It is therefore not surprising that the *nagas* should decorate the avenue connecting the secular area of the old city of Yashodharapura and the sacred area of Suryavarman's new capital-temple.

After taking the causeway, halfway down which is a cruciform platform with stairs that descend to the water and become jetties, you will see the front side of the outer enclosure wall, which consists of a sandstone gallery with a corbeled vault that rests on a blind wall and a row of square pillars. The portico, which is 771 ft (235 m) long, has animated molding decoration and is preceded by a half-nave on a lower level, only a few pillars of which have survived. In the middle is the theatrical main entrance, which is elevated and anticipates the one of the third gallery, and which consists of three cruciform *gopuras* surmounted by other turreted structures connected to one another by a series of chambers. The central *gopura* is larger than the side ones and is preceded by a double hypostyle portico. At either end of the front of the gallery are two other passageways for the animals and vehicles, while on the three other sides of the fourth enclosure walls there are three axial *gopura* passages that have simpler structures. If you can do so, it is worthwhile spending some time to admire the exquisite relief sculptures of women dancers and the friezes of horsemen in the lower part of the blind wall, the rose windows under the lintels, and the beams that end in grotesque masks. In the *gopura* to the right of the

***153 top** Guardian lion and gopura of the fourth enclosure.*

***153 center** Multi-headed naga.*

***153 bottom** Gopura of the fourth enclosure and access.*

154 top South 'library' in the fourth enclosure.

154-155 View of the north side of the third gallery.

154 bottom left Gopura of the cruciform cloister of the third gallery.

154 bottom right Stupa built in a later period on the east side of the third gallery.

central one there is a statue of Vishnu with eight arms, which experts think may have belonged to the main *prasat*; there are two other statues of the eight-armed Vishnu, but they are less important.

Once past the entrance, on the walls you will see the carvings of the *devata*, female deities with complex hair-dos who smile enigmatically against a backdrop of trees with flowers: there are more than 1,500 of them in Angkor Wat.

Inside the enclosure of the sacred city another paved avenue, almost 33 ft (10 m) wide and elevated 5 ft (1.5 m) above the ground, extends for 1150 ft (350 m), flanked by *nagas*. At regular intervals of 165 ft (50 m), six stairways per side descend to ground level, where the houses once stood. About halfway down are two 'libraries,' the north one of which is now being restored. These structures have a cruciform plan with a triple nave and hypostyle porticoes on the four

sides accessible via stairways, and are covered with corbeled vaults or half-vaults with very smooth inner surfaces.

A little farther on are two rectangular pools about 165 ft (50 m) wide that were added in a later period. From the northwest corner of the north pool there is a splendid overall view of the monument reflected in the water.

The construction next to the pool is a Buddhist monastery, with *stupas* dating from different periods, which was part of the previous complex.

The causeway leads to a cruciform terrace with two levels, the lower one of which has a courtyard and short, thick columns that serve as supporting elements.

On the platform – which measures 846 x 1090 ft (258 x 332 m), and is about 3.2 ft (1 m) high, and is accessible by means of three

***155 bottom** Detail of one of the gopuras of the third gallery.*

156 top Panoramic view of the first gallery, with corner devatas.

stairways per side – is the temple proper, which has three stories surrounded by three galleries. Built on a tall base with elaborate molding and covered with a corbeled vault, the third gallery, 613 ft (187 m) long and 705 ft (215 m) wide, has a blind inner wall and an outer arcade with piers that supports a hypostyle half-nave. Four axial entrances open into the gallery: the west one is articulated in three cruciform pavilions that can be reached by means of stairways

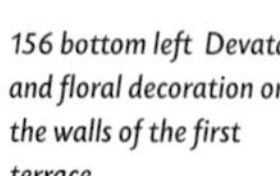

156 bottom left Devata and floral decoration on the walls of the first terrace.

156 bottom right Decoration with female divinities among foliage.

and are connected by rectangular chambers: the central *gopura* is preceded by the porticoes as well as by a vestibule. The same structure is repeated symmetrically on the east side, while on the other two sides the entrances consist of a single cruciform pavilion preceded by a vestibule and with porticoes and stairways. The expedient of the cruciform pavilion with stairways was skillfully adopted also in the corners of the perimetral gallery, interrupting its horizontal movement with the vertical thrust of the superposed roofs.

The blind wall of the third gallery is the support for an incredible series of bas reliefs that unravel like illuminated manuscripts in the stone in a panel that is about 6.5 ft (2 m) high and more than 1970 ft (600 m) long, not counting the carvings on the corner pavilions. Some particularly shiny sections have led scholars to think that this was the result of a layer or protective varnish or lacquer added in a later period, rather than being caused by visitors rubbing them with their hands. The former theory seems to be substantiated by the presence in certain points of traces of red, black and gold coloring. The carvings all concern the mythology of Vishnu, with whom Suryavarman II, the builder of Angkor Wat, identified himself, and various interpretations have been given to their overall dynamics.

Given the fact that Angkor Wat was a mausoleum, many scholars affirm that the bas-reliefs should be read counterclockwise, that is, they should not be at the viewers' right – as the traditional circumambulation of the temple, the *pradakshina*, requires – but should be at the left. In fact, in their funerary monuments the Hindus replace the *pradakshina* with the *prasavya*, that is to say, the counterclockwise circumambulation during ceremonies.

Proceeding in this manner, and going through thresholds that are very tall in order to block the entrance of evil spirits, once in the entrance pavilion you turn right, into the west gallery of the south wing: here there is a representation of the battle of the Kurukshetra, the

157 Devata holding a mirror and doing her hair.

158 top Gopura of the third gallery.

field north of Delhi, which was the arena of the struggle between the Pandavan and Kauravan armies, the protagonists of the great *Mahabharata* epic. Almost in the middle of the panel is the hero Arjuna, who is shooting an arrow from his chariot, and his charioteer is the four-armed god Krishna, the incarnation of Vishnu.

In the southwest corner pavilion, now being restored, there are Vishnuite scenes and others from the *Ramayana*, another fundamental epic poem that celebrates Rama, an earthly incarnation of Vishnu. A particularly fine and touching episode – in the south wing of the pavilion, on the east side above the window – is the battle between the two monkey kings, Sugriva and Valin, and the death of the latter mourned by his wife.

In the west wing of the south gallery, Suryavarman II is seated at a royal audience: the king has decided to wage war, and his army begins to march. Standing out from the other soldiers because of their attire are the mercenaries or conscripted soldiers from provinces not inhabited by Khmers, as is the case with the Thai contingents from Lobpuri in Thailand. In the middle of the panel we again see the Khmer king preceded by a standard with Vishnu mounted on Garuda.

158 bottom Corner pavilion of the third enclosure and the prasat in the southeast corner of the second enclosure.

The redone lacunar ceiling shows how this section was roofed originally.

In the east section Yama, the god of the dead, on his buffalo oversees the judgment of the souls, in which the damned are rendered in almost cruel detail.

The corner pavilion has no decoration, but the east gallery in the south section boasts the spectacular Churning of the Ocean of Milk, whose representation drew on the *Mahabharata* and the *Bhagavata Purana*. The lower register has carvings of the inhabitants of the ocean, both real and fantastic. In the middle register the gods and demons – the former with elongated eyes and the latter with round eyes – are arranged on either side of Vishnu, who is riding on the

158-159 and 159 top The wall of bas-reliefs in the third gallery, west side: the Battle of Kurukshetra.

160 top Third gallery, west side, south wing: detail of the Battle of Kurukshetra.

160 bottom Third gallery, south side, east wing: detail of the 'Judgment of the Dead.'

160-161 Third gallery, south side, west wing: the army is on the march.

161 bottom Third gallery, south side, west wing: soldiers from siamese provinces.

turtle Kurma. The upper register depicts *apsaras* born from the waves dancing in the air. The following relief representing Vishnu's victory over the demons, in the north section, was carved in a later period, sometime between 1546 and 1564, during the reign of Ang Chan I, who had moved the capital of the Khmer empire to Lovek but had continued to support the religious foundation of Angkor Wat.

After going past the northeast corner pavilion, which has nothing of any real interest, one enters the north gallery, whose east wing again

162-163 Third gallery, south side, east wing: the damned are dragged to the underworld in the 'Judgment of the Dead.'

has reliefs of the struggle against evil and celebrates Krishna's victory over the *asura* Bana, who in the end is saved thanks to the intercession of Shiva. This panel also dates to the period of Ang Chan I.

162 top Third gallery, south side, east wing: beatings and torture in the 'Judgment of the Dead.'

162 center third gallery, south side, east wing: the damned being torn to pieces by monsters in the 'Judgment of the Dead.'

162 bottom Third gallery, south side, west wing: a group of women with a child.

The west wing continues with the major theme of the battle between *devas* and *asuras*: twenty-one armed and bejeweled Hindu deities file past on their mounts among troops of humans and demons.

The pavilion of the northwest corner celebrates Vishnu and depicts some events from the *Ramayana*, while the north section of the west gallery features the crucial moment of this epic poem, the Battle of Lanka, the final clash between Rama and Ravana, the thousand-headed demon who had kidnapped Rama's consort. Here the monkeys are depicted biting the demons and their mounts in fierce hand-to-hand struggles.

The composition of the reliefs is continuous; it is the viewer's eye that defines the individual scenes, which in any case are gauged precisely to coincide with the viewer's visual field, and skillfully wrought details attract their attention to the main elements of the scene. Lovely friezes consisting of superposed rows of petals, rosettes, festoons and *garudas* or winged lions conclude the carvings above, while

163 bottom Third gallery, south side, east wing: the guardians of the underworld in the 'Judgment of the Dead.'

in the chamber with windows the flat maze of plants carved on the walls creates a tapestry effect that reminds one of the silk brocades with floral patterns imported from China.

Back at the main entrance, there is one of the most intriguing and brilliantly conceived elements in the entire structure – the cruciform cloister. Three parallel corridors start from the three entrances, leading to the stairways with their successive landings. These passageways are covered by corbeled vault intradoses and extradoses with pediments inserted into one another and are the 'porches' of the three cruciform entrance pavilions on the upper level; the extradoses are exact reproductions

164 top Third gallery, south side, east wing: the Judgment of the Dead, sedan-chair.

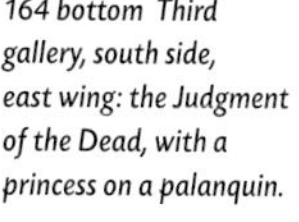

164 bottom Third gallery, south side, east wing: the Judgment of the Dead, with a princess on a palanquin.

165 top Third gallery, south side, east wing: the Judgment of the Dead, the chosen few being taken to heaven.

of the roof tiles, imitating even their tiniest details to the last degree of accuracy. A fourth, three-nave corridor with four rows of pillars – the central nave with a corbeled vault and the side ones have half-vaults – is perpendicular to the other three, thus delimiting four small inner courtyards. The tall platform on which these courtyards lie and the step leading to ground level, show that they are lustral water basins used for the temple ceremonies. The south side of the cloister was formerly known as the Hall of the Thousand Buddhas because it once housed a huge number of statues of the Enlightened One, only a few of which remain. Be sure to observe the details of the cloister closely:

165 center Third gallery, south side, east wing: the Judgment of the Dead, a scene of tribute.

165 bottom Third gallery, south side, east wing: the Judgment of the Dead, the procession towards heaven.

166 top Third gallery, east side, south wing: top, Vishnu in the middle of the Churning of the Ocean of Milk.

pillars whose base has representations of ascetics, friezes of *apsaras* on the inside walls and of ascetics on the outside ones, groups of *devatas*, and sinuous multi-headed *nagas* that frame the pediments, softening their profiles. The traces of painting date to the 16th century.

As for the pediments, the one of the corner stairway in the left-hand cloister has a beautiful Vishnu on Garuda. Other outstanding elements are the lintels at the junction point of the four galleries: above the west entrance is the Churning of the Ocean of Milk; on the north one Vishnu is vanquishing the *asura* Bana, between the sun and the moon; the lintel on the east entrance has a carving of Vishnu on Garuda among adoring deities; the south one again depicts Vishnu, this time lying on the serpent Ananta, while Lakshmi massages his feet.

Before going up to the second level, you may find it interesting to exit from the door on the north

166 bottom left The gods and Hanuman in the Churning of the Ocean of Milk.

166 bottom right The god Shiva.

167 top Third gallery, south side, east wing: the 'Judgment of the Dead,' with Yama on a buffalo.

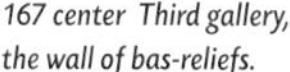

167 center Third gallery, the wall of bas-reliefs.

167 bottom Third gallery, east side, south wing: the demons in the Churning of the Ocean of Milk.

168-169 and 169 Third gallery, west side, north wing: the Battle of Lanka and details.

side to see the wall with the blind windows of the third gallery and also to visit one of the two 'libraries' that, in an elevated position on a tall foundation, provide a panoramic view.

There are three ways to get to the second level: via the cloister; from the courtyard, that is, from the entrance pavilions on the other three axes of the second gallery, with their very steep steps; and from the corner towers, which in this case are true *prasats*. However, it is advisable to go up the central stairway of the cruciform portico: once outside you will see two other small 'libraries,' with a single hall and charming groups of *devatas*, which are connected and have their entrance on a raised platform resting on short columns that probably date from a later period. This second level of Angkor Wat was off-limits for the common people, so that the dark, single-nave gallery that bounds it and that measures around 328 x 377 ft (100 x 115 m) has no openings in the

168 bottom Niches with dancing apsaras in the friezes under the ceilings.

170 top View of the northwest 'library' of the second level.

outer walls; but the overall effect is lightened by blind windows with small columns. In the interior, on the other hand, the windows are real, although they are screened by multi-faceted short colonnettes divided into ten or twelve circles that make them light and vibrant. Before going up to the third level, take a stroll around the central body to admire the *devatas* and some pediments in the second gallery, including, on the north side, scenes of battles and triumph, and on the south side the combat between Sugriva and Valin that ends with the death of the latter. Especially noteworthy are the carvings of the four *prasats* soaring over the top of Angkor Wat, in particular the glory of Vishnu on the southeast tower and two scenes of warriors and archers on chariots on the northeast tower.

In the courtyard of the second level, the base of the third tier rises up for 42 ft (13 m) divided into two profusely molded terraces. Twelve very steep stairways with a single flight and a gradient that is as much as 70°, enclosed between four pairs of massive buttresses, lead to the top square area (196 ft or 60 m per side) of the first gallery. The safest way to go up is by the south stairway, which has a handrail and

170 bottom left Cloister on the first level.

170 bottom right Buddha in the first-level cloister.

cement steps. In the outer wall there is a series of windows with colonnettes, while toward the interior the gallery, with the usual corbeled vault, rests on pillars and is bordered by a colonnade that supports a segmental half-vault.

The cruciform pavilions on the corners are *prasats*: the quincunx represents the five peaks of Mt. Meru. This third level reproduces the cruciform cloister of the first level and connects the middle *prasat* to the axial entrance pavilions by means of corridors with three

171 top Shiva dancing (third level, pediment of the east vestibule of the central prasat).

170-171 Cloister on the third level.

172 top *Gopura of the first-level cloister.*

naves on pillars, marking out four small courtyards that probably served as lustral basins. But unlike the cloister on the first level, which had no superstructure at the junction of the four corridors, here the massive central *prasat* (138 ft/42 m high) dominates the space, soaring at a height of more than 213 ft (65 m) over the plain of Angkor, overwhelming all the other structures, almost as if it sucked them into the powerful spiral thrust of its five stories, which end in a triple arched lintel of lotus petals crowned by an acroterion in the shape of a lotus bud. In the pediments of the vestibules of the *prasat* that serve as buttresses, there appears, next to Vishnuite figures such as Hanuman (to the north) – the monkey god who is Rama's companion, holding two enemies by their feet – an image of the dancing Shiva to the east.

The *prasat*, with a serrate plan and four vestibules preceded by four porticoes, originally had four real doors and housed a statue of Vishnu, which seems to be the one now in the west *gopura* of the outer gallery. After the temple was converted into a Buddhist sanctuary, the doors were walled up so that images of the standing Buddha with his right hand on his chest could be sculpted thereon. In 1908 the south doorway was opened, and archaeologists discovered, in the interior of the *cella*, a shaft 82 ft (25 m) deep under the pedestal of the removed statue of Vishnu, the foundation treasure chamber, consisting of two rectangular blocks of laterite: in a round hole of the lower block there were two gold leaves and four smaller ones covered with fine sand containing two white sapphires. Nothing else of what must have been the treasure was found.

The four corner *prasats* are similar to the central one but are smaller. In the palace of the gods on Mt. Meru, the third level could be entered only by the high priest and the king, who identified himself with the god portrayed in the statue in the central shrine. Make sure to walk around the outer gallery to enjoy the spectacular commanding view; on the west side is a Buddha seated on Mucilinda, the king of cobras.

The five prasats of the Angkor

172 bottom left *Devatas at the sides of the central prasat entrances, third level.*

172 bottom right *Devatas on the walls of the central prasat, third level.*

173 *View from the third level of the corner prasat in the second enclosure.*

Wat quincunx are not the only tower-temples there; the ones at the corners of the second gallery are also temples, as are the three that dominate the entrances of the outermost enclosure wall. Therefore the total number of *prasats* is twelve, a recurrent number fraught with astrological symbolism: there are twelve stairways in the second access causeway, and the same number on the terrace of the true temple, and twelve that lead up to the third level, while the third enclosure wall has twelve entrances.

Although there are some technical flaws in the construction, such as the unsolved problem of the vault, built by means of corbeling, and the slight attention paid to the vertical staggering of the stones that would have avoided the creation of spaces between them, from an architectural standpoint Angkor Wat is without a doubt an absolute masterpiece. Its perfection is due to the architects' use of certain stereometric expedients. For example, the causeway between the entrance pavilion and the temple proper is almost twice as long as the west façade, so that it is possible to see the entire monument, since it stands at a perspective distance that is twice its maximum size. Each of the three terraces is twice as tall as the preceding one and has a surface

174 bottom left *Detail of the extradoses of a pediment in the second gallery.*

174 bottom right *Third level: Vishnu on the pediment of the southeast prasat.*

174-175 *The temple platform viewed from the east.*

area at least two times smaller, so that the gallery on the lowest terrace will not conceal the one on the terrace above it, thus offering the sight of a perfect pyramid to the viewer. What is more, each terrace is set farther back toward the east with respect to the preceding one, that is, in the direction opposite that of the main entrance, to avoid giving the impression that the monument is jutting forward.

When your visit is over, you can exit through the east *gopura* of the third gallery, leaving a back *stupa* at your left, which will afford different views of Angkor Wat and will also give you the opportunity to pass through a pleasant stretch of greenery and to exit from the outer wall to the east, where the transport vehicles are stationed.

175 bottom *The central prasat on the third level.*

Ta Prohm Kel

Situated about 1313 ft (400 m) north of the main entrance of Angkor Wat and set back somewhat from road to the left, Ta Prohm Kel is one of the 102 chapels of the hospitals built at the behest of Jayavarman VII.

176 top A statue inside the Ta Prohm Kel.

176-177 Ta Prohm Kel, near Angkor Wat.

Visit

After the invocation to Bhaishajyaguru, the healing Buddha and the eulogy of the compassionate sovereign Jayavarman, the Sanskrit text sets forth the regulations of the hospital and provides a list of the personnel. In most cases there were 98 persons, plus an astrologist and two officiants, but as many as 200 persons worked in the hospitals in the capital. The structure seems to have been basically the same, consisting of a *prasat* with a portico or projecting body to the east and a small 'library' southeast of the tower, inside an enclosure with a *gopura*, an artificial lake lying outside this latter. To this were added the wooden structures, no longer extant, which served as lodgings for the ill and the hospital personnel. In Ta Prohm Kel there are almost no remnants of the enclosure and the *gopura*, and even the *prasat* is in a precarious state: only the north false door has survived – with two *devatas* at the tower corners, one with curls and braids and the other with a crown-like cover over the chignon – and in the three upper stories the southwest section has collapsed. The Bayon style decoration is rather crude here. A similar structure, known as the Hospital Chapel, is located near Ta Keo.

177 top Interior of the Ta Prohm Kel prasat.

177 bottom left Niches with devatas in the 'Hospital Chapel.'

177 bottom right The so-called Hospital Chapel near Ta Keo.

Ta Som

Some scholars have identified Ta Som as the Gaurashrigajaratna, the "Jewel of the Propitious White Eelephant" mentioned in the stele of Preah Khan as the home of 24 deities. Ascribed to the late 12th century, this temple is a rather small construction and is therefore easier to interpret.

178 Detail of a devata in a niche.

Visit

The Ta Som temple, at the foot of the dike east of the Jayatataka *baray*, can be reached both from the East Mebon, heading north for about 1.5 miles (2.5 km) and from Neak Pean by going east for 1.1 miles (1.8 km).

The third enclosure wall – 787 x 656 ft (240 x 200 m), made of laterite, with merlons containing images of Buddha no longer present – was added in a later period. Of the two *gopuras* on the east-west axis, the eastern one is famous for the roots of a dead sacred fig tree that frames the face of Lokeshvara, the *bodhisattva* of compassion with whom King Jayavarman VII identified

Legend

1 Gopura
2 Second enclosure
3 Courtyard of the second enclsoure
4 First enclosure
5 Courtyard of the first enclosure
6 'Libraries'
7 Peg pillar
8 Central prasat

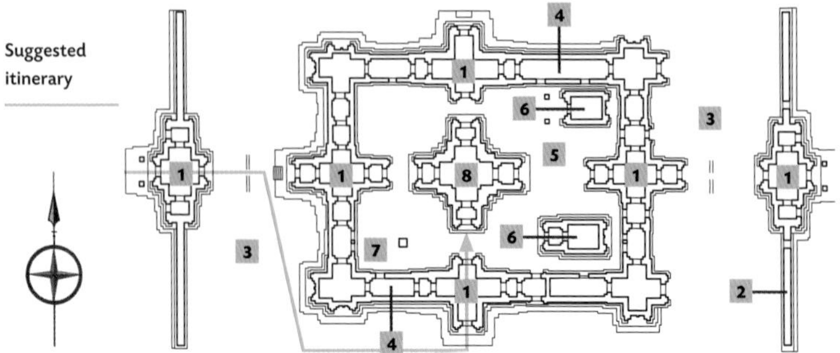

178-179 East gopura, third enclosure.

179 bottom Interior of the first enclosure.

180 top The east gopura of the third enclosure, with the faces of Lokeshvara

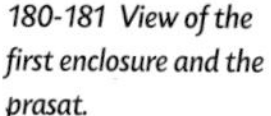

180-181 View of the first enclosure and the prasat.

180 bottom left Niches with devatas, first enclosure.

180 bottom right Devata in the niche of a gopura.

himself. Entry to the temple is from the west. The second enclosure wall is made of laterite, is surrounded by a moat and has two *gopuras*; the eastern one, preceded by a small cruciform terrace, is being restored. Once past the *gopura*, by turning to the right of the first enclosure you will come to a pediment with a lovely carving of Lokeshvara. Proceeding in this direction and keeping to the south side of the temple, you enter from the south *gopura*, which is the easiest access. The first enclosure consists of a laterite gallery with corner pavilions, sandstone doors and windows (the latter in the typical style of the time, with partly lowered curtains), and vaulted roofs with pinnacle-shaped acroteria. The south pediment of the north *gopura* has an interesting scene with Lokeshvara, at whose feet are four praying figures on four lotus buds on the same stem.

In the southeast and northeast corners there are two 'libraries,' while the central *prasat* has a Greek cross plan, and the *cella* has entrances at the four cardinal points, with the same number of vestibules, surmounted by four tiers and ending in a magnificent double lotus flower. In the southwest section of the courtyard you can see a pillar with a peg on the top – seen in other temples of the same period – whose purpose has yet to be explained.

***181 bottom** Devata doing her hair.*

Preah Khan

In ancient times the Preah Khan was known as Nagarajayashri, the "Fortunate City Blessed with Victory," and its modern name means "Sacred Sword," an allusion to the palladium of the Khmer kingdom, a more recent copy of which is now kept in the royal palace of Phnom Penh.

182 West avenue affording access to the fourth enclosure, flanked by steles.

Visit

The temple occupies an area of 138 acres (56 hectares) and lies in four enclosures, the outermost of which measures 2296 x 2624 ft 700 x 800 m) and is surrounded by a moat 131 ft (40 m) wide. The avenue that leads to its west entrance is flanked by a row of pillars crowned by an overturned

The History

The itinerary suggested here starts off from the west gopura of the fourth enclosure – which lies about 0.9 miles (1.5 km) to the right, after having passed by the North Gate of Angkor Thom – and ends at the east entrance, where you can have your vehicle pick you up. Preah Khan was built by Jayavarman VII from 1184 on and was dedicated in 1191 to his father Dharanindravarman, who identified himself with the Bodhisattva Lokeshvara, the most important of the 450 deities who had shrines here. In fact, the Preah Khan was not only a Buddhist site but also housed shrines dedicated to other gods of Hindu cosmogony, to local genies, royal ancestors, and deified human figures.

A true city with 102 prasats and several other stone edifices, Preah Khan lay west of Jayatataka, the new 'Baray of Victory,' and included other religious complexes as well. The foundation stele celebrates the gift of 5,324 villages, which were charged with furnishing ten tons of white rice per day, and states that 97,840 persons gravitated around Preah Khan. Besides its royal foundation, the Preah Khan was also a famous center of learning and was modeled after the large Buddhist universities in India.

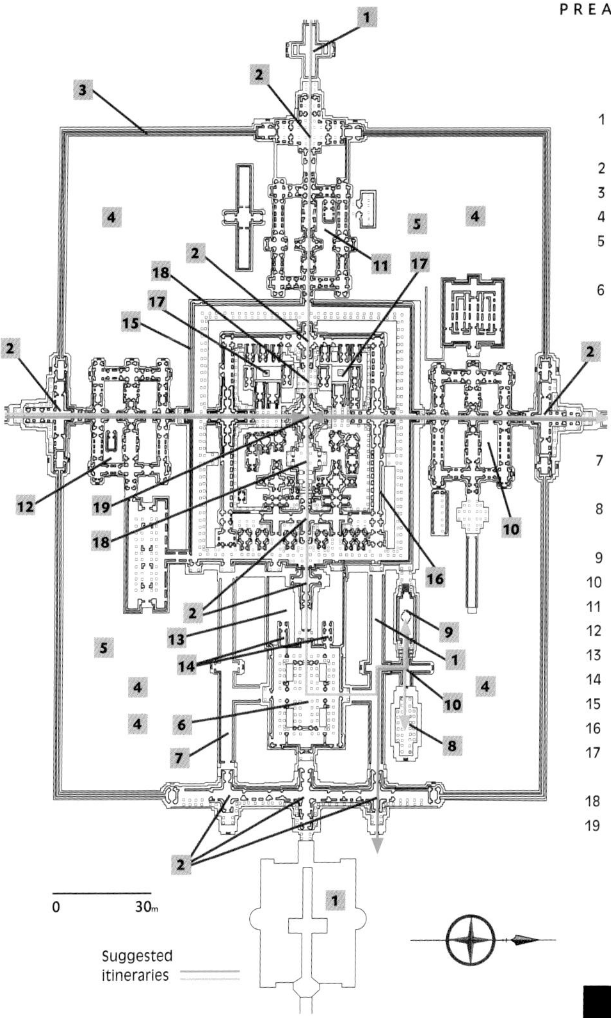

1 Cruciform platform
2 Gopura
3 Third enclosure
4 Pools
5 Courtyard of the third enclosure
6 'Hall of the Dancers'
7 Causeways lined with nagas
8 Columned pavilion
9 Laterite platform
10 Temple of Shiva
11 Temple of Vishnu
12 South temple
13 Paved courtyard
14 Chapel
15 Second enclosure
16 First enclosure
17 Cloisters in the first enclosure
18 Hypostyle hall
19 Central prasat

0 30m

Suggested itineraries

lotus acroterion: on the sides of the base four telamons with the body of a *garuda* and the face of a lion support four niches that once housed seated Buddhas which were defaced during the revival of Brahmanism in the 13th century. The avenue becomes a sort of bridge lined by rows of *devas* and *asuras*, gods and demons that support a multi-headed *naga* (see Angkor Thom)

Once at the enclosure, you cannot help noticing, on the laterite wall, the spectacular 16 ft (5 m) high *garudas* holding serpents with their claws, located on the corners and 147-164 ft (45-50 m) from one another. Above there is long crenellation that once had images of Buddha. The entrance pavilion consists of three towers, with the central entrance for elephants and

183 Steles with telamons along the west access avenue.

184 top A gigantic garuda on the wall of the fourth enclosure.

184 center Access bridge of the fourth enclosure, with nagas supported by gods.

184 bottom A chapel in the second enclosure 'strangled' by a kapok tree.

chariots surmounted by five stories and the side entrances by three. The area inside this enclosure was occupied by dwellings and is now overrun with jungle vegetation. A path 607 ft (185 m) long leads to the cruciform platform with *nagas* that affords access to the *gopura* of the third enclosure, a rectangle 574 x 656 ft (175 x 200 m). Two colossal headless *dvarapalas* guard the main entrance. The pediments are quite interesting: the middle area is dominated by Rama and Ravana, recognizable by his thousand heads and thousand arms; on the east pediment there is a relief of a boat, and in the west one the battle of Lanka is represented.

Beyond the *gopura*, a slight turn to the left leads to a pair of pediments on the ground. They are exceptionally interesting: one, with many figures, some of them praying, is dominated by a standing divinity holding two kneeling beings by the hair, while the other features the scene of Shiva cremating Kama, the god of love, who is depicted dead in his wife's arms. On the walls of this enclosure is a row of merlons with bearded soothsayers in the niches. Returning to the axial route, you will come to a cloister made up of a gallery with entrance pavilions at the four cardinal points and on the corners. This complex was dedicated to Vishnu, as can be seen in the isolated pediment just after the small entrance *gopura* that depicts Krishna, the incarnation of the god Vishnu,

raising Mt. Govardhana to protect his followers from a flood unleashed by Indra. The pedestal with three holes that lies a short distance away once had the statues of Rama, another incarnation of Vishnu, of his wife Sita, and of his brother Lakshmana, heroes of the epic poem *Ramayana*. In the northwest corner of the cloister is a small 'library,' while in the middle is a *prasat* preceded by a long hall and followed by another chamber that connects it to the second enclosure.

This enclosure is made up of a laterite wall (272 x 321 ft/83 x 98 m) without a *gopura* and corner towers, with a double colonnade that is no longer traversable. Continuing on the west-east axis, you will immediately come to the first enclosure, which is almost square (180 ft or 55 m per side) and contains various galleries. Lying against the west gallery, which is accessible only by way of the *gopura*, are six small edifices with a *cella* and porch; the north and south galleries both have a *gopura* and two doors added, as well as windows and colonnades, while the east gallery comprises a blind wall bordered by columns, with a triple entrance pavilion and two corner projecting sections between which stand six *prasats* with their porches facing east.

Past the west *gopura* of the first enclosure is a hall with twelve pillars that leads to the central *prasat*. Before entering, it is

185 West gopura in the third enclosure.

186-187 *The wall of the second enclosure.*

worthwhile visiting the two courtyards to the northwest and southwest of the columned hall. Both have a pillar in the middle topped by a peg and house three edifices with corbeled vaults that rest against the west gallery and almost look like 'oratories' (they may have been funerary chapels), as well as four other edifices, two 'libraries' and two 'oratories' against the east side. The decoration is particularly interesting, a beautiful pattern of leaves and volutes among which are *devatas* and ascetics with their legs crossed. Other noteworthy sights are the southwest corner tower, one of the best preserved, and, again in this courtyard, on the pediment of the second chapel resting against the wall, a standing Buddha; it is one of the very few that are intact. Traces of rebuilding, and above all the frequent mutilation of the images of Buddha, which were either scraped away or were replaced by *lingams*, are signs of the revival of Brahmanism after the death of Jayavarman and the attempt to convert the Preah Khan, as well as other Buddhist monasteries, into Hindu temples.

In the prasat with its four porticoes, which has a *stupa* in the middle that was added in the 16th century (once there was the statue of Lokeshvara Dharanindravarman), the

186 bottom *The 'oratory' in the first enclosure courtyard.*

187 top Buddhas transformed into ascetics.

numerous holes in the walls suggest they were dressed with bronze plates and that the outside of the sanctuary was also probably cased with bronze. Indeed, the stele of Preah Khan states that 1,500 tons of bronze were used in the construction of the temple. From the central temple turn left, behind a headless statue that may be of Jayavarman VII, to get to the north cloister, which is the complex dedicated to Shiva.

After going through the north *gopuras* in the first and second galleries and having come to a pedestal with two feet – an unusual reference to Shiva – turn right to admire the sculpture of Vishnu reclining on the serpent Ananta, which is depicted here in the guise of a dragon, while Vishnu's wife Lakshmi is massaging his feet. Now turn left and note a dancing god with several arms that has been identified as Shiva Nataraja, the "Lord of Dance." Proceeding along the south-north axis, you will exit at the north *gopura* of the third enclosure, guarded by a headless *dvarapala*. At this point it is advisable to go back to the central *prasat* and then head toward the south *gopura* of the third enclosure, passing through the south cloister, which is dedicated to the dead Khmer sovereigns. This complex is in ruins, but there are two beautiful threshold guardians on the jambs;

187 center Gallery in the first enclosure courtyard.

187 bottom Wall decoration of the 'oratories' of the first enclosure courtyard.

188 top left
A dvarapala with a gentle appearance.

188 top right The cella, with a posterior stupa, of the central prasat.

the one at right is depicted in an aggressive attitude, while his counterpart seems to be gentle. And to your right there is also a fine view of a tower with a lotus-shaped roof that is perfectly intact. The *gopura* you will exit from, which is protected by two *dvarapalas* whose heads have been cut off, appears wild and mysterious.

Back once again at the central *prasat*, you now proceed eastward, crossing through a columned hall and an area cluttered with ruins. Here, in the *gopura* of the first

portal of the *gopura* a lovely panel of dancing girls. Other noteworthy friezes of dancing *apsaras* decorate the so-called Hall of Dancers, a hypostyle structure with false doors at the corners that faces the terrace to the east: derived from the cruciform cloister, it measures 85 x 118 ft (26 x 36 m), has 102 pillars and is roofed by a corbeled vault and a half-vault.

Exiting from the pavilion through the north doorway, you will see a walkway lined with *naga* balustrades along which is an unusual pavilion resting on 32 thick, cylindrical columns 11.4 ft

189 top left Apsaras with a pointed diadem.

189 top right Kinnari holding garlands in the first enclosure gopura.

189 bottom right A ferocious dvarapala.

enclosure is a beautiful frieze under the ceiling with corner *garudas* and *kinnari*, winged females that are human for half their length, the rest of their bodies consisting of garlands of flowers, who are paying tribute to the Buddhas in the niches (which are missing).

The *gopura* in the second enclosure faces a square terrace paved in sandstone that is closed off to the north and south by a laterite wall and connected to the east to the protruding entrance of a sandstone edifice with two small chambers at the sides. Turning away from the gigantic tree that dominates the south small chamber, you will see on the side

188 bottom and 189 bottom left Frieze of apsaras in the Hall of the Dancers.

190 top Part of the gopura in the second enclosure.

190 bottom left Frieze of praying figures under the mutilated Buddha.

190 bottom right The gopura in the third enclosure.

(3.5 m) high, which now appear for the first time in Khmer architecture. This structure, with two porches at the ends, has two stories, the first consisting of a hall with five windows per façade, and had a wooden and tile roof. There is no access to the upper floor, though there may have been a wooden stairway. Many theories have been advanced concerning the purpose of this building: from a granary to a storehouse for the Sacred Sword. On the western extension of this mysterious edifice there is a massive laterite terrace with stairways guarded over by lions that was almost certainly a venue for ceremonies, perhaps even cremations. Behind the terrace, on the corner porch of the second enclosure, the guardians are in an excellent state of preservation.

Now take the *naga* walkway and head toward the spectacular east *gopura* in the third enclosure, which is 347 ft (106 m) long, compared to the 131 ft (40 m) of the other *gopuras*, and which opens outward with a double colonnade gallery. Once through this latter, you will see an impressive rectangular platform bordered by *nagas* that is 131 x 98 ft (40 x 30 m) and has stairways lined with lions. A path begins at this point. After about 492 ft (150

191 top Pavilion with cylindrical columns in the third enclosure.

191 bottom Guardian lion of the stairways.

m) you will come to a 'house of fire' (possibly connected to a fire cult) that has been beautifully restored. This consists of a vestibule and a rectangular hall whose north wall is blind, while the south one has four windows. The hall has a corbeled vault and two half-vaults on a lower level, so that from the outside it looks like an imitation triple nave. A tower topped by a double lotus rises up on the west end of this structure.

Exiting from the *gopura* in the fourth enclosure, you will see the rows of *devas* and *asuras* and the avenue lined with columns: a Buddha still stands on one of first ones at left.

Prasat Prei

Built during the reign of Jayavarman VII, it stands on an earth embankment among the ruins of a laterite enclosure, with a 'library' in the southeast corner that has an entrance facing west. The decoration is lavish, as is always the case with the Bayon style.

Visit

Once at Preah Khan, go around it up to the north *gopura*, and 2460 ft (750 m) farther on take the unpaved road at left that goes for 328 ft (100 m) right to Prasat Prei, the "Sanctuary in the Forest." In the northeast corner are the remains of a laterite foundation. The *prasat* is surmounted by a four-level tower, and a long corridor to the east leads to the *cella*, which has small corridors with blind doors on its other sides.

192 top detail of the walls made of laterite.

192 bottom The temple and the remains of the 'library.'

Banteay Prei

Banteay Prei, the "Citadel of the Forest" dates back to the reign of Jayavarman VII and, being rather small, it is possible to acquire a good understanding of its structure and of the construction methods used.

193 top View of the temple.

Visit

When you get to Preah Khan, skirt around it up to the north *gopura*, and 2460 ft (750 m) farther on take a dirt road at your left. Then 492 ft (150 m) past Prasat Prei is Banteay Prei. Once past the ruins of the third enclosure you come to the second one, which is made of laterite, is surrounded by a moat and is 262 ft (80 m) long and 196 ft (60 m) wide. The east *gopura* in the first enclosure has a cruciform plan and was made of sandstone, with the windows with imitation lowered curtains and Bayon-style *devatas*. The central *prasat* has doorways on all four sides and is surrounded by a gallery 98 ft (30 m) long and 82 ft (25 m) wide, with low corner towers and *gopuras* at the cardinal points, surmounted by a two-story tower crowned by a lotus bud.

Krol Romeas

This is a large circle made of laterite used to house animals; it is located next to the Banteay Prei.

193 center A niche with a devata.

193 bottom The gallery of the first enclosure and the gopura with a lotus bud motif.

Krol Ko

This construction, which lies in two enclosures, dates from the time of Jayavarman VII and its modern name means "Park of the Oxen." The temple is rarely visited by tourists.

194 top Detail of a pediment on the ground.

194 center Niches withe devatas and blind windows with lowered curtains.

194 bottom The 'library' in the first enclosure.

Visit

About 328 ft (100 m) west of the turnoff for Neak Pean, a path heading north leads to the temple, another 328 ft (100 m) or so farther on. You enter from the east, passing through the second enclosure wall, made of laterite. At your left, on the ground under a tree, are the remains of battlements with carvings of Buddha in thee niches. Farther along, again on the ground, is a pediment with Krishna Govardana and opposite this is another one with Lokeshvara. Beyond the first enclosure, which has a laterite *gopura*, you will see a 'library' with a portico and the *prasat* with a vestibule, the entrance facing east, and blind doors in the projecting parts on the other sides. The roof is lacking, but this makes it possible to visualize how the corbeled vault was built.

Neak Pean

Neak Pean is one of the most important monuments in Angkor. The site occupies an area about 1148 ft (350 m) per side in the middle of the Jayatataka, the baray that Jayavarman had excavated for the Preah Khan and that is now dry.

Visit

To get there, take the 656-ft (200-m) unpaved, hard-to-traverse road 1.5 miles (2.5 km) from the north *gopura* of Preah Khan.

The complex once comprised 13 pools; today 5 have been restored. In the middle of the main pond, which is square and measures 230 ft (70 m) per side, there is a round island 108 ft (33 m) in diameter whose laterite base consists of two 'entwined *nagas*', or "Neak Pean" in modern Cambodian. Dominating the islet, lying on a platform with lotus flower motifs that is 46 ft (14 m) in diameter, is a small *prasat* that was rebuilt: its original cruciform plan was turned into a round one, with the insertion of three-headed elephants surmounted by lions between the doors. Three of the four entrances were walled up and statues of Lokeshvara were sculpted on them. The pediments have carvings of episodes from the life of Buddha: in the northern one is his departure from his father's palace, the eastern one has the scene of Buddha cutting off his hair and in the western one he is seated under the *bohdi* tree, while the one on the south side is illegible. The *prasat* is crowned by four tiers topped by a lotus bud.

Next to the temple, emerging from the water is the horse Balaha, a manifestation of Lokeshvara, with the merchant Simhala and his companions holding on to his sides, as they have been saved from a shipwreck in the ogress-infested waters of Sri Lanka. The

195 top A naga.

195 bottom A Lokeshvara on the prasat.

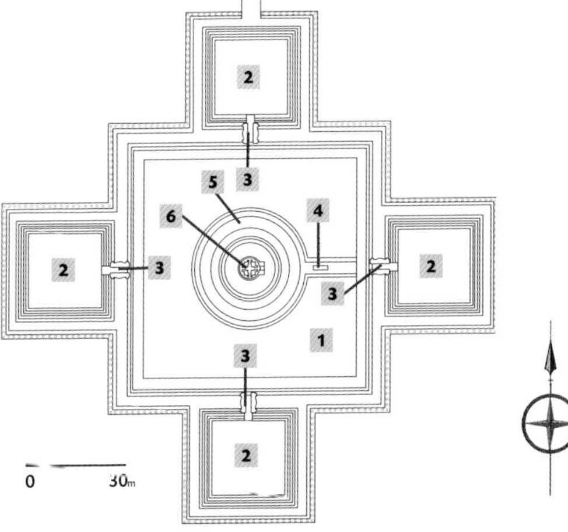

Legend

1 Central basin
2 Side pools/basins
3 Chapels
4 The horse Balaha
5 Island
6 Prasat

symbolism implied here is that of crossing over the ocean of rebirth thanks to the grace of the *bodhisattvas*, in order to attain *nirvana*.

Four smaller ponds 82 ft (25 m) per side are arranged in a cross shape around the central one, and at the axes are four vaulted edifices – added in a later period – acroteria and images of Lokeshvara. Here, when poured into a communicating receptacle by means of conduits with four carved spigots with different masks, the water of the large pool, with its healing powers, would be available to the pilgrims. One of these receptacles can be seen in the guise of a woman's bust behind the east chapel; this edifice has the mask with human features and symbolizes the element of the earth. In the north chapel the elephant mask was the emblem of water, while in the north chapel the lion sprinkling water on the ill evoked the fire, and in the one to the west the horse was the symbol of air. The fifth cosmic element, ethereal space, was probably alluded to by the central *prasat*.

The context here would seem to be that of traditional Indian medicine, Ayurveda, according to which the balanced composition of the elements in the human structure is fundamental, and any excess or flaw in one of them may bring about illness. Hence the water cure in the pool, which was connected to the 'defective' element.

A popular pilgrimage site, Neak Pean is described with a wealth of detail in the stele of the Preah Khan, which informs us that the images of fourteen gods and no less than a "thousand *lingams*" were placed there, which by no means is in conflict with the Buddhist character of the site, but on the contrary asserts its universal and conciliatory character among the faiths of the Khmer empire. Called Rajyashri at the time, that is, "the Fortune of the Kingdom," Neak Pean is also connected to Lakshmi, the mistress of royal fortune in both Buddhist and Hindu contexts.

Some scholars believe that Neak Pean is a representation of Anavatapta, the mythical Himalayan lake where the divine beings bathed and which was the fountainhead of the four great rivers of India. Thus the two *nagas* are the king and queen of the lake, whose waters were used to consecrate the *cakravartin*, the universal sovereign. Jayavarman VII therefore gave his kingdom a lake that not only had healing properties but was the source of royal power.

196 The head of a man in the east chapel (left) and the head of a lion in the south chapel (right).

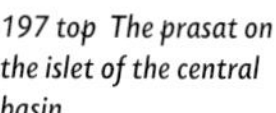

197 top The prasat on the islet of the central basin.

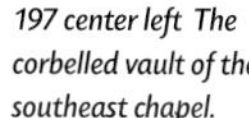

197 center left The corbelled vault of the southeast chapel.

197 center right The northwest chapel.

197 bottom The horse Balaha facing the prasat.

WHEN YOU VISIT ANGKOR THOM, THE "GREAT CITY," LOCATED ABOUT 7 KM NORTH OF SIEM REAP, YOU WILL DISCOVER MANY MONUMENTS THAT ARE RELATIVELY CLOSE TO EACH OTHER.

The Heart of Angkor

198 *Exterior of the East Gate of Angkor Thom.*

Introduction

THE HIGH CONCENTRATION OF MONUMENTS AT ANGKOR THOM AND THEIR RELATIVELY PROXIMITY TO ONE ANOTHER MAKE FOR A VISIT ON FOOT THAT OFFERS A COMPLETE, ALBEIT SUMMARY, OVERVIEW OF KHMER ARCHITECTURE AS WELL AS A PICTURE OF THE LIFE OF THAT TIME.

A walk around the walls, with their monumental gates and the divine protectors standing in front of them, reveals how the defense of the complex was based more on symbolic-esoteric elements than on military structures proper, while a walk inside the palace enclosure revolves around the Phimeanakas, an ancient legendary site. Around the Royal Square, the luxurious monuments – the Baphuon, the Terrace of the Leper King and Terrace of the Elephants, the terrace of Tep Pranam, the Prasat Suor Prat and the Khleang

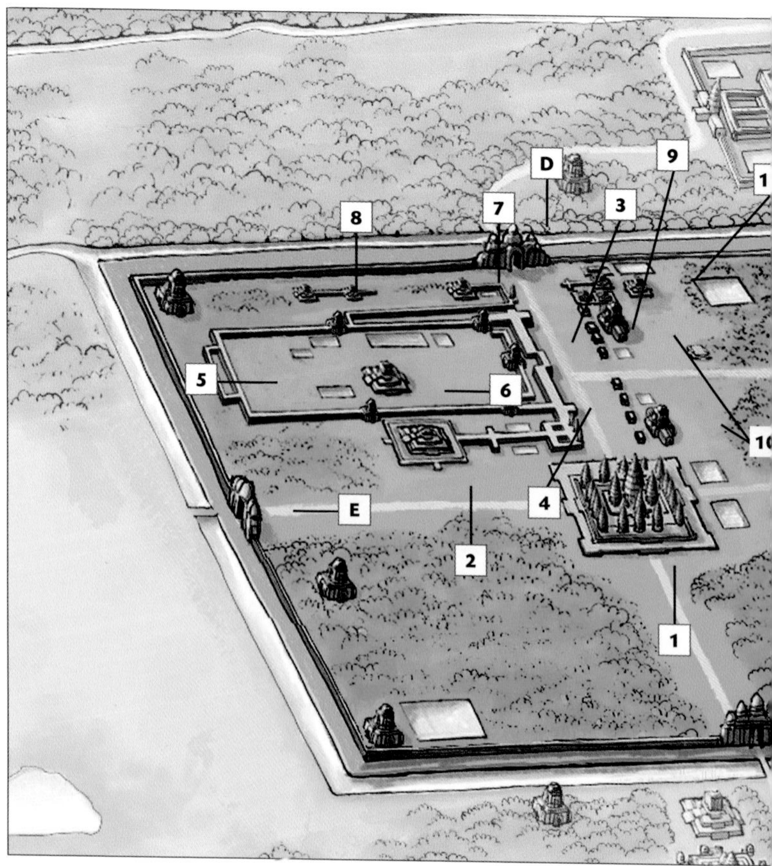

(whose function is still a mystery) – bespeak imperial grandeur. The complex and rather disturbing Bayon is the last megalomaniacal monument built to honor the deification of the king. The looming presence of these gigantic constructions is mitigated by the large areas of greenery that were once populated by dwellings and service structures and are now an oasis of dream-like silence that boasts the Preah Palilay with its carved scenes from Buddha's life and the fascinating, deserted temples of the Preah Pithu.

Legend

A South Gate
B East Gate
C Victory Gate
D North Gate
E West Gate

1 Bayon
2 Baphuon
3 Terrace of the Leper King
4 Terrace of the Elephants
5 Royal Palace
6 Phimeanakas
7 Tep Pranam
8 Preah Palilay
9 Prasat Suor Prat
10 Khleang
11 Preah Pithu

Angkor Thom

Angkor Thom, the 'Great Capital,' attracted a population of one million and within its walls were housed the court, the priests, the high officials, and the bureaucrats, while some of the common people lived outside the fortifications.

Visit

Access to Angkor Thom is afforded by five laterite causeways that cross over the outside moat and lead to five monumental gates, four on the cardinal points

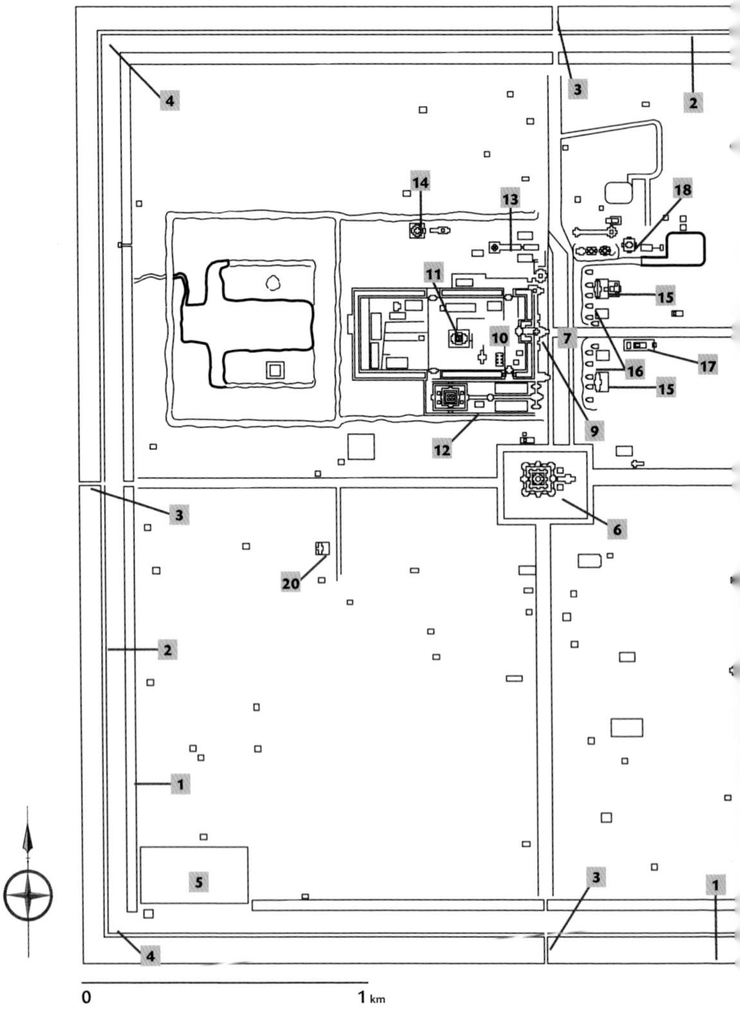

0 1 km

of the compass and the fifth, known as the Victory Gate, added on the east side to afford access to the Royal Square and the Palace. Each of the five gates, which are up to 75 ft (23 m) tall, is surmounted by a turreted structure consisting of four faces of the *bodhisattva* Lokeshvara, with whom Jayavarman VII identified himself. On the sides of the gate, Airavata, the three-headed elephant, mount of Indra, king of the gods, keeps watch with his lord on his back. Above this a series of praying figures is the frame on which the faces are placed. At the approach to the gates of Angkor Thom there are two rows of 'giants': 54 *devas* or deities at left and 54 *asuras* or demons at right, all beautifully

The History

Built over the earlier settlement founded by Udayadityavarman II that revolved around the Baphuon, Angkor Thom is enclosed by massive laterite walls that delimit a square area of 1.8 miles (3 km) per side, bordered by a moat 328 ft (100 m) wide and 20 ft (6 m) deep.

On the inside of the 26-ft (8-m) tall walls is a bastion 49 ft (15 m) wide with a parapet walk. On the corners are four small temples, all called Prasat Chrung (see below), which house stelae containing information concerning the construction of the city. About 328 ft (100 m) from the walls a 130-ft (40-m) wide canal once marked another inner perimeter, along which there was a road used to move troops and for the ritual circumambulation processions of the city.

Legend

1 Moats
2 Walls
3 Gates
4 Prasat Chrung
5 Beng Thom
6 Bayon
7 Royal Square
8 Avenue of Victory
9 Terraces
10 Royal Palace
11 Phimeanakas
12 Baphuon
13 Tep Pranam
14 Preah Palilay
15 Khleang
16 Prasat Suor Prat
17 Terrace of Buddha
18 Preah Pithu
19 Mangalartha
20 Monument 486

203 top A naga held up by the leader of the demons in front of the South Gate.

203 bottom right Interior of the east gate.

203 bottom left One of the gods in front of the South Gate.

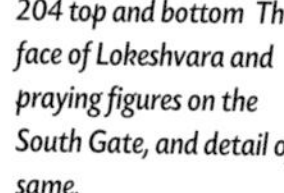

204 top and bottom The face of Lokeshvara and praying figures on the South Gate, and detail of same.

executed, holding *nagas* or multi-headed serpents.

From the gates there ran five avenues from 98 to 131 ft (30 to 40 m) wide flanked by canals 26 ft (8 m) wide that flowed in the enclosure canal. The city was divided into *padas* or residential 'squares,' in keeping with the traditional Hindu urban grid layout that had straight intersecting streets, while the location of the districts and buildings depended on their function.

Of the four gates, the south one is the most famous and best preserved.

The North Gate is usually not part of the itineraries, even though it has to be crossed to reach other temples; but it is well worth a visit, not so much for the series of giants, most of which are headless, as for the praying figures and the three-headed elephants (which are almost all intact) and for the faces of Lokeshvara decorated with crowns and jewels. The Victory Gate, which was also used as an access, has no canals and only parts of the bodies of the giants have remained. The East Gate is reached by means of an unpaved road in the brush: before crossing it and going over a fascinating and mysterious path that winds among the trees, note at your right the god Indra and two lovely praying nymphs. The West Gate is the one in the poorest state, but from there beautiful walks on the walls lead to the Beng Thom – the Great Pool, 1300 ft (400 m) long

***204-205** The South Gate is flanked by rows of gods and demons.*

***205 bottom** The last demon in the row in front of the South Gate.*

206 top left The North Gate of the complex.

206 top right The exterior of the West Gate.

and 1150 ft (350 m) wide, which collected the city's sewage and channeled it into the outer south moat by means of five vaulted canals 196 ft (60 m) long that passed under the walls – and the Prasat Chrung.

There are other ruins among the vegetation. Little remains of Monument 487, known as Mangalartha, which was the last one to be constructed in Angkor, in honor of the son of one of the tutors of Jayavarman VII; it can be reached via a path that winds through the forest about 656 ft (200 m) west of the Victory Gate.

206 bottom A demon in front of the Victory Gate.

Monument 486 is a Brahmanic construction dating from the 10th century that was transformed into a Buddhist edifice in the 13th century; it is also in the forest, and can be reached by going from Bayon toward the West Gate and turning left at about the halfway point.

After the terrible sack of Yashodharapura by the Chams in 1177, Jayavarman VII managed to drive out the enemy and ascend to the throne. He then decided to build an invincible city. The defense of Angkor Thom was not only based on the structures, but also on a complex apotropaic symbolism connected to the construction. The architects drew inspiration from Hindu cosmology: the city revolves around the Bayon, the temple mountain that symbolizes Mt. Meru, and lies at the foot of the cosmic mountain as the Jambudvipa, the 'Continent of the Rose-apple' that embraces India, surrounded by six other concentric circles of continents separated by

207 top Faces of Lokeshvara on the North Gate.

207 center The inner section of the Victory Gate.

207 bottom A row of demons in front of the South Gate.

209 King Jayavarman VII in a 12th century sculpture kept in the National Museum of Phnom Penh.

oceans. Furthermore, Buddhist cosmology also played a role in the construction of Angkor Thom, as it encloses the world in a rock wall, beyond which there is the great primordial ocean, and these are symbolized by the enclosure wall and moat.

But Jayavarman VII's city is also linked to the so-called Churning of the Ocean of Milk: the 54 deities and 54 demons total the sacred number of the 108 protectors of the city. The *asuras*, as the servants of royal power, keep evil influences and enemies far from the city. The *nagas* with their seven heads ready to spit poison initiate the rows of giants and terminate them again with their erect tails. The multi-headed serpent is both the primordial serpent Vasuki of Hindu mythology and the Khmer symbol of the rainbow, the bridge between earth and sky, the emblem of the pact of benevolence of the celestial powers that send fertilizing rain to the Earth.

The gods of the South Gate are corresponded by the demons of the North Gate and vice versa, and the same holds true for the East and West gates. The powers of light and darkness are both indispensable as polar forces, whose opposition generates the dynamism of existence. The rotation of the cosmic mountain, Meru-Bayon, results in the extraction of *amrita*, the ambrosia that makes Angkor Thom invincible. Jayavarman VII therefore built a city protected by divine powers and at the same time he utilized those powers to ensure his own immortality. Indra, the warrior god *par excellence*, the king of the celestial deities, also helps to protect the city.

Lastly, Lokeshvara is keeping watch from the top of the city gates; his attentive and compassionate faces with the features of the king look in all the directions of the kingdom, guaranteeing protection: Hindu symbolism is therefore reinforced by Buddhist symbolism, becoming more comprehensible to the people, who up to that time had no access to the innermost or most elevated parts of the temples and understood very little, if anything, of the esoteric meaning of the Indian myths.

208 Gods and demons guard the gates of the Angkor Thom complex.

Bayon

The walls of Angkor Thom itself constitute the outermost enclosure wall of this temple, which is articulated on three levels. When approaching the Bayon from the east, the first structure you see is a platform 236 ft (72 m) long and 88.5 ft (27 m) wide, flanked by two pools.

210 top A prasat with the faces of Lokeshvara.

Visit

A terrace bordered by *nagas* and lions leads to the *gopura* of the third enclosure, a rectangle measuring 512 x 462 ft (156 x 141 m), consisting of a gallery with a blind wall facing the interior and double row of columns facing the exterior, which has led scholars to suppose that a half-nave was added.

Note the graceful *apsaras* dancing on the lotuses. The corner towers and entrance pavilions in the gallery are cruciform, with broad, projecting porticoes: the four central pillars in the main hall are larger than the eight adjacent ones. These hypostyle edifices, with sides measuring 66.5 ft (20 m) had corbeled vaults and cross vaulting that collapsed because the bay was extended and because of flaws in the overall construction. The techniques adopted, borrowed from carpentry – for example, the use of superposed pediments – proved to be unsuitable to bear the weight of stone roofs.

On the blind wall, which is 14.7

210 bottom Marching to a dance step, relief from the second enclosure wall.

211 top left *Aerial view of Bayon.*

211 top right *Detail of a relief in the east gallery of the third enclosure.*

The History

The Bayon is difficult to interpret because it was altered so many times. Long considered to be a Hindu sanctuary, only in 1925 was it recognized as Buddhist.

Legend

1 Basins
2 Terrace
3 Gopura
4 Third enclosure
5 Corner pavilions
6 First level
7 'Libraries'
8 Second enclosure
9 Courtyards of the second level
10 Third level
11 Prasat
12 Protuberant section
13 Central Prasat

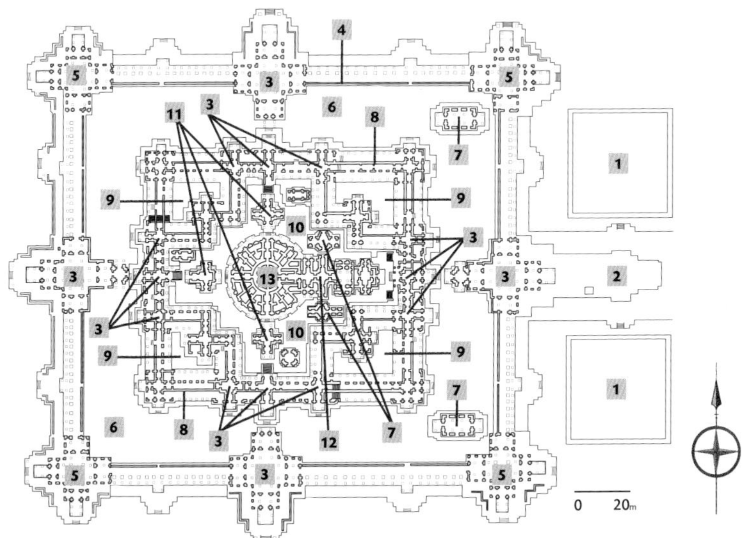

212-213 The northeast corner of the temple.

ft (4.5 m) high, is a stupendous series of bas-relief sculpture on several registers, the incomplete parts of which allow us to follow the various working stages.

Having entered by way of the *gopura*, visitors should then turn left and go through the south wing of the east gallery: in the ranks of troops that march among scenes of everyday life there are also Chinese soldiers, as well as the procession of the ark of the Sacred Fire, accompanied by bearded Brahmans; in the second register a buffalo is about to be sacrificed. In the south gallery the west wing celebrates Jayavarman VII's victory

212 bottom left The south gopura of the second enclosure.

212 bottom right The protuberant body of the central prasat.

in the naval battle of Tonlé Sap against the Chams, who wear helmets in the shape of overturned flowers. The backgrounds are fully detailed and the lake fauna is rendered with lively precision. In between the battle scenes, daily life is humming: in the houses on stilts pigs are being cooked in large

***213 bottom* Courtyard of the third enclosure.**

214 top The army marching (south wing of the east gallery in the third enclosure).

214 bottom left the supply lines (south wing of the east gallery in the third enclosure).

214 bottom right The Chams can easily be recognized by their special headdresses.

cauldrons and on skewers over the fire, and the utensils and furnishings are the same that are used to this day in the rural areas of the Khmer region. In the marketplace the men are drinking brandy and watching cock and wild boar fights, while on the upper registers there are scenes of life in the royal palace: the princesses are dressing and the nobles are playing chess. The common people proceed on foot with their possessions on their heads, and the wealthy are transported in palanquins. The military procession continues in the west wing. In the south wing of the west gallery there are many incomplete carvings, but the scene of the construction of a temple is interesting, as is the scuffle that

215 top left Detail of the Battle of Tonlé Sap (third enclosure, east wing of the south gallery).

215 top right Third enclosure, east wing of the south gallery, with the Battle of Tonlé Sap.

seems the representation of a civil war. In the north wing there are traces of inscriptions that were 'instructions' for the sculptors – and were never removed. In the northwest corner pavilion are the remains of a Buddha on a *naga*. The west wing of the north gallery contains festive scenes with acrobats, wrestlers and images of combat that continue in the east wing, where the Khmers seem to be fleeing from the Chams. The central *gopura* of this gallery is watched over by a headless *dvarapala*. Back at the east façade of the temple, the north wing has other war scenes.

In the corners of the east side of the courtyard delimited by the third gallery, there are two 'libraries.' You can also see part of the foundations of sixteen rectangular edifices that may have been demolished upon the death of Jayavarman VII; they were laid out in perpendicular fashion, four per side, between the third and second gallery, thus creating sixteen small courtyards. Simple doors in the wall with relief sculpture afforded access to them. It seems that the sixteen edifices were sanctuaries housing the images of the main Khmer deities and of those of the various provinces dominated by the Khmer empire.

You have to go up 4.2 ft (1.3 m) to reach the second gallery, which measures 230 x 262 ft (70 x 80 m). With a triple nave, it has a blind wall with a corbeled vault on the exterior that is also decorated with bas-relief sculpture and a series of columns; in the interior there is a windowed nave with a half-vault and a columned portico. On the triple *gopuras* of the four axial entrances and on the corners there are sixteen towers surmounted by the four faces of Lokeshvara.

While in the bas-reliefs of the third gallery it was not only the gods and kings who dominated the scene but also the common people, who at the twilight of the

215 bottom A devata holding a dove.

216 top *Niche with devatas and dvarapalas.*

216 center *A gopura with dvarapalas and a lintel with apsaras.*

216 bottom ***A gopura with a naga balustrade and a garuda.***

Khmer empire gained the right to appear side-by-side with their rulers, in the second gallery the subjects change. Given the prevalence of Hindu subjects, scholars feel that this reflects the return of Jayavarman VIII to Hinduism in the second half of the 13th century. Furthermore, since the walls have limited space, there are more single scenes and small sections than long panels.

Your visit begins by turning left at the east entrance. In the south wing there is Shiva among hermits; in the east wing of the south gallery – where you can see the beautiful ceiling in its entirety – troops marching and palace scenes flank the representation of the myth of a young boy saved from drowning, while in the west wing are a bearded Shiva and a four-armed Vishnu.

In south wing of the west gallery, Vishnu's combats alternate with scenes of the construction of a temple; the Churning of the Ocean of Milk is depicted in the north wing. The west wing of the north gallery offers scenes of court life and religious devotion, as well as two images of the Trimurti and one of the myth of Kama, the god of love, killed by Shiva. In the east wing we again see representations of Shiva with his consort Uma and the bull Nandi, and of Vishnu with Lakshmi. Back at the east façade of the gallery, the east wing illustrates two myths that are still a part of Khmer folklore: the liberation of a girl imprisoned in the rock and a king becoming ill with leprosy after being bitten by a serpent.

Most probably the second gallery was added to an earlier cruciform structure in order to transform it into a rectangle by means of a four square wings. In the interior, in fact, the open spaces are tiny, reduced to extremely small courtyards that look almost like wells, since the cruciform platform on the third level occupies almost all the area of the second one.

Two side stairways in the east *gopura* and one in each of the other three *gopuras* on the other sides lead to the third level, 10 ft (3 m) higher up. With a Greek cross plan, the terrace is occupied by a veritable forest of face towers

***216-217** The northeast 'library' in the third enclosure courtyard.*

***217 bottom** Lions guarding the stairways and naga balustrades in the third enclosure.*

218 bottom This elegant sculpture depicts the band that accompanies the army.

made of stone, dominated by the formidable central *prasat*, 82 ft (25 m) in diameter and 141 ft (43 m) above ground level. Four chambers, flanked by two 'libraries,' afford access to the *prasat*: a portico, a columned hall and a double vestibule. On the west, north and south sides three other cruciform *prasats* surround the central one, connecting to the outer gallery. The terrace has other structures: a square one in the southeast corner and two rectangular ones in the northwest and northeast corners.

Arriving from the east, you head right up to the 'library' and then, keeping this latter to your left, you go around it until you reach corner of the balustrade to see a beautiful Lokeshvara on the pediment of an edifice on the lower terrace. Circling around the central *prasat*, you will see faces of Lokeshvara everywhere, with the features of Jayavarman VII. According to the scholar Paul Mus there were originally 54 *prasats*, which means more than 200 faces of the Compassionate Lord that, facing the cardinal points, watched over and protected the Khmer people. However, although Lokeshvara is a *bodhisattva*, it is the symbolism of the *Buddharaja*, or Buddha-king, that is evoked here. In fact, the Bayon complex celebrates both the functional role of the king, who is identified with Lokeshvara and is therefore the thoughtful and concerned guardian of the well-

***218-219** View of a panel of the bas-reliefs in the south gallery of the second enclosure.*

***219 top** Scenes of battles against the Cham.*

***219 center** Boar combat, third enclosure, east wing of the south gallery.*

***219 bottom** A devata combing her hair and bas-reliefs in the second enclosure.*

220 top Towers with the faces of Lokeshvara in the first gallery.

being of his subjects, and his most intimate essence as Buddha, from which the *bodhisattvas* themselves emanate.

The central *prasat* has been drastically rebuilt. It has a cruciform plan, to which were added four radial chapels for a total of eight sanctuaries with porticoes, the east one extending into the projecting part. The chapels probably housed deified members of the royal family. Furthermore, among the eight rectangular chapels there are eight triangular ones, the two at the sides of the projecting porch being smaller and almost impossible to identify. Besides the solar symbolism (the eight directions of space) and lunar symbolism (sixteen digits, according to Hindu philosophy), the massive *prasat*, which in the meantime had become round, was modeled after the *stupa*, the first Buddhist monument built in India as a burial mound over the cremated remains of the historical Buddha. The eight chapels also refer to the Wheel of the Law, which consists of eight rays – the eightfold path of rectitude in faith, resolution, word, action, moderation, effort, thought, and concentration – symbolizing Buddhism.

You can enter the dark *cella*, a true cave 16.5 ft (5 m) in diameter in the prasat temple pyramid, from the east or west: all around is a dark *pradakshinapatha*, the corridor for the *pradakshina*, the ritual worship of the sacred object, which should be encircled at one's right as a sign of respect and veneration: this was a statue, 11.8

220 bottom The central prasat viewed from the gopura of the second enclosure (left); third level, the protuberant secion of the central prasat (right).

ft (3.6 m) high, of Buddha seated on the coils of the serpent Mucilinda, which used its seven heads like a baldachin to shelter the Enlightened One. He had the king's facial features. Smashed to pieces and thrown into the foundation well during the revival of Brahmanism that occurred after the death of Jayavarman VII, the statue was discovered in 1933, reassembled, and placed on a terrace east of the South Khleang.

221 The smiling Lokeshvara.

223 The goddess Tara, identified with Jayarajadevi, the consort of Jayavarman VII. Musée Guimet, Paris.

The first form of Buddhism that spread in the Khmer area was brought by missionary monks who followed on the heels of Indian merchants. This was the Hinayana or Lesser Vehicle. It is more correctly defined as Theravada, that is, the Doctrine of the Elders, the custodian of Buddha's original and succinct teachings that favored moral training and a monastic life rather than metaphysical speculation and mysticism. These two elements were, on the other hand, the basis of the schools of Mahayana or 'Great Vehicle,' which were already present in Kambuja in the 7th-8th century and were considered by their supporters to be the custodians of Buddha's true message of salvation. The vehicle is termed 'great' because it included esoteric aspects that, according to the Mahayanians, the followers of the Lesser Vehicle did not have. The Vajrayana or 'Diamond Vehicle,' an esoteric version of Buddhism that is quite complex on a ritual level, spread somewhat in the 12th and 13th century, as can be seen in some inscriptions and splendid bronzes.

When Jayavarman VII ascended the throne Mahayana Buddhism became the state religion; the new king, inspired by compassion, proclaimed himself the incarnation of the Bodhisattva Lokeshvara, Lord of the World. Although he is enlightened, the Bodhisattva purposely does not attain liberation and enlightenment in order to indicate the path of salvation to others, in keeping with the cardinal virtues of Mahayan Buddhism, benevolence and compassion. Jayarajadevi, the favorite wife of Jayavarman, was associated with the goddess Prajna or, according to another version, to the goddess Tara, the Mistress of Compassion, and other relatives of the emperor were recognized as figures in the Buddhist pantheon after their death.

But if on the one hand Jayavarman set himself up as a compassionate ruler, on the other his mania for building and eagerness to attain immortality forced his subjects to make terrible sacrifices. Thus, Mahayana Buddhism did not survive in the Khmer empire: when the king died, his kingdom, on its knees and bled dry by his obsessions, abandoned the Great Vehicle and turned to the more essential Theravada, which has continued to be practiced with extreme simplicity by some monks and part of the population.

222 Delicate figures of dancing apsaras on the columns of a gopura of Bayon.

Baphuon

Baphuon, which is situated 656 ft (200 m) northwest of the Bayon, was completed around the year 1060 and is the center of the capital of Udayadityavarman II. This exceptionally large temple mountain eventually collapsed because the engineering skills of the Khmers did not match their architectural aspirations.

224 *Causeway and basin.*

The History

The enormous weight of the galleries, *gopuras* and corner towers on the terraces of the Baphuon was too heavy to bear, even though the builders had used cramps to connect the blocks of stone. At present a grandiose restoration project is underway that will take some years to finish. The Baphuon lies in a rectangular enclosure that measures 1395 x 410 ft (425 x 125 m) and is made of sandstone, which is unusual. It is a five-tier pyramid 78 ft (24 m) high, 426 x 338 ft (130 x 103 m) at the base, and 138 x 118 ft (42 x 36 m) at the top. Counting the crowning prasats, it is probable that this temple attained a total height of 165 ft (50 m). A 656-ft (200-m) elevated approach more than 3.2 ft (1 m) above ground level on a platform supported by a triple row of round and short columns leads to the temple. The approach is flanked by four pools; the second pool to the left was restored with its sandstone steps.

Legend

1 Outer enclosure
2 Gopura
3 Causeway
4 Cruciform pavilion
5 Pool
6 Perimetral gallery
7 'Libraries'
8 Pyramid
9 Central Prasat

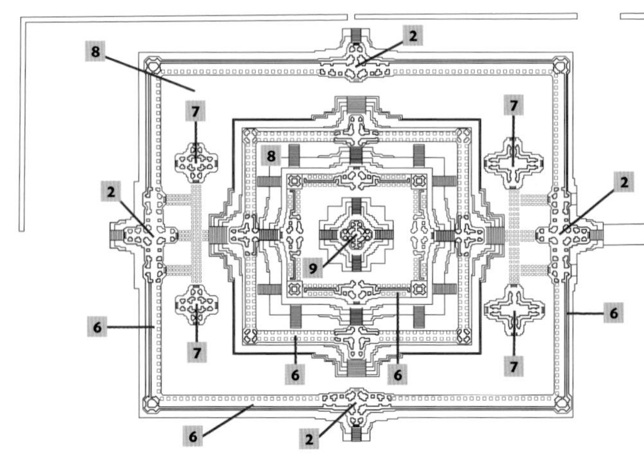

225 *Overall view from the east gopura of the outer enclosure (top) and the stilt causeway (bottom).*

Visit

Halfway down the causeway is a cruciform pavilion.

The access *gopura* on the first tier, delimited by a gallery with corner pavilions, was entirely restored and is an extremely interesting tripartite structure: the square central hall, flanked by wings whose two chambers are set into each other in a sort of tapered arrangement, is preceded by a double corridor toward the exterior and a single one facing

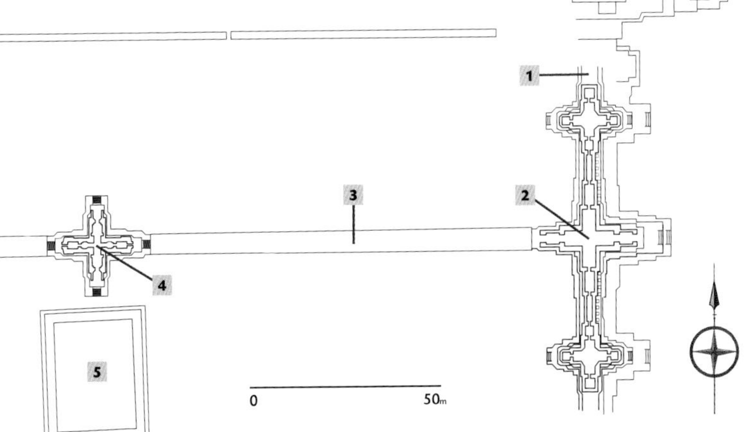

226 top *Wing of the cruciform pavilion.*

juxtaposed blocks, with real windows on both sides. The marvelous and justly famous bas-relief panels are located here; however, they cannot be seen at present because of restoration work that is in progress.

The third level was also divided into a double platform ending in a gallery. Between the second and third level there are traces of stairways on the corners that probably led to the corner towers; in any case they are impossible to use. On the top was a single cruciform *prasat*, whose structure has not yet been defined.

It is advisable to descend through the pavilion in the middle of the raised causeway (at present visitors cannot go beyond this point) by using the right-hand stairway and then go around the monument, keeping it to your left, to admire the stuccowork on the base, until you arrive at the west side of the Baphuon, where there are the remains of a colossal Buddha made in the 16th century by monks who used building material taken from the temple. Retracing your steps, at the northwest corner of the Baphuon you can enter one of the Palace *gopuras* and pass on into this other section of the monument.

the interior. The side chambers have corbeled vaults, while the central one is surmounted by a another smaller tier crowned by an unusual domed structure with a square plan known as the 'priest's chapel' or 'cloister arch,' which is topped by a lotus acroterion. The gallery, in which the *gopura* mentioned above opens out, had blind windows in the outer wall and real windows in the inner wall, all of them with baluster screening; the roof must have consisted of tiles set onto a wooden framework.

This first level of the Baphuon contains the remains of four 'libraries,' two on the east side and two on the west side, and these paired edifices were probably connected by a raised walkway. The second level was articulated in a double platform and was topped by a narrow sandstone gallery with a corbeled vault, consisting of four rows of stone blocks ending in two

226 bottom left *Window of the cruciform pavilion.*

226 bottom center *Window in the enclosure wall facing the Royal Palace.*

226 bottom right *A blind window of the first-level gopura.*

227 top Moldings of the first level and gopura.

227 bottom Decorative panels on the second level.

Terrace of the Leper King

This monument rises up north of the Terrace of the Elephants, and in its present state is not to be attributed to Jayavarman VII, but rather to Jayavarman VIII, one of his successors.

228 The outer wall of the Terrace of the Leper King.

229 top Gods of the underworld on the inner wall.

229 bottom Statue of the Leper King. National Museum, Phnom Penh.

Visit

The front of the Terrace of the Leper King facing the Royal Square is 82 ft (25 m) long, and ranged on the 19-ft (6-m) high wall are up to seven registers of divine figures; five-, seven- and nine-headed *nagas*; and sea creatures. The gods are depicted in their palaces with their consorts and attendants, and many of them appear terrifying and fiendish. Behind this first wall, entering from the southwest corner, there is a second one that was accidentally discovered during the excavations made by EFEO (École Française d'Extrême Orient), decorated with the same bas-reliefs mentioned above. This has led to various interpretations. In the opinion of some scholars, such as Philippe Stern, this wall was an enlargement of the structure that was made necessary because of a probable collapse of the wall, and testimony of this are the unfinished parts and the re-use of some blocks of stone from the old wall for the new one. Other experts, particularly Georges Coedès, think the wall was deliberately hidden by another one since it refers to the chthonic world and the underworld divinities under Mt. Meru. The latter interpretation, which is certainly the more fascinating, is based on the probably funerary purpose of the Terrace of the Leper King, whose platform was used for the cremation of the royal family. Go up the terrace by way of the stairs on the northwest corner, where you will find the statue of the so-called Leper King, surrounded by four other statues, hence the name of the terrace itself. The figure has been identified with Yama, the god of Death; the original is kept in the Phnom Penh National Museum and is dated to the 14th-15th century. The supposed representation of leprosy on this mysterious nude figure without sexual organs is really due to lichens. However, according to popular Khmer tradition, Jayavarman VII was a leper, which is the reason why he built so many hospitals. Besides Jayavarman, other Khmer kings supposedly suffered from the same terrible disease – at least according to local legends.

Legend

1 Terrace of the Elephants
2 Outer wall
3 Inner wall
4 Corridor
5 Statue of the Leper King

Corridor

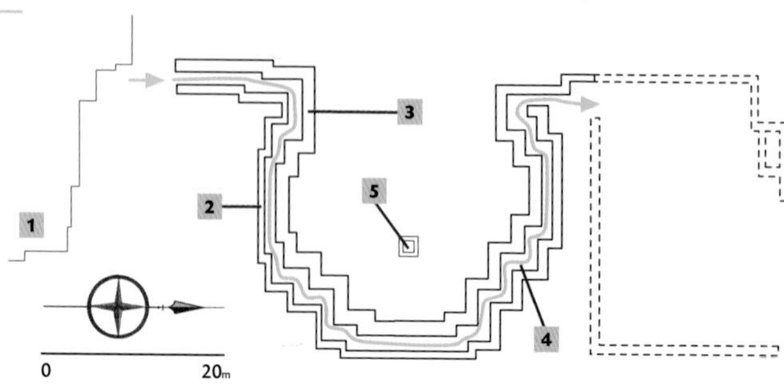

Terrace of the Elephants

The Terrace of the Elephants extends slightly beyond Bayon and looks out over the Royal Square, planned by Jayavarman VII as a theatrical venue of parades and ceremonies.

230 top The procession of elephants on the east wall.

Legend

1 Protuberant wings with stairways
2 Wall of the elephants
3 Wall of the garudas and the lion telamons
4 Circus games
5 Five-headed horse
6 Platform with lotus bud
7 Wall of the Royal Palace
8 East gopura of the Royal Palace
9 Cruciform plataform of the hamsas
10 Terrace of the Leper King

Visit

On the east side of the square is the avenue running from the Victory Gate between two rows of six towers. The Terrace is more than 984 ft (300 m) long and faces the Royal Palace, serving as a sort of 'balcony' for the king's residence, although it partly conceals the walls and entrance. Two stairways at the ends and three in the middle, all of them projecting and guarded over by three-headed elephants and seated lions, afford access to the top of the terrace, which is lined with *nagas*. On the walls, which are as much as 13 ft (4 m) high, is a long series of sculpted elephants rendered with surprising realism. The central projecting stairway has *garudas* and lion-headed figures with their legs and arms raised: four of the most beautiful of these can be seen at right by going up the stairway to the left of the central one.

There is a second raised platform on the terrace that is decorated with *kinnaris* –winged female figures – praying genies on lotus flowers (probably *yakshas*), and *hamsas*, the sacred geese that are a vehicle of Brahma. On this platform there once stood a wooden pavilion with a roof with painted tiles, some remains of

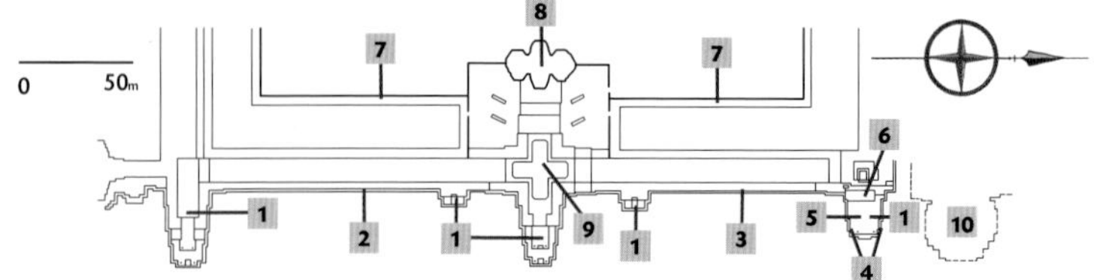

230-231 South ramp of the triple central stairway.

231 center The elephants spurred by the kornaks on the east wall.

which were discovered nearby. Farther on is the cruciform platform facing the Royal Palace *gopura,* also supported by *hamsas.*

The Terrace of the Elephants is the end result of successive

231 bottom View of the central protuberant section.

232 top left *A five-headed horse in the excavation behind the north buttress.*

232 top right *Circus scenes on the north buttress.*

alterations, and evident traces of this can be seen at the northern end, which has further enlargements and a different stairway arrangement: two very steep ones lie to the east and one to the north. On the north and south sides of the wall there are extremely lively scenes of circus games – acrobats, wrestlers, and chariot races – and on the upper register is a game of polo, a sport imported from India. Behind this complex, archaeologists brought to light another wall whose sculptures are in a fine state of preservation because they had remained buried. Going down the stairway that allows you to approach them, you will see a majestic five-headed horse among warriors and women dancers, while in the northeast corner an elephant is holding two figures upside down with its trunk. Going up the stairway again and heading toward the Palace wall, you will see a balustrade with *nagas* whose bodies are decorated and a wall framed by two three-headed elephants, with a swarm of divine figures around Rahu, the demon who causes eclipses: above this buttress is a platform in the shape of a lotus bud.

232 bottom left *The lotus bud platform.*

232 bottom right *Lions and garudas serving as atlases at the sides of the north buttress stairway.*

233 *Detail of a god in front of the lotus bud platform.*

The Royal Palace

The construction of the Royal Palace was probably begun by Rajendravarman in the 10th century; the edifice was enlarged by Suryavarman I and later totally rebuilt by Jayavarman VII in the 12th-13th century.

234 top Two pools: the one in the back is known as the Queen's Bath.

Visit

This 34-acre (14-hectare) area is bounded by a laterite wall – 16 ft (5 m) high, 807 ft (246 m) long from north to south and 1920 ft (585 m) from east to west – that in turn is surrounded by a moat to which another wall was added in a later period. You will find your visit an extremely pleasant walk among the greenery in search of idyllic spots, entering by way of the east *gopura* on the Terrace of the Elephants and exiting at the second gopura on the south side to go to the Baphuon, or at the second *gopura* on the north side to proceed to Preah Palilay and Tep Pranam. The royal palace has five *gopuras*, one to the east and two on both the south and north side.

As the east entrance is the main one, the *gopura* on that side is an important structure with harmonious proportions that overlooks a terrace supported by rampant lions and *garudas*. The only remains of its elegant decoration are some lintels with sinuous floral motifs. Inside west vestibule of the *gopura*, on the upright of the left-hand window and partly on the one on the right-hand window, there is a famous inscription containing the text of the oath of allegiance of the court dignitaries to their king, Suryavarman I.

The palace was divided into quarters, but there are no traces of houses because even the king's were made of perishable material; these were wooden pavilions set on tall stone bases,

234 bottom North gopura of the Royal Palace.

235 East gopura of the Royal Palace.

with axial stairways and balustrades, and the roofs had several gables, one set into the other, creating a tapering effect, with polychrome terracotta tiles, which were found during the archaeological excavations.

In the palace enclosure, if you turn left, to the south, you will see an edifice with part of a corbeled barrel vault and blind windows with slender columns, another structure made of laterite and sandstone, four small towers, and a cruciform terrace with columns at its base,

Legend

1 Moat
2 Enclosure wall
3 Gopura
4 Terrace of the Elephants
5 Phimeanakas
6 Pools
7 The Bath
8 Terrace
9 Prasat

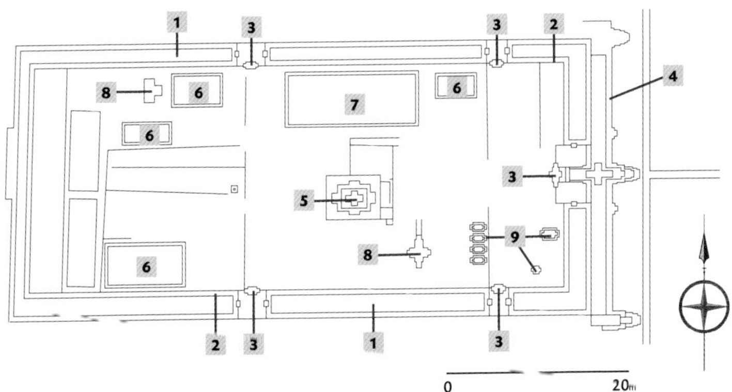

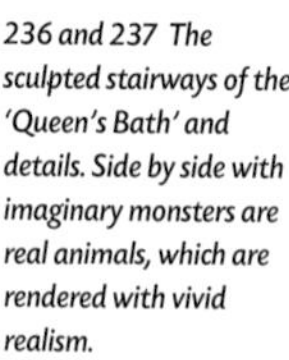

236 and 237 The sculpted stairways of the 'Queen's Bath' and details. Side by side with imaginary monsters are real animals, which are rendered with vivid realism.

probably a support for structures made of perishable material that has been dated to the 14th century. At this point, to your right is the Phimeanakas; leaving it to your left, proceed northward until you reach the pond area. The first pond, called Srah Srei or 'women's bath', is 98 x 164 ft (30 x 50 m) and is surrounded by tiers of steps made of sandstone. But it is the second that is noteworthy. Known as the Srah Pros, or 'men's bath', this measures 410 x 147 ft (125 x 45 m) and is bordered by terrace walls with relief carvings of *garudas*, *nagas*, fish and other aquatic animals which, in the southwest corner, are in an excellent state of preservation.

Beyond the 'bath,' proceed to the west, where you will come to another pond with a terrace partly covered by vegetation, with carvings of elephants and horses and a lovely frieze of *hamsas*, the sacred geese that are a symbol of the soul, which date no earlier than to the 14th century. Farther along are two other ponds that are not very interesting. At this point, retrace your steps and you will come to the *gopura* that leads into the Preah Palilay area. By reversing the order of your initial itinerary, that is, by going at once to the pools and then heading south, you can exit from the south *gopura*, which faces the Baphuon.

Phimeanakas

The name Phimeanakas derives from the deformation of the Sanskrit terms *vimana* and *akasha*, "palace of the gods" and "sky" respectively, and according to the Chinese emissary Zhou Daguan this temple was made of gold. So its dome must have been gilded.

238 The east gopura of the Royal Palace.

Visit

This sanctuary can be reached by going up the central stairway of the Terrace of the Elephants, going beyond the Royal Palace *gopura*, and proceeding eastward for 820 ft (250 m). Scholars disagree about whether to ascribe this edifice to Rajendravarman II or Suryavarman I. The sanctuary is a rectangular temple about 118 x 92 ft (36 x 28 m) at the base, 98 x 75 ft (30 x 23 m) at the top and 39 ft (12 m) high, set on a three-tier pyramid made of laterite and crowned by a single *prasat* that was partly built with re-employed blocks. The four axial stairways are extremely steep, and the best-preserved one faces west. The stairway buttresses have carvings of guardian lions, and some remains of elephants are on the corners of the terraces.

The gallery around the last level of the pyramid, interrupted by real and blind windows, was the first to be completely made of sandstone, including the roof, which consists of three rows of corbeled stones crowned by another stone. The bell-shaped extrados is carved to imitate the tiles. Being so small – 3.3 ft (1 m) wide and 5.5 ft (1.67 m) high – the gallery most probably had no practical purpose. The corners on the east and west sides are marked by blind doors. On this third level is a five-cornice pyramid in poor shape with four axial stairways that lead to the ruins of a pavilion. Probably, the upper gallery and small pyramid

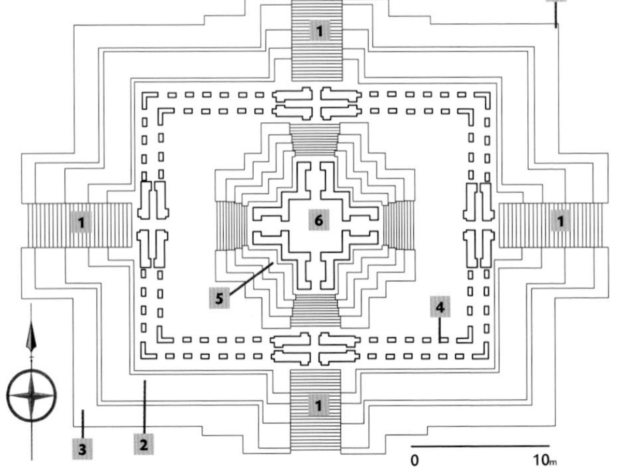

Legend

1 Axial stairways
2 Pyramid
3 Elephants Perimetral gallery
4 Foundation of the prasat
5 Prasat

with the pavilion on the top terrace did not exist in the 11th century and were added later.

Zhou Daguan relates the story of the union that took place in the Phimeanakas between the king and the Nagini, the girl with a serpent's body – a familiar figure in Indian culture. The king had to lie with her every night before going to his wives and concubines, because if he failed to do so his kingdom would be beset by misfortune. And if she did not appear at the nocturnal appointment, this meant that the king's death was imminent.

Influenced by the fact that many royal families in India believed they were the issue of the union between a prince and a *Nagini*, the Khmer also espoused this belief: the first dynasty of Funan rulers, in fact, traced its origin to the Indian Brahman Kaundinya and the *Nagini* Soma, the daughter of the king of the *Nagas*, who in Khmer culture is the dragon lord of the land. In order to conserve his power and guarantee the fertility of the kingdom, the king had to propitiate the *genius loci*, and this operation was symbolized by the union with his daughter, the many-headed, serpent-shaped *Nagini* mentioned by Zhou, whose account reiterates the importance of the female element in the legitimization of royalty.

239 top The east side of the temple.

239 bottom One of the two south gopuras of the Royal Palace.

Tep Pranam

Tep Pranam has nothing of any particular artistic worth, but is a place of worship. It seems the site once included a monastery built by Yashovarman I at the end of the 9th century, of which there are hardly any remains: what you will see is the result of construction work in the late 12th century and the 16th century.

241 top Threshold of the terrace guarded by lions and nagas.

Visit

You can get to Tep Pranam by turning left after the Terrace of the Leper King.

A laterite causeway 246 ft (75 m) long leads to an elegant terrace with a cruciform platform 98 ft (30 m) per side

240 One of the guardian lions.

with a lovely base with sandstone molding and Buddhist stelae on the corners and along the axes. Four proud, seated lions in the Bayon style guard the east entrance, flanked by a *naga* balustrade. To the right is a series of modern *stupas*. The statue of Buddha, which is still a popular object of worship, consists of re-used stones, while the head dates from a much later period. The Enlightened One is in the *bhumisparshamudra* position, his legs crossed and his right hand touching the earth, calling it to witness his victory over Mara, the god of love and death, and his consequent enlightenment.

The wooden pavilion that houses the statue was made in the ancient style, but it is unfortunately preceded by an ugly sheet-metal veranda. Farther on, under another modern and squalid building, is a large standing Buddha.

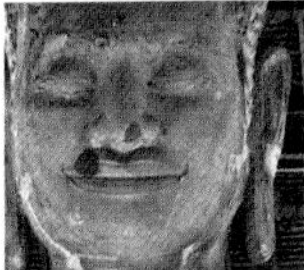

***241 center and bottom* Buddha under the central pavilion and detail.**

Preah Palilay

The Preah Palilay was supposedly built between the late 13th and early 14th centuries, because the images of Buddha were not mutilated, as occurred in the early 13th century during the revival of Brahmanism. This temple is interesting precisely because of its intact Buddhist iconography.

242 top West side of the gopura, south gable.

Visit

This idyllic Buddhist sanctuary can be reached by passing over the Terrace of the Elephants, turning left, proceeding past the Tep Pranam and continuing for a several hundred feet, or by entering the Royal Palace from the east and

242 bottom East side of the prasat.

exiting from the second north *gopura*.

A 108-ft (33-m) causeway leads to the temple by way of a double cross-shaped terrace supported by a based decorated with *hamsas*, the sacred geese, and bordered by a balustrade with splendid *nagas*. The east stairway is watched over by sculpted lions. Before reaching the temple, there is a large, modern Buddha made of sandstone, protected by an elegant wooden canopy. The temple itself is surrounded by a single laterite wall 164 ft (50 m) long with a single cruciform *gopura* made of sandstone to the east; only the feet of the *dvarapala* statues have survived.

The beautifully sculpted lintels and pediments narrate episodes from the life of Buddha. On the east side of the central body, Buddha on a pedestal receives the homage of the praying figures in the pediment, while on the lintel he is seen reclining in a state of *parinirvana* (see glossary). On the right-hand pediment to the north, the Enlightened One is receiving offerings from the animals of the Parilliyaka forest, after which the temple may have been named. On the left-hand pediment facing south, Buddha is seated on a throne under the tree of illumination. On the north gable, the lower pediment shows Buddha placating the elephant Nalagiri, which Buddha's envious cousin Devadatta had intoxicated so it would attack him. On the west side of the *gopura*, in the central pediment, some women are bringing children to be blessed by Buddha, while underneath is a row of elephants. On the right-hand gable, two superposed pediments have scenes of disciples venerating their Master, while the left-hand one shows Buddha receiving a bowl of rice from the shepherdess Sujata.

The Preah Palilay sanctuary consists of a tall terrace that supports a tapering sandstone *prasat* 62 ft (19 m) high that is literally besieged by tall trees. The lintel inside the corridor, showing a *makara* with its jaws wide open supporting Indra seated on Airavata, is a splendid sculpture.

243 West side of the gopura, south pediment: Buddha under the Tree of Enlightenment and detail.

Legend

1 Terrace
2 Avenue
3 Gopura
4 Enclosure
5 Pyramid
6 Prasat

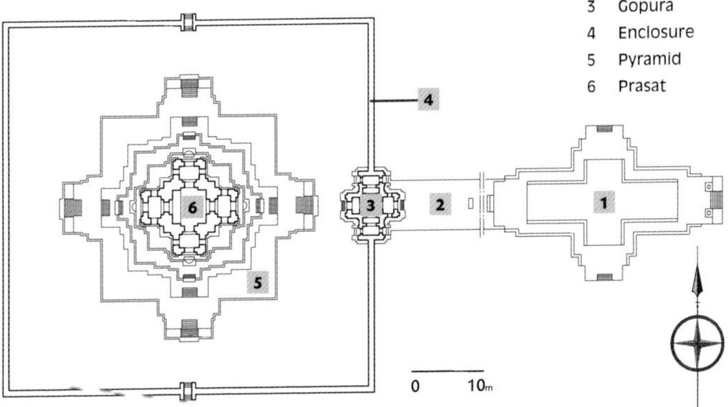

Prasat Suor Prat

Since the Suor Prat towers face the Royal Square, some scholars have advanced the theory that they were viewpoints for the high officials and ambassadors during parades. However, their purpose is still a moot question.

244 top and bottom right The Suor Prat Prasats.

244 bottom left Inscription in ancient Khmer.

Visit

Of the twelve Suor Prat towers, ten are aligned on the east side of the Royal square in two groups of five, separated by the avenue that leads to the Victory Gate, with the entrances facing the square. The other two towers are set back a bit and face each other, their entrances also along the avenue.

A long terrace made of laterite and 32 ft (10 m) wide connects the *prasats* and extends into porches in front of each entrance. Built in laterite during the reign of Indravarman II (first half of the 13th century), with sandstone lintels and pediments, and crowned by two stories with antefixes in the form of *nagas*, these towers consist of a porch entrance and rectangular hall that is illuminated by large windows on three sides. According to popular tradition, the towers were used for spectacles of tightrope walkers who walked on ropes stretched from one edifice to the other, hence the modern name "Towers of the Rope Dancers."

Zhou Daguan on the other hand claimed that the litigants in a dispute were kept in the towers and after a few days the person in the wrong would inevitably come down with an illness.

Khleang

The two large twin buildings overlook the Royal Square at Angkor Thom behind the Suor Prat towers. As noted, their purpose is still being discussed by scholars and in any case it is improbable that they were 'storehouses,' as their modern name suggests.

Visit

Some say the Khleangs were residences for illustrious guests. Two pools about 295 x 157 ft (90 x 48 m) flank the edifices at the sides of the avenue that leads to the Victory Gate.

The north Khleang, built in the period between the end of the 10th century and early 11th century, perhaps by Jayaviravarman, is an unusual construction more than 197 ft (60 m) long and only 15.4 ft (4.7 m) wide, with sandstone walls 5 ft (1.5 m) thick, and is preceded by a cruciform terrace facing the square. The tall platform supporting the structure has molding decoration with garland and diamond motifs. You enter from the west side by means of a vestibule with four windows that leads to a square hall; here there are two wings, also illuminated by large windows, which end in two halls that open onto the east side through two doors. A decorated cornice on the outside indicates that there was a false story with a roof made of tiles on a wooden framework. The lintels of the east and west doors of the central halls have luxuriant floral volutes. At the east side of this hall is another corridor, which leads to a

245 top West side of the North Khleang.

245 bottom The North Khleang.

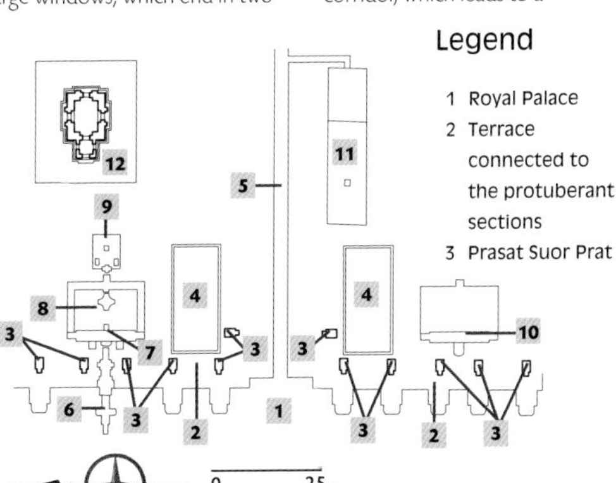

Legend

1 Royal Palace
2 Terrace connected to the protuberant sections
3 Prasat Suor Prat
4 Pools
5 Victory Avenue
6 Terrace
7 North Khleang
8 Courtyard with prasat
9 Enclosure with two 'libraries' and a prasat
10 South Khleang
11 Terrace of Buddha
12 Detail of a Prasat Suor Prat

courtyard with a small temple – note the antefixes that reproduce it – that opens out to the west and has elaborate blind doors. A little farther on, a laterite wall with a *gopura* whose west side is in very poor condition, encloses two 'libraries' and, in the middle, a small sanctuary in the shape of a Greek cross on a platform with elaborate molding, three blind doors, axial stairways and medallions with carvings of dancers.

246 Interior of the North Khleang.

The south Khleang, built a short time after the north one, is smaller (147 ft/45 m long and 13.7 ft/4.20 m wide) and is somewhat different: the platform is molded but not decorated, the structure is a long gallery-hall without the square central hall and ends with two chambers at the ends with blind doors. What little decoration it presents is of no significance except for the elegant colonnettes that frame the east doorway of the chamber added to the south. A second entrance pavilion on the east façade leads to an avenue that may have been lined with stelae.

Behind the south pool that flanks the Khleangs, along the causeway that leads to the Victory Gate, in an enclosure is a laterite terrace 420 ft (128 m) long and 115 ft (35 m) wide, decorated with lions and elephants, that houses, under an ugly modern pavilion, the large sandstone sculpture of Buddha found in 1933 in the well of the central tower of the Bayon. This is one of the most typical Khmer

representations of Buddha, who is portrayed seated on the serpent Naga king Mucilinda, which came out from the roots of the tree under which the Enlightened One was meditating to protect him from a storm. This animal symbolizes both the early chthonic religion

illuminated by the teachings of Buddha, and dangerous primeval energy that is dominated and made spiritual by Buddha. Having coiled up three times, Mucilinda serves as a throne for the Enlightened One and opens out its multi-headed hood to cover him like a canopy. The *naga*'s hood refers to the tree of illumination and wisdom or *bodhi*, and the three coils can symbolize both the three-fold world of earth, atmosphere and sky in which Buddha triumphs, and the triple jewel of Buddha, his Doctrine, and the community.

246-247 Behind a Prasat Suor Prat, the South Khleang.

Preah Pithu

The Preah Pithu complex, situated east of the northeast corner of the Royal Square in an extremely fascinating, secluded site, comprises five sanctuaries surrounded by moats and ponds that are now mostly in ruins.

248 left Many-headed nagas around Temple 484 V.

248 right and 249 top Balustrade with nagas on the terrace facing Temple 481 T and the temple pyramid.

Visit

The cruciform terraces with the classic *naga* motif, the foundations traversed by axial stairways guarded over by lions, the false doors, the gods in the niches, and the details of the decoration, all manifest great elegance and will come as a pleasant surprise for the enterprising visitor who is willing to wander off from the traditional circuits of Angkor.

The first temple, known as 481 T, is preceded by a spectacular cross-shaped double terrace that is supported by elegant cylindrical colonnettes. Past the west gopura there are many fragments

Legend

1 Pool
2 Moats
3 Terraces
4 Temple 481 T
5 Temple 482 U
6 Temple 483 X
7 Temple 484 V
8 Temple 485 Y

Suggested itinerary

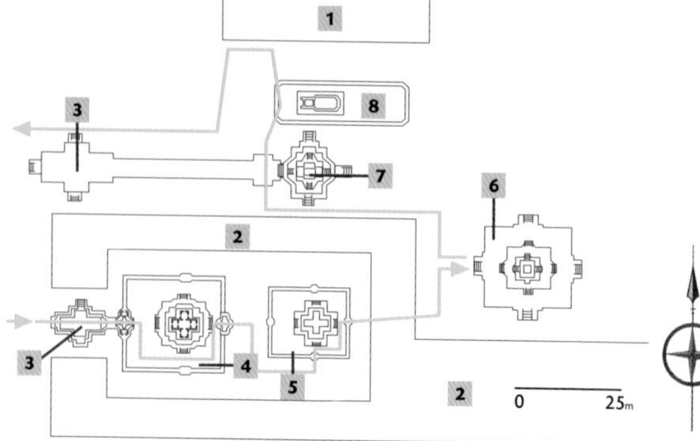

scattered all around that have interesting discoveries in store for you. The temple itself stands on a three-terrace cruciform pyramid foundation with molding decoration and axial stairways. The cella opens out on all four sides by means of four vestibules, but sadly, the tower has collapsed, as is the case with most of the temples at Preah Pithu. Charming *devatas* with flowery skirts stand out in a train of small dancing figures. The 16-facet colonnettes are particularly fascinating.

Exiting from the east *gopura* you will come upon Temple 482 U, whose wall has simpler entrances. The structure of this edifice is like the preceding one but it is smaller and here too only part of the tower has remained. The north pediment features the Churning of the Ocean of Milk motif, and the south one has Vishnu and Krishna on the monster Kala; the one facing west represents the Trimurti, the three-fold form of the Divine, that is, Brahma, Vishnu and Shiva, the latter dancing in the middle. The wall decoration is especially elegant, with a tapestry-like plant background from which *devatas* and *apsaras* emerge.

***249 bottom** Temple 482 U, southeast side.*

250 top *Cylinrical colonnettes on the terrace in front of Temple 481 T.*

250-251 *Temple 483 X, northwest corner.*

About 164 ft (50 m) east of the Temple 482 U, once past the moat, is Temple 483 X, which has no enclosure wall. A square terrace 131 ft (40 m) per side and with much molding decoration, is the foundation for two much smaller terraces that are accessible by means of four axial stairways. In the cella of the cruciform *prasat*, which is preceded by vestibules, there is a double frieze of Buddha and the Enlightened One on the east lintel. This Buddhist iconography in a prevalently Hindu context such as Preah Pithu has led the scholar Claude Jaques to date it to the 14th century. East of Temple 483 X, among some ruins and *semas*, the typical Buddhist stelae that border consecrated areas, is a stairway with two elephants that is covered with luxuriant vegetation.

Now heading westward, you will reach Temple 484 V, which also lacks an enclosure wall, but has a 230-ft (70-m) causeway that leads to a large cruciform terrace 114 x 180 ft (35 x 55 m). The temple, consisting of the usual *cella* with four vestibules, lies on a low cruciform, three-tier pyramid base made of sandstone with elegant molding decoration, with a more developed east wing. Next to the east entrance, to your left, is a noteworthy stele with Varuna, god of the ocean, on his vehicle, the sacred geese, while all around this are lovely fragments of multi-headed *nagas*.

Immediately to the north, about 50 ft (15 m) away, is Temple 485 Y on an earthen terrace. Its structure is totally different from that of the preceding temples. It is articulated in a rectangular pavilion with an entrance to the east, a vestibule with two side doors and a *cella* with a blind door facing west. This would seem to be a typical Hindu arrangement, consisting of a *mandapa*, *antarala* and *garbhagriha*. On the west side of the pavilion, the north relief represents Vishnu on Garuda fighting against the many-headed and multi-armed demon Bana; the carving facing south takes up the motif of Vishnu's three strides as he sets his foot on the lotus held up by the Great Goddess while underneath them is a palace scene (*see* Prasat Kravan).

Proceeding northward for about 165 ft (50 m) you will reach a large pond (328 x 246 ft/100 x 75 m) in a secluded, wild spot. Retracing your steps, take the causeway of Temple 484 V to get to the Royal Square.

***251 top** Foundation with a dvarapala.*

***251 bottom** Temple 484 V, south side.*

EVEN THE MONUMENTS FAR AWAY FROM THE MOST VISITED SITES OFFER AN INTERESTING VIEW OF THE ART AND LIFE OF THE KHMER PEOPLE.

The Heritage of the Khmer

252 Detail of a pediment, with the smiling Buddha from Banteay Kdei.

Introduction

Relatively isolated from the popular itineraries but still inside the Archaeological Park.

The sites suggested for visiting are grouped around two complexes, Banteay Samré and Banteay Kdei. Both are 'citadels' but differ in structure and period. The former is compact and intimate, and it is decorated with high-quality pediments – a sort of introduction to Angkor Wat – while the latter is vast and complex, another major royal foundation whose daily life was cadenced by ceremonies and rituals. A visit to Banteay Samré could also include the climb to the wild Phnom Bok (although this is rather fatiguing), while a tour of Banteay Kdei is rounded off with the romantic Srah Srang baray or reservoir and a slight detour to Kutishvara for those who want to see everything in the Archaeological Park. And after the excitement and thrills offered by the great Angkor monuments, the two long walks to the Prasat Chrung and Ta Nei in solitary and

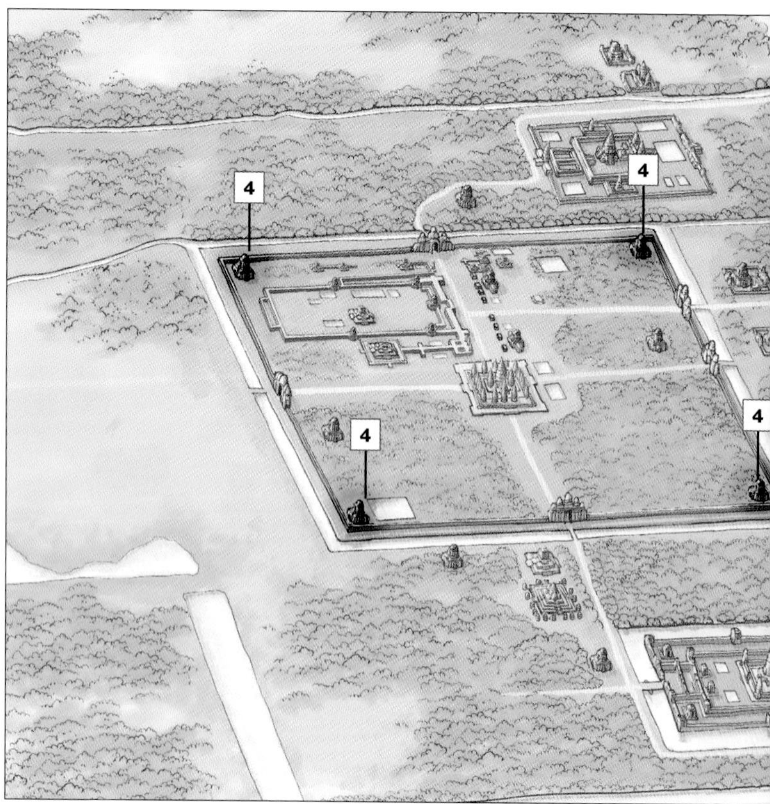

fascinating forest areas will provide visitors with moments of meditation and deeper contact with nature, nature that is the theatrical backdrop to the monuments as well as a looming, ubiquitous presence ready to reclaim its space and erase all human memories.

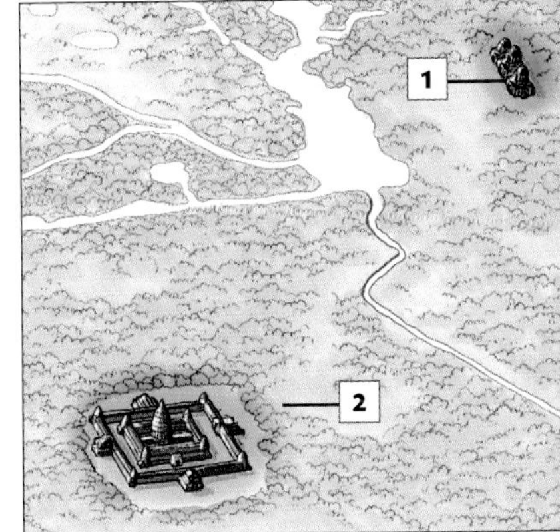

Legend

1 Phnom Bok
2 Banteay Samré
3 Ta Nei
4 Prasat Chrung
5 Banteay Kdei
6 Kutishvara
7 Srah Sang

Banteay Samré

Some scholars ascribe the construction of Banteay Samré to Suryavarman II or to one of his high officials, while others think it was partially or wholly built by his successor Yashovarman II.

The History

The temple lies on the end of the East Baray in an isolated zone. At a point 984 ft (300 m) before the East Mebon, take the road heading east, cross the village of Pradak and proceed for about 1.2 miles (2 km).

After Angkor Wat, Banteay Samré is the most significant example of the period and in this complex the structure of the temple, with a horizontal rather than vertical layout, achieves perfection. The name of the site, which means "Citadel of the Samré," links it with the Samré population, which lived in the region around Phnom Kulen.

256 top The plinth of a column, with a praying ascetic in the niche.

256 bottom Detail of the decoration, with a central kala.

Phnom Bok

About 2.5 miles (4 km) past Banteay Samré is the village of Tcherey, where you must take a rather difficult path to get to the top, at an altitude of 770 ft (235 m). Probably built at the same time as Bakheng and dedicated by Yashovarman I to the Trimurti, Phnom Bok is surrounded by an enclosure wall and consists of three laterite *prasats* on a common platform that have been ruined by the elements, and four other edifices, two made of bricks and two built in sandstone. The rectangular moat to the east of the towers was probably a reservoir. The most significant part of this site is a *lingam* – placed on a laterite base that is 13 ft (4 m) high and has a diameter of 3.9 ft (1.20 m) – that is unfortunately shattered.

Visit

Arriving from the north, go around the temple to enter the complex from the east and admire the 460-ft (140-m) processional avenue, which may have had wooden roofing, is on two levels, is lined with serpentine balustrades and ends in a stairway flanked by seated lions. On a laterite terrace stands the base of the east *gopura*, which opens into the outermost

enclosure, a rectangle 272 x 252 ft (83 x 77 m), with axial accesses marked by cruciform *gopuras* with elongated wings and flanked by two other chambers. The laterite wall is made up of galleries that originally had wooden and tile roofs and a solid wall on the

257 top Aerial view of the temple.

257 bottom Detail of blind door.

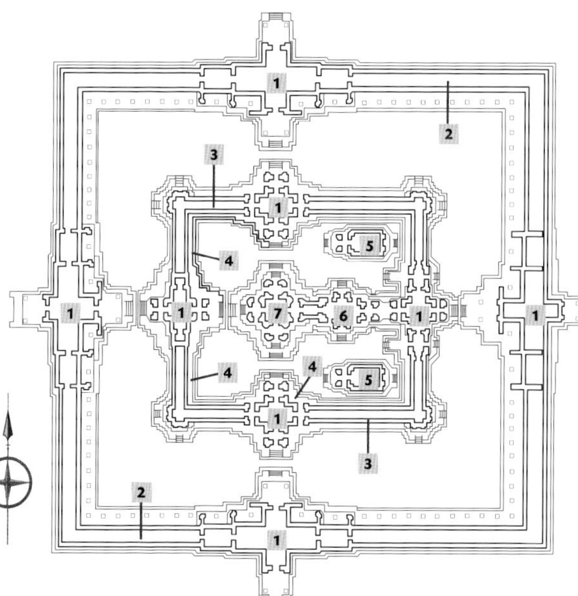

Legend

1 Gopura
2 Second enclosure
3 First enclosure
4 Platform
5 'Library'
6 Mandapa
7 Prasat

0 20m

258 top left Detail of a multiheaded naga.

258 top right Stairway of the terrace facing the east gopura.

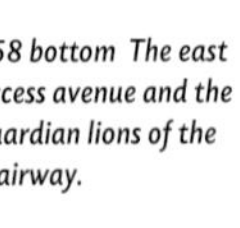

258 bottom The east access avenue and the guardian lions of the stairway.

exterior and one with windows with small columns in the interior. Resting on a tall base, the galleries are flanked toward the temple by a colonnade that supported a portico made of perishable material. On the east side there is neither a gallery nor a portico. Going around the temple by following the gallery of the second enclosure and keeping it to your right, you will see some remarkable pediments. At the south *gopura* there are scenes from the *Ramayana* on the pediment on the outside of the second enclosure, while the one on the first enclosure *gopura* is rather deteriorated, but you can make out Ravana on a chariot drawn by lions. On the west side, the pediment of the *gopura* opening onto the second enclosure has other scenes from the *Ramayana* on the exterior (from where you can see another cruciform terrace with a connecting avenue), as well as two beautiful dancing Shivas on the interior pediment. At the entrance to the first enclosure the central pediment has reliefs of deities with their vehicles, including a strange three-headed animal; on the left-hand pediment there is a superb battle between a demon and some monkeys.

Now back at the east entrance,

after going down and then up the steep linking stairways, you pass into the first enclosure, comprising a laterite gallery 144 x 125 ft (44 x 38 m) with an axial *gopura* made of sandstone and covered with corbeled vaults. The corners are highlighted on the exterior by overhangs with stairways and blind doors topped by pediments. The

259 top The southwest corner of the first enclosure.

259 bottom South gopura of the second enclosure.

galleries, whose roofs are intact, have a blind wall and a wall with columned windows toward the interior, though there are no doorways. Situated on tall bases, like all the other edifices in the enclosure, they are lined with a continuous inner platform with *nagas*, which allows for circumambulation around the temple.

During the monsoon period the temple rises up bewitchingly from the water that is collected in the laterite basin bounded by the enclosure walls. In the northeast and southeast corners, which are connected to the temple by a walkway on stilts, there are two 'libraries' preceded by porticoes, with corbeled vaults and blind triple naves. On the pediment of the entrance porch of the south 'library' is a lovely scene of adoration, while in the north one Vishnu is depicted reclining on the serpent Ananta.

Among the noteworthy elements here, mention should be made of the decoration of the blind doors and also the stairways, which are lined with exquisitely wrought multi-headed serpents.

In order to see the inner pediments in the first enclosure you must stand beside them and observe them obliquely – because there is no room to do otherwise. The following works are well worth seeing: on the main portico of the east *gopura* is a scene of the battle between the deities and demons, and the left-hand portico has a relief featuring Krishna Govardana; on the pediment of the central portico of the south entrance is a prince on horseback; the pediment of the main portico of the west *gopura* has a representation of the sun and moon, and on the pediment behind this one is Skanda on a peacock. Finally, the central pediment of the north entrance – from which you will exit – has a view of the women's apartments with a harpist, and on the pediment behind this is Shiva with Uma.

Although no inscriptions have been found on this site, the temple seems to have been dedicated to Vishnu. It is made of sandstone and is articulated with the usual elements of clearly Indian inspiration: the *ardhamandapas* (portico), the *mandapa* or pavilion, *the antarala* (vestibule), and the *garbhagriha* or *cella*. A rectangular

260 left Colonnettes in the windows of the second enclosure.

260 right Detail of the pediment of the west gopura in the first enclosure, inner side.

structure with a corbeled vault, the pavilion was made lighter through the use of columned windows in the walls next to the side doorways. The portico of the *mandapa* is almost merged with that of the *gopura*, which accentuates the sensation of longitudinal extension in the temple. The *prasat*, with three blind doors and double pediments, has a very tall first floor that rises above the pediments of the porticoes, and four other strongly serrate stories that have a round crown in the form of a lotus that is 69 ft (21 m) above the ground.

***261 top** Interior of the first enclosure, bordered by a continuous platform with nagas.*

***261 bottom** Inner side of the west gopura in the first enclosure.*

Ta Nei

The temple has no truly special features, except for some pediments, but its secluded and wild location makes it particularly fascinating. An observatory was recently installed there to ascertain the impact of the climate on the stones.

Legend

1 Third enclosure
2 Gopura
3 Pools
4 Second enclosure
5 First enclosure
6 "'Library'
7 Tower
8 Connecting chamber
9 Central prasat

Visit

The Ta Nei temple (12th century) lies on the northwest corner of the East Baray, 492 ft (150 m) from the west dike. In order to get there you have to walk for about 0.9 miles (1.5 km) in the forest, since in general entering with vehicles is not allowed.

The path leading to Ta Nei starts a short distance past the southeast corner of Ta Keo and arrives at the temple from the southwest, near the west *gopura* of the third enclosure, which is almost totally ruined: by skirting round the temple, which is bounded to the north and south by two elongated moats, you will arrive at the east side, at the end of the roadway coming from the east *gopura* of the third enclosure.

The second enclosure now measures 180 x 154 (55 x 47 m), with one entrance per side, except for the east side, which has five: a triple *gopura* and two side entrances. The two north and south pavilions of the central *gopura* are connected to the north and south wings of the first enclosure, which therefore shares the triple *gopura* with the second enclosure. This inner section of the sanctuary was enlarged a few times, becoming a rectangle 88 x 150 ft (27 x 46 m) and extending toward the west side of the second enclosure. This led to the transformation of the old west

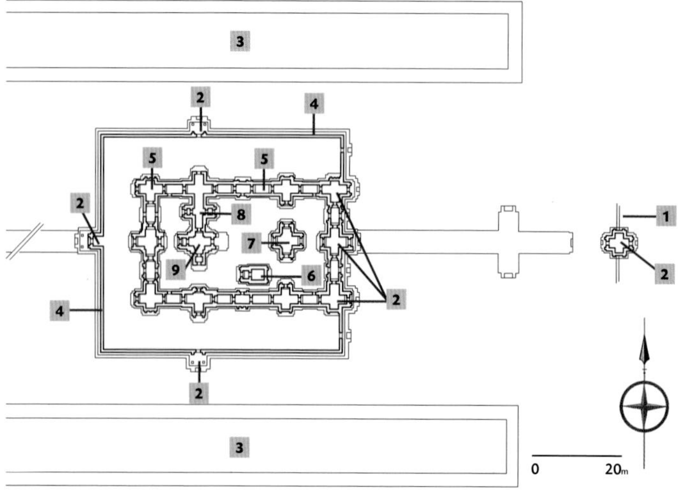

gopura – which measured 88 x 115 ft (27 x 35 m) – into the central cruciform *prasat* with four vestibules. What was once a wing of the west gallery became a connecting structure that also had two side entrances. Beyond the *prasat*, in the first enclosure, stand an isolated tower and a 'library.'

Among the relief carvings, which do not seem to have been affected much by the fanatic revival of Brahmanism after the death of Jayavarman VII, are the following noteworthy elements: on the north vestibule of the *prasat*, a figure on a canoe giving a blessing; in the middle hall of the south façade of the north gallery, the lower part of Lokeshvara; in the hall at the southwest corner of the north façade of the south gallery, a panel of warriors; on the south façade of the northwest *gopura* (connected to the side hall of the *prasat*), a horseman wielding a sword; on the north façade of the southwest *gopura*, a figure in a palace who seems to be blessing some children. On the ground in the west *gopura* is a pediment with the portraits of two donors above the head of Kala, and a Buddha and other images of the Enlightened One are on a ruined pediment in the pavilion in the southwest corner.

Prasat Chrung

Past the South Gate of Angkor Thom, you immediately enter on a little path at your right that leads to the ramparts, then take the parapet walk among fascinating greenery, and after about 0.6 miles (1.5 km) you arrive at one of the Prasat Chrung, or Corner Temples, at Angkor Thom. This is surrounded by an enclosure wall with a single entrance facing west, a simple sandstone cornice with a pediment containing carvings of multi-headed *nagas* at the ends. A paved avenue leads to an elevated terrace that is connected to a cruciform *prasat* on a foundation with molding; this pyramid temple has a *cella* and four vestibules, the ones facing east and west with entrances and the other two with blind doors. In front of the east corridor there is an extension of the base where there was once a small shrine with a foundation stele, now kept in the Conservation Office. The roof of the *cella* is in good condition and has a lotus on the top and lintels with carvings of Lokeshvara, some of which were mutilated and converted into *lingams* during the Brahmanic revolt against Buddhism. Another Prasat Chrung "corner temple" can be reached via the West Gate (see Angkor Thom).

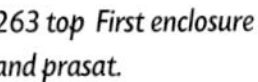

263 top First enclosure and prasat.

263 bottom The remains of an entrance to the second enclosure.

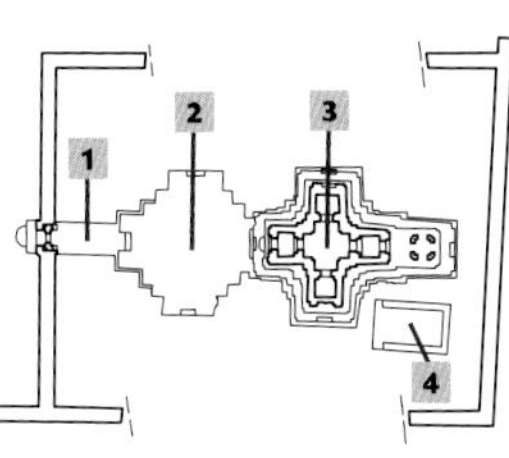

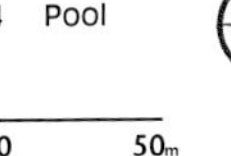

Legend

1 Gopura
2 Terrace
3 Cella
4 Pool

0 50m

Banteay Kdei

Banteay Kdei, whose modern name "Citadel of the Cells," referring to what were supposedly monks' dwellings, was built in 1181 by Jayavarman VII, probably over the ruins of a Buddhist temple constructed by the famous architect Kavindrarimathana during the time of Rajendravarman.

The History

Although the foundation stele has not been found, it is thought that Jayavarman dedicated Banteay Kdei to Buddha, thus rounding off the homage to the Buddhist triad consisting of Buddha, Prajnaparamita – after whom the Ta Prohm was already named – and Lokeshvara, venerated in the Preah Khan. The last two temples celebrated the mother and father of Jayavarman. However, some scholars have proposed the theory that the Banteay Kdei was built in honor of the king's tutor.

264 top Apsaras from the Hall of the Dancers.

Visit

The complex lies within four enclosure walls. The outermost one, measuring 2300 by 1640 ft (700 x 500 m), included the residential area: added in a later period, it is in the classical Bayon style, that it to say, with four axial *gopuras* surmounted by face-towers with the visages of Lokeshvara and *garudas* on the corners.

Entering the complex from the east and taking a path for about 656 ft (200 m), you will pass by the remains of two edifices made of laterite and sandstone and will then arrive at the usual cruciform terrace with *naga* balustrades facing the third enclosure, which is 1050 by 985 ft (320 x 300 m), has a laterite wall and is surrounded by a moat. Another terrace above the first one leads to the beautiful and spectacular

264 bottom Detail of the east gopura in the fourth enclosure.

265 top Aerial view of the temple.

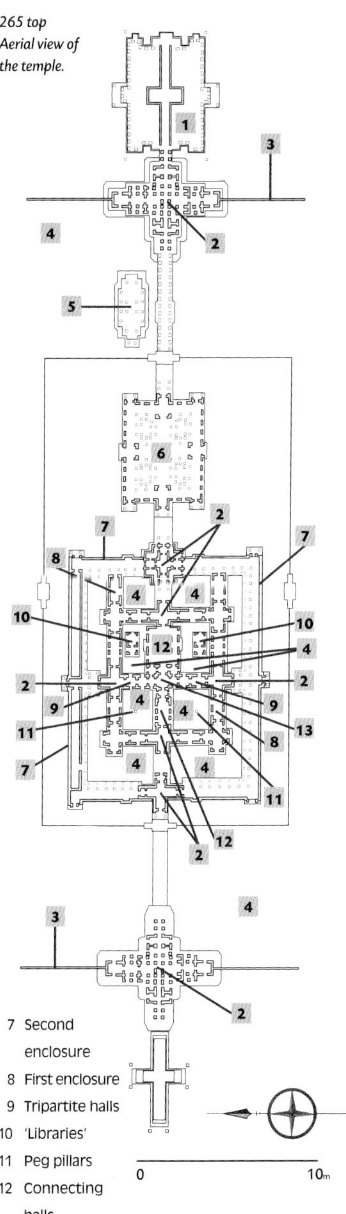

265 bottom The tapestry-like decoration.

Legend

1 Terrace
2 Gopura
3 Third enclosure
4 Courtyard
5 Columned edifice
6 'Hall of the Dancers'
7 Second enclosure
8 First enclosure
9 Tripartite halls
10 'Libraries'
11 Peg pillars
12 Connecting halls
13 Central prasat

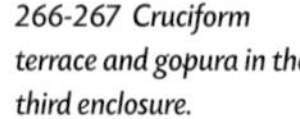

266 top Balustrade with a garuda on a multi-headed naga.

266 bottom A recent Buddha in the cella of the main prasat.

266-267 Cruciform terrace and gopura in the third enclosure.

267 bottom The east gopura of the fourth enclosure.

cruciform *gopura* with attendant buildings and porticoes, whose east lintel has a carving of Rama with his inseparable bow and his consort Sita; in the middle of the main hall is a seated Buddha. Once past the *gopura* there is another stretch of causeway flanked by *nagas*, and to the right is a pillared edifice that probably had a roof made of perishable material, and then the so-called Hall of the Dancers, a name given because of the carvings of dancing *apsaras* in the interior. This is in fact a square structure bounded by an enclosure wall, 69 by 85 ft (21 x 26 m), that has three portico entrances on the east and west sides and one on the north and south sides, watched over by gate guardians and with *devatas* in the niches of the profusely decorated walls. In the interior, the cruciform arrangement of the pillars marks out four small cloisters. The traces of red on the stone are not the remains of painting but are due to oxidation.

In the second enclosure, 165 by 206 ft (50 x 63 m), the east *gopura* has an unusual double concentric Greek cross plan, while the west one is much simpler; furthermore, the wall

268-269 The west side of the second enclosure and the prasat of the first one.

has four other doorways on each of these sides, plus one to the north and south, with porticoes. Toward the interior the enclosure opens out into a double colonnade, whose second row of columns is lower, except for the north side, where the columns were incorporated into a laterite wall. The roof of the gallery consists of a corbeled vault between the wall and the first

268 bottom Gopura with protuberant wing.

row of columns and a half-corbeled vault between the two rows. The pinnacle acroteria on the roofs are in a good state of preservation.

The first enclosure, which is 101 by 118 ft (31 x 36 m), is connected to the second on its east façade by the *gopura* and two extensions of the corner pavilions and comprises eight minor *prasats*, four on the corners and four on the axes, that serve as *gopuras* and are connected by

269 top Avenue lined with nagas in the third enclosure courtyard.

269 center Galleries with half-vaults in the second enclosure.

269 bottom Columned building in the courtyard of the third enclosure.

***270-271** Courtyard of the first enclosure.*

long halls. Once past the east *gopura*, you enter a pavilion that is connected to the central *prasat* by three small chambers. There are two 'libraries' in the side courtyards. The central *prasat* is 57.5 ft (17.5 m) high and is topped by five stories that end in a large lotus flower. A triple series of chambers connects it to the south and north *gopuras*, while it is connected to the west *gopura* by a long hall that creates two other small courtyards with pillars ending in a peg in the middle whose purpose is unknown. The courtyard at right has a beautiful view of the central tower.

Beyond the west *gopura*

***270 bottom left** Halls connected to the prasats.*

***270 bottom right** Chambers connected to the cella of the main prasat.*

is a spacious courtyard. If you choose not to exit from the west, since the route is rather rough, you can go back to where you came from by staying outside the temple to the left and following the moat.

The decoration is typical of this period: rather hastily built windows that imitate partly lowered curtains, *devatas* inserted in profuse floral decoration, niches with traces of the Buddhas that were damaged during the revival of Brahmanism that followed the death of Jayavarman VII.

Kutishvara

Go 656 ft (200 m) past the north *gopura* of Banteay Kdei and then turn left, where you will cross a rice field and see the ruins among the vegetation on an earthen bank. They consist of three brick towers with sandstone doorways facing east. The most interesting part of this site is a lovely pediment, lying on the ground, with a relief of the four-headed god Brahma (only three heads are visible).

271 top Niches with devatas and other figures visible among the creeping plants.

271 bottom The Hall of the Dancers with images of apsaras.

Srah Srang

This *baray*, which lies east of Banteay Kdei, is thought to have been designed in the 10th century by Kavindrarimathana, the architect of Rajendravarman, as an annex of a Buddhist temple that no longer exists. The lake was rebuilt and its present size and shape – 1148 x 2296 ft (350 x 700 m) with sandstone lining – date from the time of Jayavarman VII.

272 top Central stairway of the landing stage.

Visit

Some ruins in the middle of the lake seem to indicate that an islet with a pavilion made of perishable material once stood there.

On the west side of the *baray* is a splendid landing stage. It has been carefully restored and gives us an idea of what the many landing stages at Angkor must have been like. Also built by Jayavarman VII, it consists of a laterite terrace that once supported a pavilion made of perishable material, and by a cruciform structure with three platforms on a level with the water. The two blocks are connected by a stairway on whose sides are guardian lions, while all around this is a beautiful *naga* balustrade: the three-headed cobras stand at the ends, mounted by *garudas* with outspread wings; on the back are three other serpent heads being crushed between the bird's wings and its stylized tail.

The Srah Srang *baray* is extremely beautiful and at sunset the soft hues make it an ideal place for meditation.

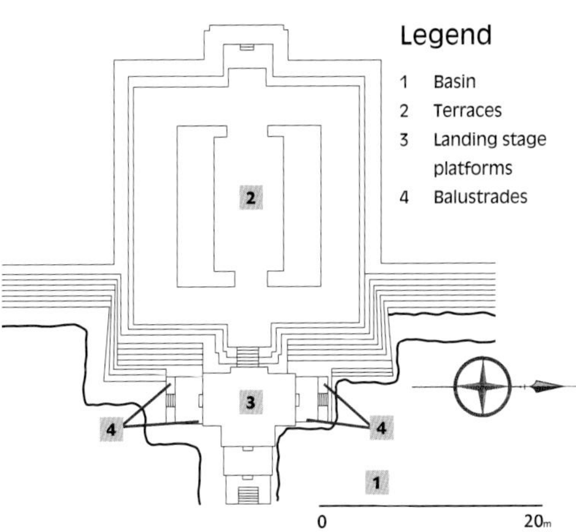

272-273 Sunset at the Srah Srang landing stage.

273 top The back of a multi-headed balustrade naga.

273 bottom The remains of a naga in the pool.

THERE ARE ALSO RUINS OF GREAT INTEREST OUTSIDE THE ARCHAEOLOGICAL PARK. A BOAT TRIP ON THE WEST BARAY TO THE WEST MEBON GIVES YOU AN IDEA OF THE VASTNESS OF THE RESERVOIR.

Itineraries Outside the Archaeological Park

274 *Statue of Vishnu anantashayin found in West Mebon.*

Introduction

ALTHOUGH THEY ARE NOT AWE-INSPIRING COMPARED TO THE GREAT MASTERPIECES OF ANGKOR, THE RUINS RECOMMENDED HERE FOR VISITS WILL STILL BE INTERESTING FOR THOSE WHO HAVE SEEN EVERYTHING INSIDE THE ARCHAEOLOGICAL PARK.

In Siem Reap, the Wat Preah Indra Kaorsey, situated in a popular religious complex, reveals how life in a temple and its annexes must have been during the Khmer age.

A trip by boat on the west *baray* to visit the West Mebon provides an idea of the vastness of the large reservoirs of the past, and a stop at the nearby Ak Yum complex will satisfy those who are intent upon seeing every vestige of Khmer architecture.

An excursion to the austere Phnom Krom, which faces the Tonlé Sap, will show how life along the banks of this vast lake is in many respects the same as that immortalized on the bas-relief sculpture at Bayon. Lastly, the long rugged stretch

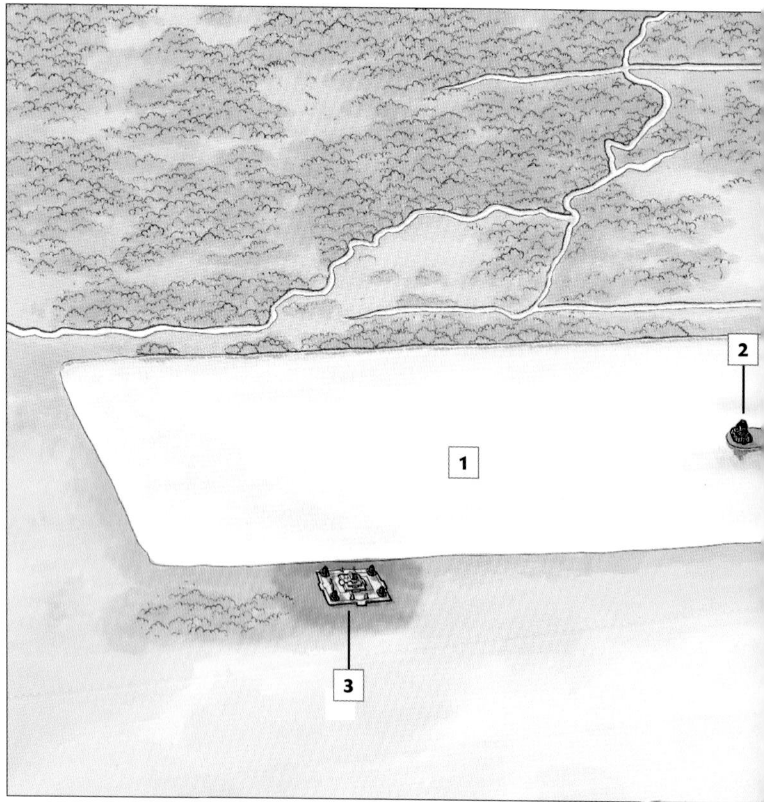

the visitor must cover in order to reach the Chau Srei Vibol passes through countryside whose rural landscapes are the same as those of the glorious heyday of Angkor.

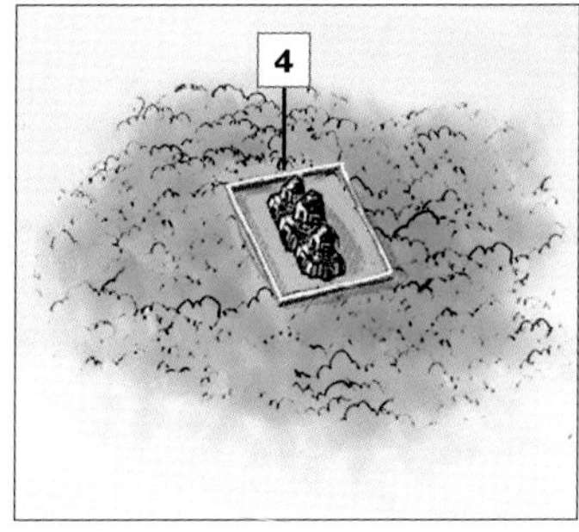

Legend

1 The West Baray
2 The West Mebon
3 Ak Yum
4 Phnom Krom
5 Chau Srei Vibol

The West Baray

The Khmer cities rose up in a vast alluvial plain with rivers that flow into the Tonlé Sap or Great Lake south of Angkor. Taking advantage of the slight declivity of the land from north-northwest to south-southwest, the Khmer rulers built a complex system of lakes and canals to collect the water that irrigated the land downstream. The nerve centers of this hydraulic system were the barays, the large reservoirs that collected rainwater and water that drained from the rivers.

278 View of West Baray.

After leveling the ground on the site of the future basin and marking out its boundaries, the embankments were built by using the earth obtained by digging on either side of the marked out perimeter. In this way the embankments were flanked by two canals, an inner one to keep the largest possible amount of water, and the outer one used for drainage and to collect floodwater. The current flowing into the *baray* was kept at the same level as the maximum quantity of water that was to be stored in the reservoir, that is, about 3.2 ft (1 m) below the top of the lowest dam, and dikes and levees were used to maintain the inflowing water a level higher than that of the plain. Dikes and levees were constructed below the water intake point. The water issued into the *baray* from the highest section and flowed out of the lowest part, thus irrigating the rice paddies.

This system was obtained with much less cost and effort than that required for the excavation of a basin, and the agricultural surplus thus resulting was able to support a strong and efficient bureaucracy and army, promote public works, build architectural complexes and maintain religious foundations that did not pay taxes.

The hydraulic network also played a fundamental role in town planning: the boundaries of the capitals were marked by wide moats with causeways, while a network of orthogonal canals delimited the areas inhabited by the various social and professional groups. Conduits that lay partly underground provided clean water and got rid of dirty water. Modeled after the Indian system, the roads intersected at right angles, the main one, known as the royal way, running from east to west. The junction with the other axial artery symbolically represented the center of the universe and hence the perfect site for the main temple, which was the symbol of the cosmic mountain and connected the cardinal points as well as linking the world of humankind with the world of the deities. Pleased with this, the gods granted humankind rain and the king distributed water throughout his kingdom. A testimony of the sacred nature of this procedure were the moats and pools that lay around the temples, underscoring the fact that the gift of water was due to the divine virtues of the king.

Only a strong and highly organized central power could guarantee the smooth operation of this hydraulic system, since the *barays* silted up and required continuous upkeep work. Accustomed as they were to the collective labor required, from ancient times on, for rice production, the people probably accepted the fatigue demanded of them most willingly. But the excessive building works and perpetual warfare that characterized the last period of the Khmer empire brought about a paucity of natural resources and weakened the rulers' charisma. After the 12th century more canals were excavated and more dams and bridges were built, especially outside Angkor, as they were prey to floods and collapses. The most ingenious irrigation system in Indochina was beginning to fail.

The Indratataka or Pool of Indra at Lolei was built by Indravarman I in 877. Completed in 889, this *baray* is 12,470 ft (3800 m) long and 2625 ft (800 m) wide and was laid out perpendicular to the course of the waterways and to the natural declivity of the plain; by exploiting the waters of the Roluos River through a canal system it provided water for the rice paddies and the temple complexes (including their urban district annexes) of Preah Ko, Bakong and Prei Monti, the last of which is the temple around which Indravarman's palace was probably erected. Now this *baray* is dry.

The Yashodharatataka, known as the East Baray, was begun by Indravarman I and finished by Yashovarman I in 890. More than 22,965 ft (7000 m) long and 5905 ft (1800 m) wide, it was fed by the Siem Reap River, which, partly transformed into a canal, was the east moat of the new capital, Yashodharapura. This i s also completely without water.

The colossal West Baray, fed by the O Klok River and 26,246 ft (8000 m) long and 7212 ft (2200 m) wide, was begun by Suryavarman I and completed by Udayadityavarman II. It is still about three-quarters full.

The Jayatataka, the Baray of Victory (11,482 x 2952 ft/3500 x 900 m), was the work of Jayavarman VII and provided water for a network of canals that met the needs of the new city of Angkor Thom by making use of the natural declivity of the plain: the water flowed from northeast and exited toward the southwest, where a lake, Beng Thom, took in the sewage water and dumped it into the outer moat. The moats, canals, and water intake and outflow points were all clad in laterite and made up one of the most perfect hydraulic systems in Indochina.

Wat Preah Indra Kaorsey

This monument lies outside the archaeological park, in Siem Reap, in the southern zone along the river and east of the Angkor Conservation Park. Placed inside a modern monastery, it has traces of an enclosure with a *gopura* and houses two aligned *prasats*, one with five stories and the other with four, with the base of a third tower adjoining it. Recent *stupas* stand nearby. Particularly noteworthy is the frieze representing the Churning of the Ocean of Milk on the lintel of the main *prasat*. Clearly identifiable figures are the four-headed Brahma and Shiva on his bull, followed by the serpent, Vishnu on the turtle, and a row of gods and demons. The lintel is also a fine work, even though Indra is missing.

Legend

1 Ancient course of the O Klok River
2 Supposed moats of Yashodharapura
3 Visible moats of Yashodharapura
4 Water level in the dry season
5 Water level in the monsoon
6 West Mebon
7 Probable 7th-8th century settlements
8 Ak Yum
9 Modern water intake landing stage

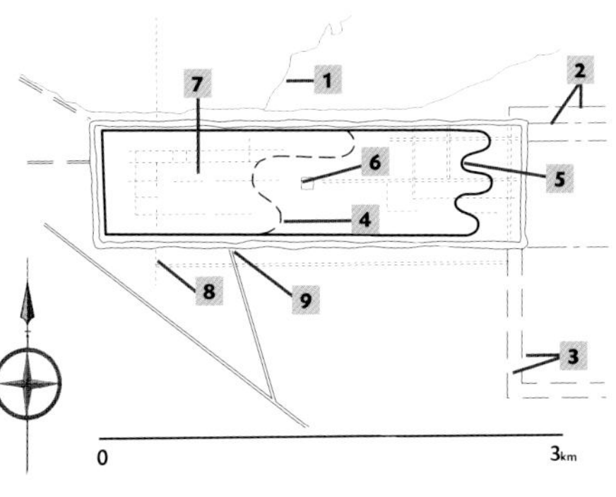

The West Mebon

On an artificial island in the middle of the colossal West Baray, the West Mebon can be reached by taking a motorboat from the Baray dam. Udayadityavarman II probably built this temple of which, unfortunately, very little remains.

280 top Wall and passage towers of the east side.

280 bottom An acroterion in the shape of a lotus bud on one of the towers.

Visit

This was not a sanctuary in the true sense of the word, but rather a square enclosure 229 ft (70 m) per side laid out on an artificial elevation 32.8 ft (10 m) above the Baray. The stone wall ended in a large cornice made to look like a corbeled vault, with a dripstone in the shape of a lotus bud. On each side were three small passageway towers interspersed with five windows. At present, part of the east side is still visible, where the tower pediments, and above all the panels with lively, realistic carvings of animals, give us an idea of how splendid the decoration must have been.

In the middle of the inner space there was a sandstone terrace, on which stood a pavilion made of perishable material, connected to the east side of the enclosure by a causeway 141 ft (43 m) long and initially 26 ft (8 m) wide, narrowing to 13 ft (4 m). In the middle of the terrace was a stone structure consisting of a series of spiral stairways around a well 6.,56 ft (2,70 m) deep in the shape of an overturned *linga*, preceded to the east by a square moat and fed by a bronze tube placed under the ground. The well was probably used to gauge the level of the reservoir. The entire complex was surrounded on three sides by a U-shaped pool. In this area archaeologists found the remains of a colossal Khmer bronze statue of Vishnu Anantashayin, that is, "reclining on the serpent Ananta," which is now in the Phnom Penh National Museum. Only the head, two right arms and the upper part of the bust of the god have survived, and their size indicates that this fine bronze piece was 19 ft (6 m) long.

Legend

1 Wall with passage towers
2 Pool
3 Avenue
4 Terrace
5 Well
6 Square moat

0 30m

Ak Yum

Ak Yum, or 'Weeping Bird,' belongs to a complex of pre-Angkor temples that lies partly under the dike. It is the most ancient temple mountain known to us, but it is by no means easy to interpret.

Visit

Once at the bank of the West Baray, turn left and proceed westward for about 1300 ft (400 m) to arrive at the ruins of the temple, which are at a lower level at left

It consisted of an elevated base with corner towers and six other towers on the first terrace, the middle of which was dominated by the main *prasat*, standing above two other terraces and made of bricks like the other structures. In the *cella* was a *linga*, under which a shaft about 43 ft (13 m) long led to an underground foundation offerings storeroom (pillaged). The lintels with arches, medallions and pendants are features of the pre-Angkor style. The date of the structure ranges from the 7th to the 9th century, since some parts are clearly built from re-used material taken from an earlier temple.

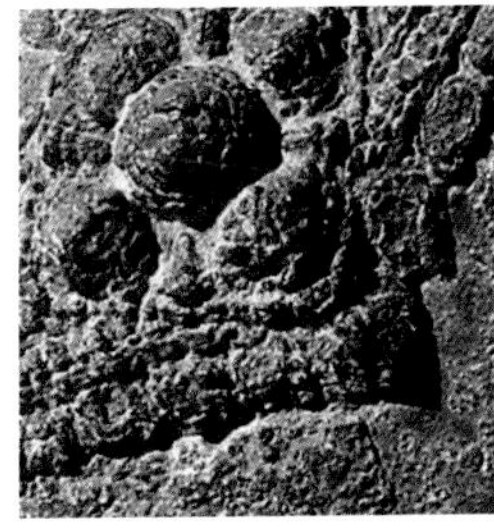

281 Vishnu Anantashayin, National Museum, Phnom Penh, detail.

Legend

1 Foundation
2 Corner prasats
3 Prasat
4 Terraces
5 Central prasat
6 Linga and well

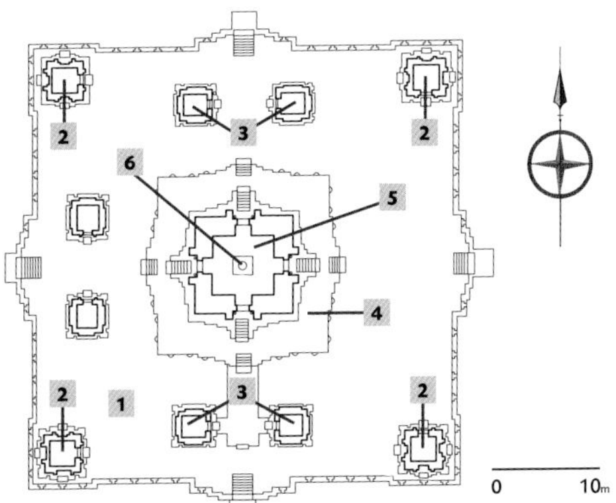

Phnom Krom

Contemporaneous with the temples of Phnom Bakheng and Phnom Bok, and also dedicated by Yashhovarman I to the Trimurti, Phnom Krom is surrounded by a laterite wall traversed by four cruciform *gopuras*.

282 top One of the pedestals of the statues from the cella.

282 bottom The three prasats on the same foundation.

Visit

About 6.8 miles (11 km) southwest of Siem Reap, Phnom Krom lies on a rise 449 ft (137 m) high. The remains of ten rectangular edifices made of laterite are laid out inside the walled enclosure, four on the east side and two on each of the other sides, that once had wooden and tile roofing. Again on the east side, there are four 'libraries,' two made of bricks on the ends and the other two built in sandstone. On a common platform accessible by means of stairways guarded over by sculpted lions, are the three sandstone *prasats*, unfortunately in a poor state of preservation, that have entrances to the east and west and blind doors on the other two sides. There are traces of decoration and of the pedestals that supported the statues of Shiva in the central tower, Vishnu in the north tower, and

Brahma in the south prasat: the foundation of this latter has a lovely frieze of *hamsa*, the sacred goose. The slightly gloomy atmosphere that prevails and the lake under this site make it particularly fascinating.

Chao Srei Vibol

This monument, located outside the Archaeological Park, beyond the Banteay Samré, is in a poor state of preservation, but the trip through the countryside you have to make to get there, is quite lovely.

283 top The ruins of Chau Srei Vibol.

283 bottom The remains of one of the rectangular edifices and the 'library.'

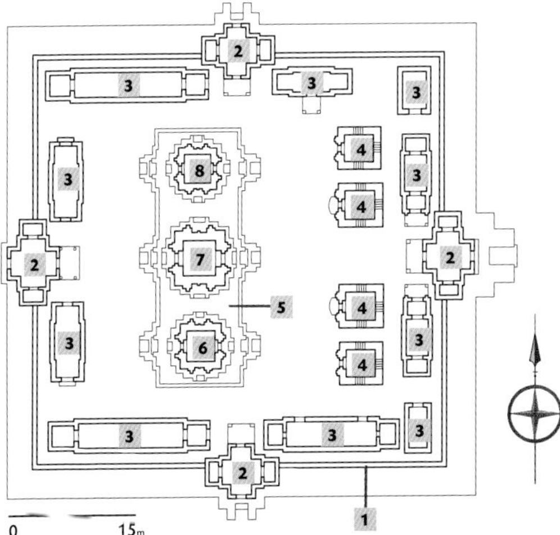

Legend

1 Enclosure
2 Gopura
3 Rectangular buildings
4 'Libraries'
5 Platform
6 Prasat of Brahma
7 Prasat of Shiva
8 Prasat of Vishnu

TRAVELWISE

PLANNING YOUR TRIP

Year after year, more and more visitors are attracted by the splendid temples of Angkor. The temple complex is undoubtedly one of the main tourist attractions of Cambodia. In the last decade alone, the number of visitors has risen by almost 190percent, reaching 2.4 million people.

Climate / When to go

The Cambodian climate is warm and humid and it is characterized by monsoon winds and high temperatures. The hottest month is April, when the average temperature can be as high as 30° C. The coldest month is December, when, in any case, the temperature in Phnom Penh is almost 26° C. In the period between May and October, the so-called rainy season, the southwest monsoon wind brings masses of humid air into the country. In the remaining months, with the arrival of the northeast monsoon, the climate is dominated by currents of dry air from the continent.

The best time to visit the country is the beginning of the dry season (November, December and January) when low temperatures and low humidity make it easier to visit the great temple complexes. In this season, you can enjoy the spectacle offered by a lush and green Nature, in stark contrast with the months when the landscape appears barren and dusty. The downside is that in this season hotel prices reach their highest levels, so it is advisable to plan your trip and book your accommodations well in advance.

During the rainy season, tourism declines and the landscape is magnificent to behold in all its green splendor. During this period, the days are often bright and sunny. On the other hand, there is the risk of prolonged periods of rain. During these months, if you are traveling with a rental car, it is better to avoid the dirt roads that soon fill up with mud and become unusable.

Insurance

The level of health care offered in Cambodia does not meet European standards. It is therefore of primary importance to take out a private health insurance policy that is valid all over the world as well as insurance for medical evacuation in case it becomes necessary to interrupt care in Cambodia and resume it later at home. It is also advisable to carry a small "traveling pharmacy" to deal with any emergencies. You should store drugs in a place where they cannot be damaged during transport and where they are protected from direct sunlight and heat.

Unfortunately, crime, and in particular, petty crime, are fairly widespread in tourist centers such as Angkor, and it is therefore advisable to take out insurance against theft. Extra care should be taken when using moto-taxis and tuk-tuks, because it is very easy for pickpockets on bikes to snatch bags and backpacks by coming up alongside your vehicle. If you need to have theft of this kind recognized by your insurance company at home, it must be reported to the Cambodian police. an operation which may well prove to be never-ending.

Vaccinations

It is advisable to find out in advance about the recommended vaccinations for the country. The only compulsory vaccination is the one against yellow fever, but only for travelers coming from areas at risk of transmission (see also www.who.int). Health care organizations and the Foreign Ministry also recommend vaccination against tetanus, diphtheria, polio and hepatitis A. In addition, for stays of longer than four weeks or in the event of personal exposure, vaccination against hepatitis B, rabies, typhoid and Japanese encephalitis is also recommended.

HOW TO GET TO CAMBODIA

Customs

There are no maximum limits for importing foreign currency. However, it is obligatory to declare sums in excess of 10,000 U.S. dollars upon entry or when leaving the country. Each traveler over the age of 18 is entitled to bring into the country the following quantities of products purchased at duty free shops: 200 cigarettes or 100 cigars or 40 grams of tobacco, one bottle of spirits or two bottles of wine, 350 milliliters of perfume and new products with a maximum value of 100 U.S. dollars. In addition, medicines can be brought in if accompanied by a regular prescription. All new products exceeding the fixed limit must be declared at customs.

If you plan to enter the country overland and travel for the duration of your stay with your own car or your motorcycle, you must obtain authorization in advance from the *General Department of Customs and Excise* (6-8 Norodom Blvd., Phnom Penh, Phone: 00855-23-214065, www.customs.gov.kh).

Entry Formalities

Passport and visa

To enter Cambodia, you must possess an entry visa (tourist visa or business, cost 20 to 25 U.S. dollars, payable in cash) that can be obtained prior to travel at a Cambodian Embassy or Consulate. To apply for a visa, you must have a valid passport.

Recently, the Cambodian Ministry of Foreign Affairs (www.cambodiaonarrival.com) set up a service whereby you fill out forms to request an entry visa, at a cost of $10 (payable by credit card), which you will then find available upon arrival in the country. Handling requires three working days. In addition, up to two weeks before your trip, you can request an online tourist visa (a so-called electronic visa) on the website of the Cambodian Ministry of Foreign Affairs (evisa.mfaic.gov.kh). The electronic visa allows you to enter the country once only, for a maximum period of 30 days; the appropriate fees must be paid online by credit card. The photograph to be affixed on the visa must be submitted in JPEG format. Tourist visas are valid for four weeks. Upon arrival, the visa is stamped with an entry date, which certifies the beginning of your stay. In the event of overstaying your visa, there is a fine of $5 for each day you overstay. However, if the visa has expired for more than a month, the penalty rises to $6 per day. The term of validity of a visa can be extended once for up to 30 days, by application to the Immigration Office of the Ministry of the Interior in Phnom Penh (Tel. 00 855 (0) 12-854-874 or 00 855 (0) 12-581-558), located opposite the airport. The extension of validity can also be obtained (upon payment of a commission for administrative costs) from one of the travel agencies that are found in the large cities that specialize in these procedures.

If you arrive by plane at one of the two international airports of the country, Pochentong Airport in Phnom Penh (www.cambodia--airports.com/phnompenh) or, if your destination is Angkor, at Siem Reap Airport (www.cambodia-airports.com / Siemreap), on board the plane you will receive a form that you must fill in and submit at the visa counter at the airport, together with the photo to be affixed to the visa and the passport / passport for children that must have a residual term of validity of at least six months.

The same documents and visas need to be shown when you arrive in Cambodia by land from one of the three neighboring countries (Laos, Thailand and Vietnam). In the latter case, the operations of issuing visas and customs formalities may take longer.

TRAVEL INFORMATION ANGKOR

Admission: to visit the temples of Angkor Archaeological Park, there are three different types of admission tickets: day tickets (20 U.S. dollars), three-day tickets (40 U.S. Dollars) or seven-day tickets (60 U.S. dollars). Day tickets can be purchased at the temple of Banteay Srei. Multiday tickets are sold only at the south entrance of the park (photo-passes are issued). Admission tickets are valid for all the monuments and must be shown at the various entrances. The only temples that require a separate ticket are those of Mealea Beng (extra charge of 5 U.S. dollars), Koh Ker (10 U.S. dollars) and Phnom Kulen (20 U.S. dollars). Tickets can be valid on the following day. When you purchase a ticket after 17.00 hrs, you can also use it the next day.

Guides: many hotels and local travel agencies offer tour guides whose fees varies between 20 and 25 U.S. dollars.

Location: Angkor is located near the town of Siem Reap and its airport, Siem Reap-Angkor Airport. The city and its surroundings are an ideal base for exploring the monumental temple complex of Angkor. The airport is located about 10 km to the northwest of the city. The entrance to the archaeological park is located about five miles north of the city. If you arrive by plane, it is better to arrange for hotel transfers in advance with your hotel, alternatively you can take a taxi to wherever you are staying, which should cost about 7 U.S. dollars. Transfers in tuk-tuks (about 5 U.S. dollars) or motorcycle taxis (about 1-2 U.S. dollars) certainly cost less, but are less convenient if you are traveling with heavy luggage.

Other attractions

Angkor National Museum, *968 Vithei Charles de Gaulle, Tel. 855-063-966 501, www.angkornationalmuseum.com, open daily 9-19, admission 12 U.S. dollars.*
The museum, which was inaugurated in 2008, is rich in exhibits from the time of the Khmer. You are not allowed to take pictures inside the museum; however, for 2 U.S. dollars you can buy a pass that allows you to take a limited number of photographs.

Angkor Wat by night (*Phum Thnal Village, Khum Sror Nge, Siem Reap, Tel. 855-(0)13-656-600, www.angkorwatnighttours.com*).
A visit to the magnificent temples of Angkor by night is a romantic and unforgettable experience. After the visit, you will be served a traditional Khmer dinner accompanied by sword-fighting and Apsara dance performances.

Angkor Wat in Miniature (*north of NR 6, on River Road, admission 1.50 U.S. dollars*).
This scale model of the colossal temple complex is useful to get an idea of the position of the various temples and an overview of the area.

Balloon flights (*on the road to Angkor; Cell 012-520810*). On board the balloon, which is anchored to the ground, you can enjoy a panoramic view of the complex of Angkor Wat and take memorable photographs from a breathtaking height of 200 meters.
Cambodia Helicopters (*offices at the airport arrivals terminal and near the Old Market, mobile 012-814 500*). Flying over the temples and the surrounding area by helicopter, you can enjoy truly unique and spectacular views. Not exactly cheap, but worth it.

PRACTICAL ADVICE

Clothing

If you decide to make the journey during the monsoon season it is essential to pack rainproof clothing and a pair of good waterproof shoes. In the winter months, you must not forget to pack sweaters and a jacket. It is not uncommon for cheap hotels, or even medium category hotels, not to have any heating.

When you visit Buddhist temples and monasteries and public buildings, it is advisable to cover your shoulders and knees. It is best to forgo skimpy shorts and low-cut tops and wear modest garments that cover legs and shoulders. In principle, you should always take off your shoes before entering a convent or even private homes. Wear shoes that are easy to slip on and off, for example, sandals.

However, you will be better off wearing stronger shoes for walking around the temples of Angkor as the pathways are rather rough and there are also many rough edges here and there among the ruins. You should always carry sunscreen and insect repellent.

Credit Cards

Major credit cards: MasterCard (MC) and Visa (V) are accepted as a rule only in hotels, restaurants and major shops in the large resorts and in tourist centers.

It is only possible to withdraw money from ATMs or banks in tourist centers. ATMs usually dispense U.S. dollars.

Currency

Despite the fact that the country's official currency is the Riel, most payments, or, in any case, those of a certain magnitude, are made in U.S. dollars. The national currency is usually used for change and for paying very modest amounts.

Banknotes of 50, 100, 200, 500, 1000, 2000, 5000, 10,000, 20,000, 50,000 and 100,000 Riel are in circulation. There are notes of various sizes and colors, and their value is written both in Cambodian and English. The most common bills are the 100, 500 and 1000 Riel.

It is recommended that you keep to hand, in a separate wallet, some small change to pay for snacks, drinks, or souvenirs, or even, a ride in a tuk-tuk. We recommend that you never show that you have brought significant amounts of cash or Traveler's Checks. It is better to keep money and other valuables in the safety of your hotel room.

Do not accept very dirty or damaged or torn notes.

Danger of land mines

Even though tourist areas, the city of Angkor and above all, densely populated regions, have by now been largely cleared of land mines, grenades and unexploded ordnance, the threat of land mines remains high in the border areas and in rural districts. It is advisable to remain on the beaten track, avoid metal objects and be very careful.

Electricity

In Cambodia, the electricity network operates at 230 volts with a frequency of 50 Hz. To use electrical equipment that complies with European standards, it is necessary to use a transformer.

Embassies & Consulates

The Royal Embassy of Cambodia to the United States of America is located at
4530 16th Street, NW
Washington, DC 20011,
tel: 202-726-7742;
e-mail: camemb.usa@mfa.gov.kh.

The Embassy of the United States of America in Cambodia is located at #1, Street 96, Sangkat Wat Phnom, Khan Daun Penh, Phnom Penh, tel: (855-23) 728-000.

The e-mail address for the embassy's American Citizen Services is: ACSPhnomPenh@state.gov.

Embassy of Cambodia in the United Kingdom
64 Brondesbury Park
Willesden Green
London NW6 7AT - UK
tel: +44 (0)20 8451 7850
fax:+44 (0)20 8451 7594
Email: cambodianembassy@btconnect.com
Website: http://www.cambodianembassy.org.uk

British Embassy in Phnom Penh, Cambodia
House No. 27-29, Street 75, Sangkat Srah Chak, Khan Daun Penh, Phnom Penh, Cambodia
tel: + 855 (0) 23 427124/428153
fax + 855 (0) 23 427125
email: britemb@online.com.kh

Health

Useful updated health care information can be found on the MD Travel Health website (www.mdtravelhealth.com/destinations/asia/cambodia.php) and on the WHO website (www.who.int.)

The Royal Angkor International Hospital, in Angkor, near the airport, is a good hospital (Phone 855-063-761888 or 855-063-399111, www.royalangkorhospital.com; 24 hour service).

Holidays

January 1st - New Year
January 7th - Celebration of the fall of the Khmer Rouge regime

February - Makha Bucha Day; on the occasion of the first full moon of the month, there is the commemoration of the spontaneous gathering of 1250 monks, without prior notice, to hear the word of the Buddha.
March 8th - International Women's Day
13th to 15th April - Khmer New Year
1st June - International Children's Day
1st May - International Workers' Day
May 13th to 15th - Celebrations for the birthday of King Norodom Sihamoni, whose birthday is on May 13th.
May - Royal Plowing Ceremony; beginning of the planting season
May - Feast of Visaka-Buja; the celebration of the birth and enlightenment of Buddha
June 18th - Birthday of Queen-Mother Norodom Sihanouk Monineath Sihanouk
24th September - Constitution Day
End September - Early October - Celebrations of Pchum-Ben; Ancestors Day
29th October - Coronation Festival of King Norodom Sihamoni
31st October - Birthday of former King Sihanouk
9th November - Independence and National Day
November - Water and Moon Festival
10th December - International Human Rights Day

Photographs

It is recommended that you never take photographs of locals without first asking for permission. To take pictures of monks is considered improper.

Pharmacies

Although you can find pharmacies all over the country, you are advised to carry a well-stocked "traveling pharmacy" with you and to pack enough medication for your needs. Unfortunately, Cambodian pharmacies often sell counterfeit drugs at the price of original products.

The U-Care pharmacy chain sells imported original products. Another problem: many of the pharmacies' staff members speak and understand little or no English.

Security

The population of Cambodia is predominantly poor. Especially in large cities and tourist areas, pickpockets are no longer a rarity. It happens increasingly often that unsuspecting tourists have bags snatched by skilled pickpockets on motorcycles and tuk-tuks. Be alert and always keep any valuables in the hotel safe. Do not carry large sums of money or, if this cannot be avoided, keep the money close to your body in a neck wallet or a money belt. Also be careful in extremely crowded places, where it is not uncommon to see children engaged in pickpocketing. You are also advised not to travel alone at night. This is imperative for women traveling alone.

To contact the tourist police call the following mobile numbers: 012-402424, 012-969991 and 012-838768.

Telephone

The international code for Cambodia is +855. To call Cambodia from the U.S.A. the international code is 011 855 . To call the U.S.A. from Cambodia the international code is 001. An easy and convenient alternative for calls to foreign countries is provided by the Skype international telephone service (www.skype.com). In 2008 the 3G standard for mobile phones was introduced in Cambodia. It is recommended that you obtain a tourist SIM card, available at airports and in many hotels and shops. These cards are valid for only 12 days and cannot be recharged.

Time Zone

Cambodia is seven hours ahead of Greenwich Mean time. The country does not observe DST (Daylight Saving Time). For more information see www.worldtimezones.com.

Tipping

The increasing number of visitors has meant that tipping has acquired greater importance. Giving a tip that is in keeping with the service received is a courteous gesture but not an obligatory one. Bear in mind that in many cases, the daily wage of the employee providing the service is roughly equivalent to 1 U.S. dollar.

Tuk-tuks

The tuk-tuk, the colorful three-wheeled taxi, can also carry luggage, and is a popular means of transport for short trips in towns and surrounding areas. A ride in a tuk-tuk is a unique and unforgettable experience. During the dry season, it is advisable to be adequately protected from dust or ask the driver to lower the side curtains. As the tuk-tuks do not have meters, you should inquire in advance about prices and agree on the fare with the driver.

Water

Never drink tap water or use it to brush your teeth. It is also better to avoid ice cubes in drinks. Fruit and vegetables should be eaten only when peeled. Drink only bottled water that you can buy anywhere in the country in stores, restaurants and street stalls.

Hotels & Restaurants

After the civil war, Cambodia and, in particular, Angkor were once again popular tourist destinations. Since the '90s there has been a steady increase in the number of tourists, accompanied by development of the tourism infrastructure. In Siem Reap, the existing hotels have been refurbished and extended, and new hotels and accommodations, ranging from basic guest houses to luxury international hotels, have been built. There is also a wide range of restaurants where you can enjoy both international dishes and traditional Cambodian cuisine.

HOTELS

AMANSARA

$$$$$

ON THE ROAD TO ANGKOR
Tel. 855(0)63-760-333
www.amanresorts.com

Aman Resort Group hotels are synonymous with exclusive luxury. The Amansara Hotel, a former palace, built in the ,60s by Norodom Sihanouk, offers guests all the services you can imagine. The suites with private pool, to relax after a busy day of sightseeing, are particularly sought after.
The hotel naturally offers guided tours of the temple complexes and, often, interesting lectures on Cambodian culture and the masterpieces of Khmer architecture.

RAFFLES GRAND HOTEL D'ANGKOR

$$$$$

1 CHARLES DE GAULLE ST.
Tel. 855(0)63-963-888
www.siemreap.raffles.com

A true classic, today as in the past. Even in the 1930s this luxury hotel was the favorite among the first wealthy visitors to the temples of Angkor Wat. Today, the hotel spoils its guests with all the services and pampering typical of 5-star hotels.
There are excellent restaurants where you can enjoy exquisite traditional Khmer dishes. As you sip tea in the afternoon, you can immerse yourself in the history of this beautiful ultra-octogenarian hotel. Your evening can start with a drink with the delicate notes of the piano bar in the background. The hotel also boasts the best wine cellar in the country.

SOFITEL ANGKOR PHOKEETHRA GOLF AND SPA

$$$$$

VITHEI CHARLES DE GAULLE;
KHUM SVAY DANG KUM
Tel. 855(0)63-964 600
www.sofitel.com

This 5-star hotel is regularly ranked among the best in town. Located just 20 minutes from the airport, the hotel, which opened in 2000, is a fascinating mixture of French and Khmer styles. The splendid English gardens boast the largest freshwater pool in the country, an ideal place for relaxing and regenerating oneself.
And if, after the exploits of a day of sightseeing, you still have some energy left for sports, you can avail yourself of the wonderful 18-hole golf course at the Phokeethra Country Club.

SOJOURN BOUTIQUE VILLAS

$$$$-$$$$$

TREAK VILLAGE RD.
Tel. 855(0)-12-923 437
www.sojournsiemreap.com

Away from the chaos and dust of the city, this small hotel near Wat Athwea offers peace and relaxation. The hotel consists of 10 elegantly furnished bungalows overlooking a swimming pool in a relaxing tropical garden.
Excellent service and absolutely exquisite food.

ANGKOR CENTURY RESORT & SPA

$$$$

KOMAY ROAD;
KHUM SVAY DANG KUM
Tel. 855(0)63-963 777
www.angkorcentury.com

This 4-star hotel is an excellent choice because of its location and a good quality to price ratio.
It has the additional attractions of a swimming pool, a beautiful garden and a fitness and wellness center. In the evening, a five-course dinner is served in the restaurant, accompanied by Apsara dancing.

ANGKOR SPIRIT PALACE

$$-$$$

PHNEACHEY VILLAGE;
SVAY DANG KUM
Tel. 855(0)-63-760 029
www.angkorspiritpalace.com

Excellent value for money. The hotel, built in 1988, was originally a cultural center.
It features many elements of traditional Khmer architecture. The rooms are comfortable and guests can enjoy the beautiful salt water pool in the garden.

GOLDEN BANANA BOUTIQUE HOTEL & RESORT

$$-$$$

NEAR WAT DAMNAK
Tel: 855(0)-63-969 888
www.goldenbanana.info

Do not be fooled by the name. Just a five-minute walk from the Old Market, this boutique-style hotel (also resort and bed & breakfast) that opened recently offers a good and reasonably priced alternative near the center.
The building and rooms overlook a salt water pool.
The hotel offers good service with friendly helpful staff.

RESTAURANTS

CHAO PRAYA

$$$

Nr. 64 ANGKOR WAT STREET;
KHOM STAR KRAM
Tel. 855(0)63-964 666

In the buffet restaurant you can enjoy good quality Thai, Vietnamese, Japanese, Mongol and Cambodian dishes.
In the evening there is a dance performance included in the price of the menu.

🕒 18-22.30

TELL RESTAURANT

$-$$$

SIVATHA RD.
TEL. 855(0)63-963 289

In addition to typical traditional Khmer cuisine, this restaurant serves German and Swiss dishes. If you cannot do without a *Wiener Schnitzel* while on vacation, this air-conditioned restaurant is the place to go.

🕒 11-22

DEAD FISH TOWER

$-$$

SIVATHAT BLVD.
Tel. 855(0)63-012-630 377
www.deadfishtower.com

This is a very pleasant restaurant that occupies several floors offering a wide range of Asian dishes. The menu is dominated by Khmer cuisine, but it also features excellent meat dishes. In the evening there is live music and traditional dancing.

🕒 10-24; osed on Saturdays and Sundays

JOAN YEN LAU RESTAURANT

$-$$

NR. 13, NATIONAL ROAD NR. 6
TEL. 855(0)63-760 269

A simple restaurant, on the third floor of the very busy Angkor Shopping Center, that serves Chinese delicacies and the classic dishes of Hong Kong cuisine. The restaurant bar is perfect for a refreshing drink.

🕒 11-21

VIVA

$-$$

OLD MARKET AREA
TEL. 855(0)63-209 154
www.ivivasiemreap.com

This is a Mexican restaurant where the thriving clientele enjoys cocktails, margaritas and a vast range of tequilas. On the big screen, you can
see CNN or sports programs. It is a very popular
meeting place for locals and tourists.

🕒 11-24

ANGKOR CAFE

$

IN FRONT OF ANGKOR WAT
www.artisansdangkor.com

After visiting the temples you can relax and enjoy an ice cream or a coffee with biscuits in this beautiful cafe, or admire and purchase beautiful items of artisan craftsmanship in the adjacent Khmer Art de Vivre Boutique.

🕒 8-17

BUTTERFLY GARDEN

$

ON THE EAST BANK OF THE SIEM REAP RIVER
TEL. 855(0)63-761 211

A true oasis of peace in a beautiful tropical garden, surrounded by countless brightly colored butterflies. You can enjoy delicious dishes from Khmer and international cuisine at leisure. The menu also includes vegetarian dishes, fresh fruit, juices and other delicacies. On some evenings there is also a dancing show that lasts about 45 minutes. A portion of the proceeds from the adjoining gift shop is donated to local charities.

🕒 9-22

SWENSEN'S

$$-$$$

POKOMBOR AVE.;
ANGKOR TRADE CENTER

A paradise for ice cream lovers. On a cone or in a cup, the many flavors of Swensen's ice creams are a real treat for the palate.

🕒 10-21

PRICES

HOTELS

The number of **$** signs indicates the price range of a double room in the high season as follows:

$$$$$	Over $125
$$$$	$76-$125
$$$	$51-$75
$$	$26-$50
$	Under $25

RESTAURANTS

The number of **$** signs indicates the price range of a three-course meal excluding drinks, as follows:

$$$$$	Over $125
$$$$	$76-$125
$$$	$51-$75
$$	$26-$50
$	Under $25

Glossary

amrita: the ambrosia or nectar of immortality
antarala: vestibule
apsara: celestial dancer nymphs
ardhamandapa: a half pavilion, portico
ashrama: hermitage
asura: demons or anti-gods
atman: soul
avatara: the divine descent to Earth
baray: (Khmer) artificial reservoirs
bodhi: enlightenment
bodhisattva: he whose essence is bodhi
brahmana: Brahmans belonging to the first Hindu caste, that of priests
Buddharaja: Buddha-king
cakra: wheel, circle, sharp disc used as a weapon by Vishnu
cakravartin: the universal sovereign, the "lord of the wheel", that is, of order
deva: the power of light, god
Devaraja: God-king
devata: divinity
devi: goddess
dvarapala: guardian of the gate
garbhagriha: chamber of the embryo, womb, the temple cella
Garuda: a lesser deity, a vehicle of Vishnu that is part bird and part man
genius loci: tutelary divinity of the territory
gopura: monumental pavilion above the entrances to the temple enclosure walls
guru: spiritual mentor
hamsa: goose with a striped head or goose-swan, a vehicle of Brahma
Ishvara: Lord
Kala: all-devouring demon
Kamrateng: (ancient Khmer) Lord
kinnari: winged female beings
kudu: horseshoe arch
lingam: phallic stone symbolizing the god Shiva
loka: world-paradise
makara: mythical aquatic monsters with a trunk and horns
mandala: symbolic and initiation route that reflects the arrangement of the cosmos and of the psyche
mandapa: pavilion
naga: mythical creature, partly cobra
nagara: capital city
Nagaraja: king of the Nagas
Nagini: the naga's consort
narasimha: man-lion, the avatara of the god Vishnu
nirvana: the ineffable state of extinction of existence
parinirvana: entry of the Buddha into final nirvana, the death of Buddha
phnom: (Khmer) mountain
pradakshina: circumambulatory ritual in which the object to be worshipped is always at one's right
prasat: pyramid temple
prasavya: funeral rite carried out with counterclockwise circumambulation
raja: king
rajavihara: royal monastery
rajya: regality
saptaloka: the seven heavens of the Hindu gods
snanadroni: the round base of the lingam, which ends in a lip, the symbol of the Female Principle
stupa: tumulus built over the remains of the cremated Buddha and the most distinguished monks; reliquary
Trimurti: triple form that the Absolute takes on as the creator, preserver and destroyer of the cosmos in the figures of Brahma, Vishnu e Shiva
ushnisha: the cranial protuberance of Buddha
vahana: vehicle or mount of the gods
varaha: incarnation of Vishnu as a boar
varman: armor, protection; 'protected by' in a ruler's name: Jayavarman is 'protected by victory', or jaya
vrah guru: (Khmer+Sanskrit) holy spiritual master
yaksha: tree genie
yantra: esoteric diagram
wat: monastery in the Thai language

Bibliography

Architecture

Dumarçay, J., *Phnom Bakheng: Etude architecturale du temple*, EFEO, Paris, 1971.

Filliozat, J., *Le Symbolisme du monument du Phnom Bakheng*, in BEFEO, XLIV, 1954.

Finot, L., Goloubew V., Coedès G., *Le temple d'Içvarapura (Banteay Srei)*, EFEO, Paris, 1926.

Finot, L., Goloubew V., Coedès G., *Le temple d'Angkor Vat*, EFEO, Paris, 1927-1933.

Mus, P., *Les Symbolisme à Angkor Thom: le grand miracle du Bayon*, in Comptes rendus de l'Académie des Inscriptions et Belles Lettres, 1936.

Nafilyan, G., *Angkor Vat: Description grafique du temple*, EFEO, Paris, 1969.

Parmentier, H., *Angkor*, Portail, Saigon, 1950.

Stierlin, H., *Angkor*, Architecture Universelle, Office du Livre, Fribourg, 1970.

Stierlin, H., *Le monde d'Angkor*, Princesse, Paris, 1979.

Stern, P., *Les monuments du style khmer du Bayon et Jayavarman VII*, Paris, 1965.

Stern, P., *Le Bayon d'Angkor et l'évolution de l'art khmer*, Annales du musée, Bibl. de vulgarisation, t. 47, Librairie orientaliste P. Geuthner, Paris, 1927.

Vann, Molyvann., *Les cités khmer anciennes*, Toyota Foundation, Phnom Penh, 1999.

Ceramics

Groslier, B. P., *Introduction to the Ceramic Wares of Angkor*, in "Khmer Ceramics 9th-14th Century," Southeast Asian Ceramic Society, Singapore, 1981.

Rooney, D., *Khmer Ceramics*, Oxford University Press, Kuala Lumpur, 1984.

General Works

Albanese, M., *Angkor: fasto e splendore dell'impero khmer*, ed. White Star, Vercelli, 2002.

Angkor et dix siècles d'art khmer, Catalogue de l'exposition à la Galerie nationale du Grand Palais, Réunion des Musées Nationaux, Paris, Jan.-May 1997.

Boisselier, J., *Trends in Khmer Art*, tr. by Natasha Eilenberg and Melvin Elliot, Ithaca, Cornell University, 1989.

Boisselier, J., *Le Cambodge*, in "Manuel d'archéologie d'Extrême Orient, Asie du sud-est, Tome I," Picard et Cie, Paris, 1966.

Coedès, G., *Angkor, an Introduction*, Tr. by Emily Floyd Gardiner, Oxford University Press, Hong Kong, London, 1963. (A translation of *Pour mieux comprendre Angkor*).

Coedès, G., *Angkor, an Introduction*, Oxford University Press, London, 1963.

Coral-Rémusat, G. de, *L'art khmer: Les grandes étapes de son évolution*, Vanoest Editions d'art et d'histoire, Paris, 1951.

Dagens, B., *Angkor: Heart of an Asian Empire*, tr. from the French edition by Ruth Sarman, Harry, N. Abrams, New York, 1995.

Le Bonheur, A., *Art khmer*, RMN, "Petits guides des grands musées" n. 60, Paris, 1986.

Mazzeo, D. and Silvi Antonini, C., *Civiltà khmer*, in "Le grandi civiltà," Mondadori, Milan, 1972.

Zéphir, T., *Khmer: Lost empire of Cambodia*, Thames and Hudson, London, 1998.

Guides

Comaille, J., *Guide aux Ruines d'Angkor*, Hachette, Paris, 1912.

Glaize, M., *Le guide d'Angkor: les monuments du groupe d'Angkor*, Maisonneuve, Paris, 1963.

Jacques, C., *Angkor*, Bordas, Paris, 1990.

Jacques, C., Freeman M., *Angkor, cité khmer*, River Books Guide, Bangkok, 2000.

Laur, J., *Angkor, temples et monuments*, Flammarion, 2002.

Lunet de Lajonquière, *Inventaire descriptif des Monuments du Cambodge*, EFEO, vol. IV, VIII et IX, Leroux, Paris, 1902-1911.

Marchal, H., *Nouveau Guide d'Angkor*, Phnom Penh, 1961.

Marchal, H., *Les Temples d'Angkor*, Guillot, Paris, 1955.

History

Briggs, L. P., *The Ancient Khmer Empire*, White Lotus, Bangkok, 1999.

Chandler, D. P., *A History of Cambodia*, Westview Press, Boulder, Colorado, 1983.

Chou Ta-Kuan, *The Customs of Cambodia*, The Siam Society, Bangkok, 1992.

Coedès, G., *Un grand roi du Cambodge: Jayavarman VII*, Phnom Penh, 1935.

Dauphin-Meunier, A., *Histoire du Cambodge*, PUF, Paris, 1968.

Frédéric, L., *La vie quotidienne dans la péninsule indochinoise à l'époque d'Angkor: 800-1300*, ed. Hachette, Biarritz, 1981.

Giteau, M., *Histoire de Cambodge*, Didier, Paris, 1957.

Giteau, M., *Histoire d'Angkor, Que sais-je?*, Paris, 1974.

MacDonald, M., *Angkor and the Khmers*, Oxford University Press, London, 1990.

Sahai, S.: *Les institutions politiques et l'organisation administrative du Cambodge ancien (VI- XIII siècles)*, EFEO, LXXV, Paris, 1970.

Thierry, S., *Les Khmer*, Le Seuil, Paris, 1964.

Miscellaneous publications

A l'ombre d'Angkor: Le Cambodge années vingt, Musée Albert Kahn, Paris, 1992.

Coedès, G., *Inscriptions du Cambodge*, 8 volumes, EFEO, Hanoi and Paris, 1937-1966.

Jacques, C., *Conservare l'impossibile*, in Archeo, XI n. 3, March 1996, Rizzoli-De Agostini, Rome.

Garnier, P., Nafilyan G., *L'art khmer en situation de réserve*, Éditions Européennes, Marseille, 1997.

Groslier, B. P.: *The Arts and Civilization of Angkor*, tr. by Eric Ernshaw Smith. New York, Praeger, 1957.

Groslier, B. P.: *Mélanges sur l'archéologie du Cambodge*, 10th printing, Presses de l'École Française d'Extreme Orient, Paris 1997-98.

Groslier, B. P., *Archéologie d'un empire agricole. La cité idraulique angkorienne*, in "Le Grand Atlas Universalis de l'archéologie," 1985.

Le Bonheur, A., *Cambodge, Angkor, temples en péril*, Herscher, Paris, 1989.

Roveda, V., *Khmer Mythology: Secrets of Angkor*, River Books, Bangkok, 1997.

Sculpture

Boisselier, J., *La statuaire khmere et son évolution*, Pub. de l' EFEO, vol. XXXVII, 2 tomes, Saigon, 1955.

Dupont, P., *La statuaire préangkorienne*, Artibus Asiae, Ascona, 1955.

Giteau, M., *Khmer Sculpture and the Angkor Civilization*, tr. by Diana Imber, Harry N. Abrams, NY 1966.

INDEX

The page numbers refer to the text, those in italics refer to pictures and maps

PHOTO CREDITS

Front cover pictures clockwise from top left: Livio Bourbon/Archivio White Star; Livio Bourbon/Archivio White Star; Livio Bourbon/Archivio White Star; Antonio Attini/Archivio White Star
Back cover from left: Livio Bourbon/Archivio White Star; Archivio White Star; Antonio Attini/Archivio White Star

All photographs are by Livio Bourbon/ Archivio White except for the following:
Stefano Amantini/Atlantide: page 11
Archivio White Star: pages 72-73, 73
Antonio Attini/Archivio White Star: pages 1-3, 34-35, 45, 54, 55, 60, 62 bottom, 63 top, 62-63, 64, 65 top, 65 center, 64 bottom, 102, 134, 143 top, 142 bottom left, 142 bottom right, 152 bottom, 153 top, 153 center bottom, 154 top, 154 bottom left, 155, 156 bottom left, 156 bottom right, 158-159, 158 top, 160 top, 160 bottom, 160-161, 161, 162 top, 162 center, 163 bottom, 162-163, 162 bottom, 164 bottom, 164 top, 165 top, 165 center, 165 bottom, 166 top, 166 bottom left, 166 bottom right, 167 top, 167 center, 167 bottom, 170-171, 170 bottom left, 170 bottom right, 170 top, 172 top, 173, 172 bottom left, 172 bottom right, 182, 183, 184 top, 184 bottom, 185, 186-187, 192 top, 192 bottom, 193 top, 193 bottom, 193 center, 197 bottom, 198, 203 bottom right, 204 top, 205 bottom, 204 bottom, 206 top left, 206 bottom, 207 top, 207 bottom, 212 left, 212 right, 213, 216 center, 216 bottom, 216 top, 217 bottom, 219 top, 220 bottom right, 221, 231 bottom, 232 top left, 234, 235, 236 top, 236 center, 236 bottom, 236-237, 240, 241 top, 241 bottom, 243 top, 242, 257 top, 263 top, 266 top, 266 bottom, 267 bottom, 269 top, 269 bottom, 271 bottom, 282 bottom, 283 bottom
Thomas Beringer: pages 139 bottom, 278 (Detail)
Marcello Bertinetti/Archivio White Star: pages 34 bottom, 114, 122 top, 122 bottom left, 124 top, 127 bottom, 129, 154-155, 156, 158 bottom, 175
Leonard de Selva/Corbis/Contrasto: page 77
Ecole Nazionale Superieure des Beaux Arts, Paris: pages 74-75
Michael Freeman/Corbis/Contrasto: pages 28, 32, 33, 42 (Detail), 43, 66-67, 223, 237
Richard Lambert/RMN: page 8
Erich Lessing/Contrasto: page 274
Chris Lisle/Corbis/Contrasto: page 283 top
Chrisobenhe Loviny/Corbis/Contrasto: page 265 top
Kevin R. Morris/Corbis/Contrasto: pages 70, 139 top, 176-177, 177 top, 178-179, 194 (Detail), 194 bottom, 272-273, 280 top
Thierry Ollivier/RMN: pages 36, 66
Luca I. Tettoni/Corbis/Contrasto: pages 13, 18, 24 left, 24 right, 25, 27, 29, 30, 31, 68, 71 left, 71 right, 194 center, 209, 229 bottom
Luca Tettoni Photography: page 19
Kimbell Art Museum/Corbis/Contrasto: page 69

Drawings and maps:
Aurora Antico/Archivio White Star: pages 93 top, 101 bottom, 103 right bottom, 108-109, 136, 138 bottom, 178 bottom, 228 bottom, 230 bottom, 235 bottom, 243 bottom, 245 bottom, 262 bottom, 263, 273 top, 279, 280 bottom, 281 bottom, 283
Armundo Borrelli/Archivio White Star: pages 37, 38, 44, 56-57 bottom, 58-59
Angelo Colombo/Archivio White Star: pages 16-17, 20-21, 23, 46 bottom, 46, 47, 49, 53, 54 bottom, 56-57 top e center, 70-81, 82, 87 bottom, 95 top, 106, 110 bottom, 116, 117 top e bottom, 118-119, 133 bottom, 141, 148-149, 151 bottom, 183, 195 bottom left, 200-201, 202-203, 211 bottom, 224-225, 238 bottom, 248 bottom, 254-255, 257 bottom, 265 top left, 276-277

Text: Marilia Albanese
Editorial Coordination: Laura Accomazzo
Graphic Designer: CLP Carlo Lauer & Partner

Via G. da Verrazano, 15
28100 Novara, Italy
www.whitestar.it - www.deagostini.it

New extended and up-dated edition

Translation: Richard Pierce
Translation of chapter *Trawelwise*: Catherine Howard

ISBN 978-88-544-0616-2
2 3 4 5 6 17 16 15 14 13

Printed in China